INSIDE THE SONY HACK

INSIDE THE SONY HACK

The Story Behind America's Most Notorious
Brink-of-War Cover-up

KENT HECKENLIVELY, JD

Waterside Productions

First Printing, 2024

ISBN-13: 978-1-962984-43-0 print edition
ISBN-13: 978-1-962984-44-7 e-book edition

Published by Clear Lantern Media
An imprint of:

Waterside Productions
2055 Oxford Ave
Cardiff, CA 92007
www.waterside.com

"Nobody knows anything."

William Goldman, *Adventures in the Screen Trade*

TABLE OF CONTENTS

PROLOGUE
THE WRITER'S DILEMMA

How does the writer begin this fractured fairy tale of Hollywood, international affairs, and cyber-criminals?

There is an objective reality of what took place on November 24, 2014, when Sony Entertainment in Culver City, California reported a digital break-in of their network and the events which followed. It began with the image of a stylized skull on the computer screen of every employee and long skeletal fingers pointing at the viewer with the warnings "This is just the beginning," as well as "we've obtained all your internal data."

The cyber-hackers (who called themselves the "Guardians of Peace") claimed if their demands weren't met, that they would release the company's "top secrets." Sony did not pay the ransom and the embarrassing internal emails were released, resulting in Sony Pictures co-chairman, Amy Pascal, losing her job. Some suggested Sony was later handed more than a hundred million dollars by private insurers and a government terrorism risk insurance program, solving their financial problems, as a result of the United States government intelligence community claiming the attack originated from North Korea.

But was that the truth?

And if not, how might an intrepid journalist go about finding the truth?

Should the writer begin with the September 28, 1989, sale of the former Columbia Pictures to the Japanese electronics giant, Sony, for $3.4 billion dollars,[1] setting up an inevitable clash between the corporate way of doing business as practiced in Japan, and the free-wheeling ways of Hollywood? An article in the *New York Times* a year before the sale of Columbia Pictures to Sony detailed some aspects of this culture clash in a different company purchased by Japanese owners:

> The most widespread complaint among American managers is that their nationality keeps them from the top of the Japanese corporate hierarchy – a complaint echoed by Japanese managers working for American companies in Japan…

> In fact, the men contend nearly every aspect of the Japanese company's business here, from hiring to marketing and finances, is run with a dictatorial and arrogant hand from afar by its parent company, NEC Corporation of Tokyo. NEC denies the charge.

> The Japanese, Mr. Neubauer said, "essentially don't trust anyone who doesn't speak the language, who is not of the same race, or has been out of Japan for too long.[2]

Might the easy riders and raging bulls of Hollywood have chafed under the corporate rule of their new Japanese owners? Could it be that the buttoned-down, insular culture of the Rising Sun did not easily mesh with the lotus land ethos of talking like hippies in public, but behind closed doors talking like the gangsters of their favorite film, *The Godfather*?

Perhaps one could see the genesis of this problem in a pattern of abusive behavior by the Hollywood Sony executives towards their employees as detailed in an October 6, 2011, email from an unidentified female employee shortly after she was terminated, regarding her boss, Keith Le Goy, the President of International Distribution at Sony Pictures Television. In one part of the email, she states:

"I am offended by the language and manner that Keith speaks to me and usage of the constant 'F' word, his derogatory language, once calling a married President [of the United States] a [Expletive] faggot, and another high level executive a 'dyke,' 'Forty year old women need tits,' regarding a high executive, 'Was that before or after she wiped the coke off her upper lip,'" accused another married high level executive of sexual dalliances with an international star, his own indiscretions and "calling me a 'Bitch,' referring to me as a 'Dumb Bitch' and calling me 'Queen B' out in the open for years, despite my telling him that it is his covert and now over way of calling me a Bitch."[3]

Could a culture of abusive actions by American executives towards their employees have lit the fuse which resulted in the hack and release of Sony's internal communications?

Or perhaps it would be more appropriate to start with the October 15, 2004, theatrical release of *Team America: World Police*. This adult puppet comedy satirized action films in its depiction of a paramilitary intelligence force which recruits a Broadway actor to help save the world from North Korean leader, Kim Jong-Il. The communists of North Korea were joined by an unlikely cabal of Islamic terrorists and liberal Hollywood actors.

A 2014 article in the prestigious publication *Foreign Policy*, quoting James Andrew Lewis, director of the Strategic Technologies Program at the Center for Strategic and International studies, suggested "*Team America: World Police* came out in 2004," Lewis added, referencing a film that depicted the death of Kim Jong-un's father, Kim Jong Il. 'It drove them wild but there was nothing that they could do. Now they have the capability to do something back.'"[4]

Might this be a tale of a dictatorial regime pushing back against the freedom of the West?

Or should we date the start of this disaster to March 21, 2013, when an article in *Vulture*, a website devoted to the arts published the news of a new movie to be called *The Interview*. The article began:

> Seth Rogen and Evan Goldberg are getting ready to direct their second movie together. THR [The Hollywood Reporter] reports that Rogen and his longtime writing partner Evan Goldberg have signed on to direct, write and produce a comedy called *The Interview*, with Rogen playing one of the two lead roles. James Franco is the top choice for the other main character, but he hasn't become involved officially yet. *The Interview* follows a good-looking talk show host (Franco, if he signs on) and his producer (Rogen) who accidentally get caught up in a plan to assassinate the Prime Minister of North Korea.[5]

Did Kim Jong-un decide that even a fictional account of his assassination by the CIA was a threat to those in his regime who might desire a change?

Were the events of November and December of 2014, when Sony's internal emails were dumped onto the internet a display of Kim Jong-un's increasing cyber-warfare abilities, and determination that North Korea would no longer be made the laughingstock of the world?

Or was North Korea simply a convenient scapegoat?

Although this book will examine the perspective of many of the key players, I have decided to begin this story with a couple of innocents, two individuals of a cyber-security company called Norse Corporation, based at that time out of Foster City, California, who prior to the release of the data had been called in to perform an analysis of the cyber-vulnerability of Sony's computer network.

For purposes of anonymity, I will give these individuals the pseudonyms, Mr. Grey, an older man in his mid sixties, a former music industry professional, and Eric, his digital bloodhound, an Einstein of understanding the internet universe, as well as a Mozart of designing systems to track and identify those who wished to remain hidden, as they tried to avoid the looming crisis.

Chapter One
The Door to the Computer Network was "Wide Open"

Like many of the good things in Mr. Grey's life, it started with a call from his long-time friend and well-known entertainment lawyer, Mickey (Michael) Shapiro.

Sony Pictures needed help with their computer network, which they believed might be vulnerable to outside attack.

Shapiro was a legend in Hollywood, getting his law degree in 1975, and having represented artists such as the Kinks, Wilson Phillips, the Alan Parsons Project, Mama Cass Elliot, Air Supply, Bobby Caldwell, and is credited with putting together the supergroup, Fleetwood Mac.[6] As an example of Mickey's knack to be close to the center of earthshaking events, he was about twenty-five feet away from Senator Robert Kennedy, in the kitchen of the Ambassador Hotel, when the 1968 Presidential candidate was gunned down by the assassin, Sirhan Sirhan. (In 2023, Mickey would also be instrumental in organizing the presidential campaign of Robert Kennedy, Jr., the namesake of the late senator and a long-time environmental lawyer.)

Mr. Grey had been in Los Angeles since the early 1970s in the music scene, where as Mr. Grey tells it, "I was probably one of the five people in the music business who wasn't stoned all the time." The two had become fast friends after meeting in the early 1980s, both were highly intelligent, clear-eyed about human nature, and excellent judges of talent.

Shapiro says of Mr. Grey, "To me, he's a brother. He's the closest person I have in my whole life. We've known each other since 1982. I have two friends I've known longer, Mick Fleetwood who I met in 1973, and another guy with whom I went to Harvard Law School. But Mr. Grey is my closest, dearest friend. At the darkest points of my life, he kept the light on, and kept me going. When Norse got started, anything I could do to steer them business, I was happy to do so."[7]

While Shapiro climbed the legal ladder, from representing artists to litigating issues of intellectual property, Grey moved from being a songwriter, to a stint setting the playlist of the nation's largest chain of black-owned radio stations (despite being a Jewish guy from Brooklyn), becoming the manager of top talent like Laura Branigan, to founding Big Deal Records which released several #1 hits with artists such as Peter Cetera, Amy Grant, Boz Skaggs, Neil Diamond, and Alicia Keys.[8]

Cyber-security might seem a world away from the music industry, but there were similarities. The best techs were often like the best musicians, quirky, emotional, prone to highs and lows that a good manager knew how to smooth out.

Mickey was the one who first put Mr. Grey in contact with Eric, his star developer at Norse Corporation, which they had founded in 2010. Mr. Grey had flown to the Midwest to meet this supposed internet genius, and their first conversation was a two-hour argument.

Eric didn't have much patience for people who didn't understand the new digital age which was dawning. Mr. Grey was used to dealing with temperamental artists, so despite the argument, he recognized the genius of the young man. "I'm not an idiot, I just don't know this area," Grey had told Eric, calming the young man down so Grey could better understand the idea he was working on at the time, keeping kids safe while they surfed the internet.

After their first meeting, Grey became convinced he'd discovered his greatest artist. Eric wasn't a musician, but he understood the vast network of the internet infrastructure because he'd built part of it, as well as having a visionary mind which could see what needed to be built in the future.

During this time, Mickey was becoming even more well-established in the entertainment industry, seeking a spiritual grounding as an antidote to the emptiness of just worldly success. He was one of the founders in 1993 of the Ohr HaTorah synagogue (the name means "Light of the Bible") in southern California. As their website explains:

> Our mission is to encourage and to include those who choose Judaism as their faith, religion, and spiritual path. We are especially supportive of those that hope of becoming a Jew by choice in the future.

> Like those in the Reform and Reconstructionist movements, we believe that Judaism is evolutionary and developmental; we do not believe that Halaka – Jewish law – is the direct will of God. Jews have the responsibility in each generation to add to this development and evolutionary growth.[9]

Mickey served as President of the Congregation for several years, and it became very popular with Jewish members of the entertainment community who sought a more liberal outlet than their traditional Jewish upbringings. In California, everything got reinvented, including Judaism.

It was in his position as President of the Ohr HaTorah synagogue that Mickey first met Amy Pascal. "From time to time I'd talk to Amy," said Mickey. "She was kind of like a fan. Everybody was aware of my music background, from Fleetwood Mac to Eric Clapton, and others. My music background seems to attract everybody, from conservatives like Congressman Dana Rohrabacher, who some consider to be ten degrees to the right of Atilla the Hun, to liberals like Congressman Adam Schiff. It makes me kind of like the pretty, curvy girl who gets accepted by everybody. People bond over music."[10]

And he also knew Michael Lynton, the CEO of Sony Pictures, although not as well. "Lynton was a member of the same congregation. At the time I was president of the congregation, so people had the pleasure of hearing me speak regularly, welcoming them and other things. As I recall, Lynton was Dutch or something. Very cordial. He was always a gentleman, but I just didn't know him that well."[11]

Somewhere in August of 2014 as Mickey remembers, he was at the synagogue, got talking to Amy and mentioned he was involved with a cybersecurity company which could probably make sure Sony was well protected in that realm, especially given the fact that the Sony PlayStation had suffered a devastating hack in 2012.

A few weeks later, Amy called Mickey and invited his team to make a presentation at Sony.

The company founded by Eric and Mr. Grey, Norse Corporation, had a unique suite of internet tools to provide internet security to businesses. An article from December of 2013, eleven months before the Sony hack, detailed some of their capabilities:

Norse, a leading provider of live threat intelligence solutions, today announced availability of Norse IPViking&trade 2.0, the next generation of its cloud-based IT security solution, which provides context-rich, dark-threat intelligence about the darkest segments of the internet. New to IPViking are unique threat intelligence capabilities that can detect malware while it is in the development phase, before cybercriminals can use it as part of an attack. Norse has also added capabilities that identify mobile and desktop devices, appliances, servers, and even satellites in space attempting to connect to networks via malicious IP addresses...

"The threat landscape evolves faster than most IT security solutions can keep pace with. Intelligence and visibility into what is taking place in the darkest corners of the internet is an essential component of any effective security strategy," said Richard Stiennon, noted cybersecurity expert, author and IT-Harvest analyst. "As a start-up, Norse is providing innovative and effective threat intelligence solutions that allow their customers to strengthen their defenses against the most advanced threats."[12]

One doesn't need to understand much about the technological space to realize that cybersecurity is akin in many ways to traditional security and investigative practices, just that it exists in the digital realm. Like fingerprints and DNA analysis revolutionized police work, companies like Norse were at the forefront of developing new investigative tools to track cybercriminals.

And in a tip of the hat to its creator, Norse's newest product, IPViking&trade 2.0, was named in honor of Eric's Viking heritage. Eric grew up on farm in Bergen, Norway which raised eggs, chickens, and milk cows. Up until the age of eight years old, he was usually assisting in those chores, but then he found computers. As he recalls, "I just became more and more curious about computers and what makes them work. I took my first computer apart to see how it works, but then couldn't get it back together again."[13] When his parents bought him a second computer, it came with a promise not to disassemble it.

The computer lines at the time used phones, and Eric was doing just what you might think a young boy set loose with a computer would do, getting in trouble. "I was dialing satellites. What I was doing was randomly dialing, having my modem dial numbers, and seeing when a computer answered. Then I'd try to break into the systems and explore around. But sometimes I broke into the wrong systems, like banks and infrastructure."[14] Although Eric generally avoided legal trouble, he often got into trouble with his parents because of the exorbitantly high phone bills.

When asked what makes him such an exceptional cybersecurity sleuth, Eric replied, "I think it's my analytical mind, meaning I'm curious about what's behind stuff and what makes things tick. And then there's a logical understanding of what happens in code and how that translates into how a computer operates. That gives you an advantage when you understand how a computer actually works and functions. It's important that you understand the principles of the internet, and the consequences of clicking a button on the keyboard."[15]

Eric's skill is in finding the bad actors of the internet. "If you're looking for a bad guy, everybody makes mistakes. Everyone makes bad choices. Everyone does stupid things sometimes. When we're looking for a hacker, that's what we're looking for, the little mistakes they make. I can give you a great example from an actual case I worked where we found a corporate blackmailer. This guy was a really proficient hacker. However, six years earlier he had an account on Adult Friend Finder. That site got hacked. His password was publicized on the internet, because it was attached to an email with his username. However, he signed the blackmail email to the corporation with the same username he'd used on the Adult Friend Finder site. I was able to correlate and backtrack the password to his current LinkedIn account, where he reused the password. And the password was so complicated and then you consider the other evidence, such as the fact he was Russian, and he was involved with some of the other people in the case."[16] Eric's point to me was that in finding the identity of a hacker, you're always relying on several pieces of evidence.

In the interest of full disclosure, there were several questions I asked Eric which he declined to answer, citing security oaths he signed with various government agencies, when he had worked for them on cases brought to him. Some might question whether this casts doubt on his claims he makes.

Perhaps I am being fed disinformation.

However, I always found Eric to be as open as he believed it was possible for him to be, as well as very free in sharing his general opinions about the way in which various government agencies operate. An additional factor to consider is that at the time of these events, Norse had a contract with a U.S. government agency to provide a significant percentage of their signal intelligence (known as SIG-INT in the trade), as well as analysis of that data.

One might liken the digital landscape to that of the Wild West, with vast distances, and instead of bandits wearing masks, the cybercriminals tried to conceal their identities by bouncing the signal off of different machines, located in different countries around the world, maybe even using machines of people they'd like the authorities to suspect of the crimes.

By June of 2014, the upstart Norse Corporation had made such a splash they were even being profiled by *Smithsonian* Magazine:

> The rise of the internet has given rise to a new battlefield. Whether across the country or across the world, hackers work to penetrate the digital defenses of nations, corporations, organizations, and individuals.
>
> In a wonderful, animated map, computer security company Norse shows who's hacking who in real time. These hacks aren't the ones going after the Pentagon, of course. Instead says Quartz, Norse's map shows hacking attempts against a "honeypot" network set up by Norse. This isn't all the world's hacking, but it could be a representative view of what the hacking ecosystem looks like …
>
> According to Nextgov, hackers try to break into the Pentagon 10 million times every day. The National Nuclear Security Administration fends off the same. The *New York Times* says that America's universities are facing millions of hacking attempts each week, while way back in 2011, Facebook was facing 600,000 hacking attempts every day.[17]

For those unfamiliar with the terminology, a "honeypot" is traditionally an attractive woman, used by an intelligence agency to entrap a target into revealing secrets. In the digital realm, a "honeypot" is what looks like an attractive digital target for penetration, but is in fact an information gathering device for Norse. The number of daily hacking attempts per day in 2014 was remarkable and have only increased in the past decade.

Who were the good guys and who were the bad guys in this new battlefield? Norse's map provided some clues.

Though Norse's map shows shots fired both against and from the United States and a load of other countries, it also seems to show China's dominance in this space. If you watch long enough, you'll see bursts of massive, coordinated attacks springing out of China, like this one from this morning. [Author's note – The image looks like computer maps from the 1980s or 1990s, showing simulated exchanges of nuclear missiles between the United States and the Soviet Union. But instead of nuclear bombs, these are daily hacks.]

"At any given time during business hours on Monday in Hong Kong, China led the list of countries where attacks originated, and the US was China's top target," says Heather Timmons for Quartz. "But the US was a steady number two on 'attack origins' list, though the targets varied."[18]

The picture of the world in 2014 becomes clear. China was the world's number one hacker, but the United States wasn't far behind.

They say in war, truth is the first casualty.

The executives at Norse liked to tell prospective clients they were "like Switzerland," neutral like a baseball umpire, calling balls and strikes, without fear or favor.

But what happens to the truthteller when he is surrounded by liars, both foreign and domestic?

Unlike many industries, in Hollywood it is possible for the same year to be very good, as well as very bad.

2014 was a year like that for Sony Pictures.

Consider this *Variety* article from early 2014 with the title, "Sony CEO: I'm Not Entertaining Even the Notion of Selling Our Entertainment Assets."[19] If you were an employee of Sony Pictures, is that the kind of talk which would fill you with hope or dread? The article began with the good news about Sony in early 2014, as it looked forward to the Oscars.

> Kazuo Hirai has circumnavigated the globe 12 times since becoming CEO of Sony Corp in 2012, but he's about to embark on what could be his most entertaining voyage yet: to the Academy Awards.

> The 53-year-old executive, known to all as Kaz, is quick to acknowledge the significance of his upcoming maiden sojourn. Sony Pictures Entertainment, the Hollywood studio owned by the Japanese electronics giant he heads, is basking in the glory of having earned multiple Oscar nominations for its movies "American Hustle" and "Captain Phillips," each of which has grossed more than $215 million worldwide to date.

> "It is very important to me and the management in Tokyo," says Hirai of being part of the industry's most prestigious awards race. "We understand how important recognition is for our creative work and how that corresponds to increased revenue."[20]

Variety wanted their readers to have a friendly view of Sony CEO "Kaz" excitedly looking forward to going to his first Academy Awards. Could the critical recognition of Oscar victories give a boost to the struggling Sony? That was the question on the minds of many as the Academy Awards drew near.

> This is a rare celebratory moment for Sony Pictures, which for nearly a year has been under harsh scrutiny for its poor

financial performance, bloated overhead, and some questionable movie choices. The studio's leaders are in the throes of recalibrating their struggling movie business in hopes of boosting the bottom line and shifting models in an increasingly tough economic climate. In the process of rethinking its strategy, SPE has shaken up its top executive ranks with high profile firings in publicity, marketing, home entertainment, technology and visual effects divisions.[21]

All of this turmoil took place before the Academy Awards of 2014, which had the potential to improve the bottom line of Sony Pictures, as an Oscar win often generates significant additional revenues for these films, either in theaters, or in home entertainment.

However, *American Hustle* and *Captain Phillips* would be shut out of the major awards at the Oscars, with the lion's share going to *Twelve Years a Slave* (Best Picture, Best Supporting Actress, and Best Adapted Screenplay), *The Dallas Buyers Club* (Best Actor and Best Supporting Actor) and *Gravity* (Best Director, Best Sound Editing, Best Film Editing, and Best Visual Effects).

Sony CEO Kaz was certainly not happy to have his studio losing both money and the Academy Awards, which were held on February 22 of 2014.

By March, the ax had started to fall on the employees of Sony because of the bad decisions made by their executives. Another article in *Variety* detailed the upcoming layoffs.

Sony Pictures Entertainment has begun layoffs for hundreds of employees, including approximately 216 people in its Culver City headquarters and its entire interactive team, which numbers more than 70 people, both in California and elsewhere ...

Additional layoffs are expected this week across all divisions of the company, both domestically and internationally. Sony topper Michael Lynton [Chairman and CEO of

Sony Pictures Entertainment] told Variety that both the $250 million the studio identified and the additional $100 million that it worked with Bain and Co. to cut has been determined. That additional slashing will happen over the next two years.[22]

In 2014, Sony Pictures Entertainment was looking at $350 million in cuts it needed to make in two years. At the time of the writing of this book in 2023, the $350 million in 2014 dollars would be approximately $438 million in today's dollars.

The firing of this large number of employees would definitely engender hostile feelings on the part of some former employees, and the only question was how deep that hatred might go with some employees, and whether they possessed the skill set necessary to harm their former employer.

Or maybe it was the North Korean dictator, Kim Jong-un, who didn't like a comedy about the CIA planning to assassinate him and intended to punish the movie studio which funded the film.

It was the United States government which would provide the accepted narrative to the world press. The villain in this drama was North Korean dictator, Kim Jong-un, and that determination would allow the United States to continue its harassment of the "Hermit Kingdom" and justify additional military spending to counter the "madman of Asia."

But a small band of cybersecurity experts would continue to question that narrative.

This is their story.

In late August of 2014 Amy Pascal, the chairwoman of the Motion Pictures Group of Sony Pictures Entertainment, and the highest paid female executive in Hollywood at the time, was worried.

The layoffs had been brutal, and Hollywood people didn't have much of a reputation for being well-balanced individuals.

A lot happened in a movie studio, but over the years since she'd first joined the former Columbia Pictures in 1998, she'd gained a reputation as a smart, compassionate studio executive with excellent instincts. A glowing profile of Pascal entitled "Amy Pascal: An Untypical Leading Lady Who's Taken Sony to the Top," from *The Guardian* in 2006, explained her role at Sony and her reputation.

Like many other studios, Sony is run as a two-headed beast, with Pascal largely responsible for the creative side (commissioning movies, dealing with artists, etc) while the chief executive, Michael Lynton, a former AOL and Penguin executive, takes care of the business side. Both report to Sir Howard Stringer, the head of Sony.

A graduate of UCLA who worked her way up from her first job as a secretary, Pascal is keen to dispel the suggestion that she is the one spending the money and doing the more "girly" bits of the job. "[Michael's] not always the one who says something is too much [money]. Sometimes I do. You would be surprised," she says. Go on then, I say. Pascal starts to mention a new financing structure at the studio but then appears to think better of it. "Michael and I really do everything together," she says. "We speak to each other a thousand times a day."

There is no doubt, however, that it is Pascal who is credited with making the studio so successful in the last few years – number one at the box office in two out of three years from 2002. And it is she who bears much of the burden for dropping to number three last year.[23]

If one believed the description of Hollywood provided by *The Guardian,* it could be a rough town, but if you proved yourself at the box office, you might be rewarded with creative control over one of the biggest studios in town.

The article went on to describe how Pascal had a "loyal following among many actors and directors and had a reputation for following her instincts" as well as being a "pretty straightforward, unpolitical, artist friendly studio executive."[24]

Pascal confided these fears to entertainment lawyer, Mickey Shapiro, who assured her he knew the perfect organization to allay her fears. Norse Corporation would do a deep dive into their computer network and identify any possible vulnerabilities.

Pascal agreed and Mickey called Mr. Grey to see when he and Eric could come down to take a meeting with Sony executives.

Mr. Grey and Eric flew down to Los Angeles in August of 2014 to take a meeting with Sony executives to review the security of their computer networks.

Amy Pascal would not be at the meeting, but Mickey Shapiro would, acting as the bridge between somebody who was well-known in the Hollywood community and the two men from Norse Corporation.

Mickey recalled walking on the Sony lot with Eric and Mickey, going to the reception area to check in with the beautiful young receptionist, then having her lead them on a curious route to the conference room, which passed through the studio's computer room with their servers.

The receptionist told the three men the executives would be with them shortly and asked if they wanted water or coffee while they waited. The three men declined, and the receptionist left.

Mr. Grey quickly turned to Eric. "Did they just walk us through their fucking computer room?"

"That doesn't look like the most secure situation," Eric replied, motioning to the route the receptionist had taken to return to her desk. He patted his backpack and pulled out a flash drive. "Oh my God, what we could do to them." He said with a quiet chuckle. "You stick one of these in and – whoop! – it'll suck out everything."

The three laughed, Mickey raised an eyebrow and looked at the open door to their computer servers. "Yeah, that doesn't seem too smart," he agreed. "I can't believe they left us alone in this room." A later article recounted the incident:

> Executives from cyber-security firm Norse Corp. were shocked that they were allowed into Sony's information security office unaccompanied and could see logged in computers running in unoccupied terminals. Mickey Shapiro, an entertainment lawyer escorting the Norse team, said, "If we were bad guys, we could have done something horrible."[25]

As they waited for the executives to arrive, Mr. Grey thought about the approach he wanted to take for this meeting.

One of the most important realizations Mr. Grey had made about trying to get a company to agree to their cyber-security services was to understand that for many the information would be overwhelming. They might find the reality of the cyber world to be so disturbing that they didn't want to know much more about the subject.

And yet, for a company to fully understand the services Norse could provide, it was critical to explain their work in some detail.

Mr. Grey had learned through painful experience, that people didn't respond well to being told how vulnerable they were to being hacked. For example, in theory it seemed brilliant for Eric to set up his technology so that when a potential client walked into the office the personal information on his cellphone would be immediately hacked, and part of the presentation would include showing the client his own information which Norse had just grabbed.

However, that made people uneasy and less likely to hire them.

What people responded to much more positively was understanding how Norse caught the bad guys, or as they talked about privately among themselves, "identifying the bad actors who were trying to stay hidden."

That was Norse's mission: Bringing the bad guys into the light.

Potential clients often found Norse's "honeypot" strategy to catch the bad actors to be fascinating and wanted to know more. In traditional spy craft, a "honeypot" was a woman (but sometimes a man) who could sexually compromise a target into revealing secrets. Sometimes the women didn't even need to have sex with the target, merely raise that as a possibility. The man would go into braggart mode about how important he was and all the things he knew, never knowing the woman's interest wasn't in him, but in the secrets he held. At other times, it was only after having sex with a woman, that the man would let his guard down and reveal his secrets to his new intimate partner.

Norse's honeypots were a little different.

They would set up what looked to be tempting digital targets to hackers, maybe an ATM machine, or the cooling system of a nuclear plant, the hackers would attempt to penetrate them, then Norse would record and catalog the code the hackers used. These honeypots were stationed in more than seventy-five different countries around the world, often in coordination with Norse's clients, who tended to be large corporations or even countries. Norse could genuinely claim to have data not even in possession of our own intelligence agencies.

Mr. Grey often compares hackers to musicians.

Talent matters.

There are some musicians who have a single hit song, then are never heard from again. Some hackers might pull off a single impressive theft, but never do anything else of note.

Then there are the superstars.

The ones who can adapt to changing environments and score big successes over a period of several years, sometimes even switching genres. But even with the superstars there was a problem, one which made the game of being a hacker a losing proposition.

Eventually you start to repeat yourself, like an older musician whose new songs sounded suspiciously like his older ones from decades earlier. The codes one used could be identified like a fingerprint. It was inevitable that you would start to repeat yourself by using a similar piece of code.

And with Norse having an extensive database of codes used by hackers of their honeypots, as well as from other sources, added to the fact they had the most advanced artificial intelligence systems available commercially, which could do a lot of the searching for the bad guys, the odds are you would eventually be caught.

Mr. Grey recalls about five executives showing up for the meeting, not the top executives, but the guys making movies and those who were reporting to the top executives.

The meeting lasted about forty minutes, with Mickey making the introductions, Mr. Grey giving the general presentation, and Eric providing the technical details. Mr. Grey felt the executives were hedging their bets, not really understanding the cyber-world, but also realizing their boss, Amy Pascal, had instructed them to take the meeting.

The meeting reached its awkward end, with the Norse team having made their pitch and the executives not having any relevant questions.

As they stared at each other across the conference room table, one of the executives had a question. "Hey, do you guys know anything about North Korea?"

CHAPTER TWO
THE INTERVIEW

I have a confession.

The Interview is one of my all-time favorite comedies and Seth Rogen is one of my favorite comedic actors. I have a weak spot for oddballs, and the movie, as well as Seth Rogen's performance, certainly qualify.

I understand it's not a classic, but for some reason its combination of skewering Hollywood, international relations, and the CIA, hit something of a sweet spot for me.

An example of the negative reviews is the one which appeared in the *Montreal Gazette*, which claimed it was "Animal House Meets Rambo."[26] (That's a criticism? Sounds like an endorsement to me!)

> OK, it ain't Charlie Chaplin's *The Great Dictator*. Or Stanley Kubrick's *Dr. Strangelove*. Nor will James Franco or Seth Rogen ever be uttered about in the same breath as Chaplin's Little Tramp or Peter Sellers, the larger-than-life stars of the latter two political satire classics ...

> ... There are giggles – admittedly of the kindergarten variety – to be had, particularly as Skylark [James Franco] quizzes Kim Jong-Un on his fondness for Katy Perry and his disdain of margaritas. It seems his daddy not so dearest once mocked his offspring for being unmasculine for slurping on the cocktail. And there are more giggles – of the aforementioned variety – to be had as Rapoport

[Seth Rogen] must stash weaponry in an orifice not accustomed to handling that sort of load ...

... It is unduly silly at times, unduly gross and grisly at other times. Yet it will find its audience, particularly after one of the grandest marketing campaigns ever taken.[27]

You might call that review damning, but with some embedded praise. It was clear to me that star, co-writer and producer, Seth Rogen, was trying to make something a little different than his previous gross-out comedies. I had a good time with it, even considering the rampant partying, drug use and reliance on butt jokes as a dramatic turning point.

However, the film did get some positive reviews, such as this one from the *Independent* in England which proclaimed in its headline "*The Interview* Film Review: Controversial Gross-out Satire is Broad, Bawdy and Bad – But Undeniably Entertaining."[28]

It's a new festive tradition: by the twinkling lights of the Christmas tree, my in-laws and I gathered around a laptop to watch Seth Rogen push a large, uncomfortable object into his own anus. *The Interview,* the gross-out satire that has united Americans in support of free speech and against North Korea, is broad, bawdy and bad – but also consistently entertaining.[29]

The review discussed the film's troubled cyber-hacking history, with the initial planned Christmas release shelved, then after an outcry, a smaller release in three hundred theaters, along with an online release of the film. The "Guardians of Peace" had threatened violence at the theaters, but U.S. intelligence officials determined that the threats were non-credible. As to the merits of the film, the review had this:

Throughout, Rogen and company walk the tightrope between homoeroticism and homophobia. At least half of the film's physical comedy involves things entering or exiting characters' "buttholes", while the plot is complicated by a bromantic love triangle that develops between the heroes and Kim, who briefly convinces the credulous Skylark that he's not a monster, just misunderstood.

As the chat show host and the tyrant bond over basketball and Stalin-era military hardware, Kim admits that he likes margaritas and the music of Katy Perry, even though his father always told him they were "gay." Meanwhile, Aaron has his way with Sook (Diana Bang), a comely North Korea propaganda minister. Rogen and Franco's interplay is familiar and intermittently funny, but the film's stand out comic performance comes from Randall Park as the brattish, sensitive, scheming Kim.[30]

Randall Park did do an excellent job as the North Korean dictator, and I think it's the main reason the film works as well as it does.

The best films work on different levels, making you initially believe they're about one thing, then blowing your mind by being about something completely unexpected. Francis Ford Coppola's *The Godfather* appears to be a film about the mafia, but it's really about American capitalism, and how the government and big business operate according to their own set of rules. In a related vein, Quentin Tarantino's film, *Pulp Fiction,* appears to be a low-rent lurid crime drama, when in fact it's a profoundly moral tale, showing that believing there's a meaning to life is the way to salvation, while being an atheist leads to misery.

Similarly, the most effective propaganda works because you believe it's not propaganda.

Is *The Interview,* just a stupid, gross-out comedy?

Or is it a cleverly designed story, made to entertain you, while at the same making you not care to look too closely if a certain Asian leader ended up dead?

For those who haven't seen the film, let me give you a brief summary.

The film opens on an image of a beautiful young North Korean girl. She begins to sing in Korean. We don't know what she's saying until the subtitles appear.

> *Our beloved leader is wise. He is gentle, kind, and strong. We wish him joy. We wish him peace. We wish him love.*

> *And the one thing in our time we wish more than this ... Is for the United States to explode in a ball of fiery hell. May they be forced to starve and beg and be ravaged by disease. May they be helpless, poor, and sad, and cold. They are arrogant and fat! They are stupid and evil! May they drown in their own blood and feces!*

> *Die America, die! Oh, please, won't you die? It would fill my heart with joy! May your women be raped by beasts of the jungle while your children are forced to watch.[31]*

The camera pulls back as she sings, and it's a rally for Kim Jong-un. When she finishes, the camera pulls back even farther. About fifty yards behind her an enormous intercontinental ballistic missile (ICBM) rises on a pillar of fire and smoke as it races into the sky.

The film cuts to multiple international broadcasters announcing that Kim Jong-un now has a missile capable of reaching the West Coast of the United States and describing him as a modern-day Hitler.

James Franco appears as talk show host Dave Skylark on his show *Skylark Tonight*. Behind the scenes we see his producer, Seth Rogen as Aaron Rapoport, running an episode where the notoriously homophobic rapper, Eminem, comes out as being gay.

At the party to celebrate the show's 1,000th episode, Aaron runs into an old friend of his from the Columbia School of Journalism, who's working as a Senior Producer for *60 Minutes*. Aaron makes the mistake of telling the old friend that they both have the same job, because he's the Senior Producer for *Skylark Tonight*.

The old friend tells Aaron their two jobs are nothing alike. At *60 Minutes,* he's doing something that matters, not like at *Skylark Tonight* where the big issue is "Who has new boobs or a funny eating disorder."

Aaron feels as if he's wasting his life and complains to Dave. The next day Dave rushes into the office and shows Aaron an article which notes that while the North Korean dictator hates the West, he's a huge fan of *The Big Bang Theory* and *Skylark Tonight*.

Aaron tries to contact North Korea.

Later that night, Aaron gets a call from a woman identifying herself as a representative of North Korea, giving him the coordinates of a remote location in southern China, where they'll meet to discuss terms. Aaron travels to China, hikes into the mountains, and at the appointed time, a large North Korean helicopter approaches and lands.

Two North Korean soldiers jump out with weapons drawn, telling him to lay on the ground. He does, and out steps the sexy Minister of Propaganda, Park Sook-Yin. She says they'll have one hour with Kim Jong-un, the list of questions will be generated by the North Koreans, and Aaron has twenty-four hours to accept.

Aaron rushes back to California to share the good news with Dave.

The two party like crazy that night, ending up hungover in Dave's place.

A knock at the door is answered by Aaron who finds two CIA agents on the doorstep. There's Agent Lacey, a beautiful, voluptuous brunette woman with librarian glasses, and Agent Bostwick, a handsome black man.

Agent Lacey explains the CIA wants the pair to assassinate Kim Jong-un because of his nuclear program.

Aaron whispers to Dave he's being "honey-potted" by Agent Lacey, because she's just the kind of woman he likes, smart, sexy, big tits, and looks like a librarian.

Dave tells Aaron that's sexist, because he might as well say Agent Bostwick is there to "honey-dick" him.

Next, they're at CIA Headquarters in Langley, Virginia, receiving instructions from Agent Lacey, who's no longer wearing glasses. When asked, she explains she just had Lasik surgery. Aaron gives Dave a look to say, "They're being used." The plan is to poison Kim Jong-un through use of a poison ricin patch which will be on Dave's hand when goes to shake hands with the North Korean leader. It will kill the person it touches in twelve hours.

Dave hates the plan. He wants to have a gun and blow the North Korean leader away on world-wide television.

Agent Lacey asks how he expects to survive when the guards shoot him.

"Bullet-proof vest," he says defiantly.

Lacey tells him they can't smuggle in a bullet-proof vest, and even if they could, what would happen next?

Dave says one of the North Koreans the CIA is working with will lead them to a secret tunnel which goes to the coast where they'll be rescued by Seal Team Six with an inflatable Zodiac boat which will take them across the Sea of Japan to safety.

Lacey tells Dave North Korea is very dangerous, and there are even Siberian tigers in the woods. She also warns him that Kim is a "master manipulator."

At the airport in North Korea, they're met by a welcoming group led by the sexy Propaganda Minister, Sook, with whom Aaron falls in love.

On the drive, Sook intends to set the record straight about North Korea, claiming everybody is well-fed, and the grocery stores are full of food. The car passes a local grocery store, which appears to be stocked with food, and a fat young boy standing outside.

Aaron asks Sook about crazier stories he's heard, such as Kim does not pee or poo.

Sook replies this is true, since the North Korean leader burns energy so efficiently he does not have need of these things and as a result, has "no butthole."

When they arrive at the residence, their bags are inspected by Kim's two most loyal bodyguards, who have protected him since he was a child. Dave has secreted the ricin strip in a pack of chewing gum, which one of the guards removes. Dave tells him it's a different kind of chewing gum, and the guard pops it in his mouth and swallows it.

When Dave and Aaron are shown to their rooms, they quickly call Agent Lacey on their secret communicators and tell her the problem. The CIA quickly whips up a new batch of two ricin patches (in case something happens to one), puts it into a drone and sends it into the air above North Korea.

While Aaron is waiting for the drone to deliver its package, the heat signature of what looks like a large dog approaches Aaron.

It's not a dog, but a Siberian Tiger.

Aaron starts to run, but the drone package projectile just happens to hit the tiger precisely in the neck and kills it.

North Korean guards approach Aaron, he doesn't know what to do with the drone projectile, then Agent Lacey tells him he needs to stick it up his butt.

Aaron is captured by the North Korean guards who bring him back to his room, but they do not find the drone projectile.

As Dave and Aaron are discussing the ricin, there's a knock at the door.

The voice at the door says it's Kim Jong-un.

Dave opens to door to find the North Korean dictator standing in front of him like a star-struck fan. "Hold it together," Kim whispers to himself because he's so excited to meet Dave. Kim invites Dave for breakfast in the morning and a tour of his residence.

The next morning Kim takes Dave on a tour of his residence, showing off his collection of expensive cars. The dictator seems to share the fashion sense of a rich Hollywood executive. Dave is attracted to a tank that Kim says was given to his father by Stalin.

Sitting in the tank, Kim asks Dave if he thinks liking margaritas makes you gay.

Dave asks if that was something Kim's father had told him.

Kim says his father was worried that growing up in wealth would turn him into a homosexual.

Dave responds by telling Kim how little approval he received from his own father.

Dave accidentally hits a button in the tank and "Fireworks" by Katy Perry begins playing over the speakers. At first, Kim blames the song on his wife, then admits it's his favorite song as he and Dave sing the lyrics.

Dave asks if they can take the tank out and Kim agrees, even firing one of the shells into a stand of trees.

Back at the residence, Aaron and Sook are working out the final details of the interview and going over the questions Dave will be allowed to ask.

Dave and Kim play basketball, talk about how the media are mean to both of them.

Eventually, Dave makes his way back to Aaron where he declares maybe they're wrong about Kim. Aaron tells Dave he's crazy, because Kim is a murderer, has concentration camps, and is developing nuclear weapons.

Their argument is cut short by an invitation to a dinner banquet for Kim. Dave sits with Kim as they watch a group of young children play guitars, while Aaron sits with Sook.

Aaron watches in horror as the guard who ate the ricin patch starts to go into convulsions. The other guard tries to help, but in the panic the dying guard grabs his gun and it accidentally fires killing the other guard.

Kim has lost the two beloved guards who have protected him for his entire life.

Outside on a bench Aaron tells Dave he's not going to assassinate Kim.

But Aaron is still committed to the plan, putting the ricin patch on his hand.

Back at their residence a guard knocks on the door and says that Kim wants to spend time with Dave.

Kim is clearly in a dark mood as he drinks with Dave and his officers, lamenting the death of his guards. He starts talking about loyalty, claiming his officers are not loyal to him, thinking he doesn't have the leadership skills of his father or grandfather, and that "If a billion people need to die to prove his worthiness as a Kim, then so be it."

An officer leans over to Kim and whispers "The American idiot is here," at which point Kim tries to lighten the mood by saying he should go for a walk.

Back in the room, Dave and Sook are sharing confidences. Both talk about how difficult it is to leave strong, charismatic individuals.

They start kissing, but Aaron realizes he's still got the ricin path on his hand and if he touches Sook with it, she'll die in twelve hours. He comically tries to make out with her without using his hands.

The next scene is of Dave walking through what looks like a small town and sees the supposedly grocery store he passed on the drive in. He goes into the store and sees that all the food is fake.

Back at the residence, Aaron is about to have sex with Sook, when she stops him. She says she's a terrible person because she lied to him about potato yields. Dave bursts into the room talking about how Kim needs to be killed, then sees that Sook is in the room and says she needs to be killed.

Aaron tells Dave that Sook is on their side. Sook hears the plan, then says something along the lines of "The CIA always does it wrong by thinking they just need to kill somebody. Somebody just as bad will take their place. His people think he's a god. You need to show them that he's not."

The three of them discuss their plans.

Aaron preps Dave for his interview, reminding him that two hundred thousand people languish in North Korean concentration camps, sixteen million people are malnourished, and of the $800 million given in the previous year by the United Nations, Kim spent

$600 million of it on nuclear weapons, leaving only $200 million for food.

The two men dress for the interview. Kim straps a small revolver to his ankle, which he conceals under his pant leg. In the interview room, the two men take their seats, then Kim reaches down into a box and hands Dave a puppy.

Dave goes all gooey, kissing the puppy and telling Kim he's the nicest person in the world.

Dave begins the interview, reading the dictator's own questions, highlighting the unfairness of America's actions toward his country. Aaron and Sook are in the control room, saying it looks as if the puppy ploy worked.

But after a few minutes, Aaron sees something in Dave's eye, knowing the pivot is coming. After reiterating the dictator's words that the North Korean people have suffered under American actions, Dave asks Kim why he doesn't feed his people.

Kim is clearly shocked.

Dave continues the attack, talking about the UN money going to nuclear weapons and the two hundred thousand people in concentration camps.

Kim responds that North Korea has fewer people incarcerated per capita than the United States, and that if it weren't for the American sanctions, his people would be well-fed.

Now it's Dave's time to falter. He wasn't expecting this type of defiant response.

Kim accuses Dave of being a typical American stooge, and a joke to everybody in professional journalism.

Dave decides it's time to fight back and get personal.

Dave begins by accepting some of Kim's criticisms, nothing that his feelings of low self-esteem probably emanate from the fact that his father was a demanding man who was never proud of him. Then Dave asks if Kim has ever felt the same.

Kim is on the verge of tears, then Dave starts singing Katy Perry's "Firework", about self-empowerment. At first, Kim claims not to recognize the song, but eventually can't help but sing along as he cries copious tears.

The dictator descends into a nasty crying jag, and just as he's about to pull himself together, lets loose with an enormous fart.

"He has a butthole!" exclaims a cameraman.

We see the reaction of various North Koreans gathered around their televisions, noting that he's not a god, just a man.

A man with a butthole.

Kim stands, pulls out his concealed handgun, shoots Dave in the chest in front of the entire world, and walks out.

Aaron back at the control room is going crazy, as Sook is trying to fight off North Korean soldiers who are trying to break in.

Back in the studio, Dave moves in his chair. He stands and reveals he was wearing a bulletproof vest. Aaron rushes in and asks how in the hell he got that into the country.

They start to leave, but then Dave says he has to go back and get the puppy.

Kim's men tell him that Dave is alive.

Kim is furious, saying "I was trying to honey-dick him, but he honey-dicked me!"

The dictator gives the order to arm the nukes and fire them at the West Coast of the United States.

As Dave, Aaron, Sook, and the puppy escape, they're pursued by North Korean soldiers in jeeps with machine guns. Dave leaves them and comes back with Kim's tank, telling them to get in. They drive the tank to the nuclear missile silos, which are getting ready for launch, running over a few North Korean jeeps in the process.

Kim appears in his helicopter, telling his soldiers to fire machine guns and missiles at the tank. The nuclear warheads are ready for launch, just awaiting Kim's order.

Dave drives the tank, avoiding missiles and machine gun fire, then Sook lines up the tank and fires a shell at Kim's helicopter.

Everything moves in slow motion as Katy Perry's "Firework" plays and the shell flies into Kim's helicopter, which erupts into flame, and the dictator himself is enveloped in fire.

Almost as if Kim himself is...a firework.

They eventually abandon the tank and Sook leads them to a tunnel, which will take them to the coast. Sook won't go with them, because North Korea needs her.

Dave, Aaron and the puppy reach the end of the tunnel when what looks like a squad of North Korean soldiers captures them. However, they quickly reveal themselves to be Seal Team Six, dressed in local uniforms.

They lead Dave, Aaron and the puppy to the waiting Zodiac boat, and are soon traveling at high speed on the Sea of Japan to safety.

Aaron is reflective, saying, "Sook honey-potted me. I see that now. She learned all about me, how I would react, my plans, and how she could shape them to her plans."

In the next scene, Dave is reading from his tell-all book, Agent Lacey is in the audience, looking like she might eventually fall for him. There's a quick scene of Aaron having a friendly Skype call with Sook, who has just been elected the first democratic ruler of North Korea.

The final scene shows Dave finishing his reading and saying of the changes in North Korea, "This was a revolution ignited with nothing more than a camera and some questions."

You can understand how a writer dedicated to discovering truth might have a soft spot for such a story, right? A camera and some questions being able to topple a dictatorship?

Every writer wants to believe the questions they pose are as powerful as any weapon. The pen is mightier than the sword, and all those cherished ideals we have about the search for truth.

But had I been honey-potted, or honey-dicked?

Was I cheering for a comedy about the assassination of a foreign leader?

Was I believing the CIA was run by a bunch of genuine patriots, solely interested in making the world safe for democracy?

It raised some uncomfortable questions for me.

Was *The Interview* simply a comedy about defending freedom, along with a satire of Hollywood and the CIA? Or might it be as some have claimed "predictive programming" meant to soften the public up to the idea of assassinating the North Korean leader?

The movie was all about people having hidden agendas.

The Interview also hinted of a close connection between the intelligence agencies and Hollywood. Were they occasional allies? Hollywood loves its broad-shouldered, square-chinned spies, like James Bond and Jack Ryan.

Did the spooks love Tinsel Town right back?

Were they "in a relationship?"

I'm not certain we'll ever know the answer to these questions, but like Alice in Wonderland, down the rabbit hole we must go.

CHAPTER THREE
NORTH KOREA, THE SONY
EXECUTIVES, & JAMES CLAPPER

Most people don't realize that the Korean War, which began on June 25, 1950, when North Korean troops invaded South Korea, has never ended.

It's true that an armistice agreement was signed on July 27, 1953, between North Korea, China, and the United States-led UN effort, effectively ending combat between the two sides.[32]

I know you're thinking I made a mistake in that last paragraph. South Korea.

Surely, South Korea must have signed the Armistice?

Nope.

An article from the BBC in March of 2015, recounted the history of what had happened in the ensuing six decades since the end of hostilities.

Decades on, the truce is still all that technically prevents North Korea and the US – along with its ally South Korea – resuming the war, as no peace treaty has ever been signed.

Both sides regularly accuse the other of violating the agreement, but the accusations have become more frequent as tensions rise over North Korea's nuclear program.

When the armistice was signed on 27 July 1953, talks had already dragged on for two years, ensnared in testy issues such as the exchange of prisoners of war and the location of a demarcation line.

Military commanders from China and North Korea signed the agreement on one side, with the US-led United Nations Command signing on behalf of the international community. South Korea was not a signatory.[33]

Even an effort in March of 2021 by the President of South Korea, Moon Bae-In to get his country to sign the then 67-year-old armistice would eventually end up as a failure, as predicted by Donald Kirk in an opinion piece in *The Hill*.

It's easy, of course, for advocates and foes of a treaty to argue that the Korean War is not over. Opposing armies face each other on either side of the demilitarized zone established by the truce, the North-South line remains closed to normal commercial traffic, and North Korea threatens foes far and near with nuclear weaponry.

Moon and his ministers and advisers are imploring all sides in the Korean War to sign this piece of paper. North Korea is not going to go along with any such agreement, however, unless the U.S. renounces sanctions imposed as a result of its nuclear and missile tests, and the North is also going to insist on an end to joint military exercises staged by U.S. and South Korean troops...

...In short, there is absolutely no point in an end-of-war agreement that provides no guarantees of anything while stripping South Korea of essential defenses. Ultimately, North Korea would want a "peace treaty" that calls for dissolution of the United Nations Command and with-drawal of U.S. troops from South Korea.[34]

Let's consider the main points of this opinion piece. It admits that sixty-seven years after the end of significant combat operations the Korean peninsula remains deeply troubled and divided. President Moon seems to have believed it would be seen as a positive step for his country to sign the armistice, acknowledging the end of the war.

But even this small step towards reconciliation would be doomed to failure.

Who benefits from continued tension in Korea?

The article actually provides a helpful list.

First, the "joint military exercises staged by U.S. and South Korean troops." As if we wouldn't worry about joint Russian/Mexican military exercises held just over the border from El Paso, Texas. Regardless of the country, potentially hostile forces on your border are not something any government wants.

Second, the "United Nations Command." (More on this later.)

Third, North Korea would eventually want all U.S. troops to leave. Is this such an unreasonable request? Let's look at a comparison of the relative strengths of North Korea and South Korea, as detailed in a 2013 article in *The Guardian*.[35]

The population of North Korea was estimated at 24.72 million, while South Korea was about double in size with 48.96 million.[36]

Life expectancy in North Korea was 69.2 years, while in South Korea it was 79.3 years.[37] In addition to ten more years of life, chances are you'll be taller if you live in South Korea because of better nutrition.

The GDP per capita in North Korea was $1,800 per year, while in South Korea it was $32,400.[38] The average South Korean makes more than sixteen times what the average North Korean does in a year.

The 2012 Corruption Index for North Korea was 174 [out of 195 countries], while South Korea was 45th in corruption.[39] I'm not sure, but I think coming in at 45th in the world for corruption is not an accomplishment.

The 2013 Press Freedom Index listed North Korea at 178, with South Korea coming in at 50.[40] Do any of the advertisements for companies to do business in South Korea proclaim, "There are forty-nine other countries in the world that have more freedom of the press than we do! Locate your business in South Korea and don't worry about reporters!"

North Korea had $4.71 billion in exports in 2013, while South Korea had $552.6 billion in exports.[41] This is more than a hundred-fold difference between the two countries.

North Korea has 1,190,000 people in its army, while South Korea has 655,000.[42]

North Korea has an estimated 4,836,567 military age males, while South Korea has an estimated 10,864,566 military age males.[43] Again, South Korea seems to have a two to one advantage over North Korea.

In 2013, North Korea spent an estimated $8.21 billion dollars on its military, while South Korea spent an estimated $26.1 billion dollars.[44] South Korea's military is spending three times as much money annually as North Korea.

And that doesn't even count the generous United States military spending in the country of a couple billion dollars a year.

In South Korea, the U.S. military obligated $13.4 billion between 2016 and 2019. The army provided the lion's share of military spending there, accounting for $9.2 billion in obligations, largely at Camp Humphreys, with the Air Force's $3.9 billion to support Osan and Kunsan air bases coming in second…

…And South Korea's contributions fluctuated from $1.2 billion in 2016 to $1.7 billion the next year, before dropping to $1.3 billion in 2018 and then hitting $1.5 billion in 2019.[45]

This is the deal the United States made with South Korea, the country that's 45th for corruption in the world and 50th for press freedom: For four years the U.S. gave South Korea $13.4 billion dollars in military protection ($3.35 billion per year), and in return, South Korea give the U.S. $5.7 billion dollars ($1.425 billion per year).

How's that for a deal?

Were we genuinely handing South Korea about $2 billion dollars a year with no strings attached?

Or was there another agenda at work?

An agenda to keep the Korean conflict on a slow boil, thus requiring the United States military to remain in Asia?

Let's talk about the "United Nations Command."

It's often an underappreciated fact in the West to know that Japan controlled Korea from 1910 to the end of World War II in 1945. This was not a friendly arrangement.

In fact, it was one of the most brutal occupations in history. This is an account of the Japanese occupation of Korea which hints at some of the barbarity.

Schools and universities forbade speaking Korean and emphasized manual labor and loyalty to the Emperor. Public places adopted Japanese, too, and an edict to make films in Japanese soon followed. It became a crime to teach history from non-approved texts and authorities burned over 20,000 Korean historical documents, essentially wiping out the historical memory of Korea.

During the occupation, Japan took over Korea's labor and land. Nearly 100,000 Japanese families settled in Korea with land they had been given; they chopped down trees by the millions and planted non-native species, transforming a familiar landscape into something many Koreans didn't recognize.

Nearly 725,000 Korean workers were made to work in Japan and its other colonies, and as World War II bloomed, Japan forced hundreds of thousands of Korean women into life as "comfort women" – sexual slaves who served in military brothels.[46]

Japan sought to erase Korea's history, culture, and language, as well as enslaving its citizens into manual labor or sexual bondage.

In the wake of this history of occupation, and the damage wrought by the Korean War, what would be the worst possible location for this newly created United Nations Security Council for the Demilitarized Zone in Korea?

Tokyo, Japan.

Here's some of that history.

After the Korean War broke out on June 25, 1950, the UN Security Council adopted Resolution 84 (S/1588) on July 7, about two weeks after the start of hostilities. This resolution assigned the name of "unified command" to the unit commanding armed forces deployed from 21 countries to aid South Korea, with the U.S. government appointing its commander and permission granted to use the UN flag alongside the flags of the participating countries.

The "Unified Command" was formed in Tokyo on July 24, 1950, taking the name "United Nations Command" (UNC), and being led by General Douglas MacArthur, the famed World War II general.

Today, the United Nations Command, under the authority of the United Nations Security Council has seven battalions in Tokyo, where they work alongside the Japan Self-Defense Forces (JSDF). Can you understand why the North Koreans might be a little suspicious that the United Nations chooses to locate its troops so close to those of the hated Japanese?

Did you ever question why North Korea likes to fire their missiles over Tokyo?

It's probably because the United Nations Command for the Demilitarized Zone in Korea is in the same city once occupied by their colonial oppressors.

As the only signatory who can claim to represent the South Korean side to the Armistice Agreement of July 27, 1953, the United Nations Command has sole responsibility for managing the agreement, preventing military clashes, and spearheading any possible peace agreement.

Because Japan's constitution prevents it from having an army larger than that strictly necessary for defense, it has been hobbled in its attempt to become a permanent member of the United Nations Security Council. The argument in favor of this move was the subject of a 2007 article in the winter 2007 issue of the *Journal of International Affairs*.

> For over three decades Japan has consistently pursued its goal of winning a permanent seat at the United Nations Security Council (UNSC). Unfortunately, it has not been successful in achieving its long-standing ambition due to a number of domestic and international hurdles. This article examines why Japan deserves a UNSC permanent seat and whether its membership, in a manner commensurate with its world status as an evolving catalytic "soft power" and a major contributor to the United Nations, would make a meaningful difference for the renovated universal body in the years ahead.[47]

Japan's interest in obtaining a permanent seat on the United Nations Security Council means one thing, pleasing the United States. This will take the form of supporting the United States in its Middle Eastern and Afghan wars, as well as going on the attack against North Korea, as shown by this December 15, 2017 press conference by Mr. Taro Kono, then Japanese Minister for Foreign Affairs.

> This morning I presided over the Security Council Ministerial-Level Meeting on the North Korean issue. With the participation of foreign ministers, state ministers, vice ministers of many Council Members, we sent a clear message that we will

never accept a nuclear armed North Korea and missile development in flagrant violation of Security Council resolutions will never be tolerated. We also sent a unified message that it is essential for every UN Member State to fully implement all the relevant Security Council resolutions.

Many members also expressed their grave concerns over human rights violations in North Korea. Some members referred to other threats posed by North Korea such as the development and proliferation of chemical weapons and cyber-attacks.[48]

As a result of these actions and others in support of the Western Alliance, in June of 2022, Japan secured a record 12th nonpermanent seat on the U.N. Security council, and as of January 2023, serves as President of the Security Council.[49]

As part of its global strategy to redeem itself for atrocities committed prior to and during World War II, being tough on North Korea has worked out very well for Japan.

What type of military activity was going on in the Demilitarized Zone (DMZ) between the two Koreas in 2014?

This is what has been acknowledged publicly.

On February 26, 2014, South Korean defense officials claimed that despite warnings, a North Korean warship repeatedly crossed into South Korean waters during the previous night.

On March 24, 2014, a North Korean drone was found crashed near Paju. The recovered camera contained pictures of the Blue House and other military installations near the DMZ.

On March 31, 2014, another crashed North Korean drone was found in Baengnyeongdo.

On October 10, 2014, protestors from South Korea released ten large propaganda balloons from the border city of Paju which were intended to land in North Korea. The balloons contained 200,000 leaflets, $1000 US dollars, 400 DVDs, and 300 books depicting the better life North Koreans could expect if they defected to South Korea. North Korea responded by firing anti-aircraft rounds at the balloons. The South Koreans gave a pre-warning to the North Koreans, who then fired a barrage of 40 bullets into the air.

On October 19, 2014, a group of North Korean soldiers approached the South Korean border. The South Korean soldiers fired warning shots at the North Korean soldiers. The North Korean soldiers returned fire (presumably also warning shots as nobody is injured) and retreated to the north.

Does all of this seem like Kabuki theater to you, as if both sides were acting out a tired old script that neither believed anymore?

Let's move from Korea to Hollywood and meet some of the key players.

Let's start with Michael Lynton, the chairman and chief executive of Sony Pictures Entertainment from April 2012 until February of 2017, where in addition to dealing with the Sony hack, oversaw Sony's global entertainment business, including Sony Music Entertainment, Sony/ATV Music Publishing and Sony Pictures Entertainment.

When he left Sony in 2017, Variety named him one of the 500 most important people in the business and published a glowing profile of him, noting his acquisition of the Michael Jackson archive of music as one of his greatest successes, and the Sony hack as one of his greatest challenges.

> After 13 years in the top job at Sony Pictures Entertainment, Lynton will spend a six-month-period as co-CEO before assuming the chairmanship full time at Snap, Inc. [makers of the Snap-Chat app], where he was already serving on the board. It will mark the end of a reign that grew turbulent

in the latter years, where he saw Sony through a devastating hack that would test to mettle of even the sturdiest corporate chieftain.[50]

We see Lynton striding confidently from Hollywood into Big Tech, where he took over as the CEO of Snap, Inc, the makers of the popular Snap-Chat application, which allows people to communicate as privately or publicly as they want, then have those communications vanish. (Some have questioned whether the posts are actually deleted, or saved into another system, but we'll leave that discussion to others.) The glowing article also noted that:

Earlier in his career, he worked for Time Warner [which purchased CNN], AOL, publisher Pearson and Walt Disney Co. Lynton has undergraduate degrees in history and literature from Harvard College, and an MBA from Harvard Business School.[51]

Lynton must simply live one of those charmed lives, always being in the right place at the right time and being able to walk between the raindrops in a storm. Harvard, Time Warner, AOL, Pearson, Disney, Sony, and now Snap-Chat.

Does the man ever make a wrong move?

Well, it seemed like he was in a great deal of trouble just before the hack. As recounted in a later article:

Even before the attacks, things at Sony were so bad (budget reductions and challenges from activist investor Daniel Loeb) that Lynton sought other jobs, even ones for which he was clearly unqualified. He put his name in to be the president of Tulane and New York University, even personally lobbying NYU trustees. But his lack of a Ph.D. and any experience in higher education led both schools to terminate his candidacy very early on. He also applied to run the

Smithsonian Institution but again was rejected because of his lack of experience in that sphere.[52]

Before the hack it seemed Michael Lynton was heading for the exit. But he was trapped. There was no way to easily extricate himself from the sinking ship that was Sony.

Perhaps salvation might be found in the great man's philanthropy, especially being on the Board of Directors of The Getty Museum, a member of the Board of Overseers of the Los Angeles County Museum of Art, a member of the Board of Overseers of the Rand Corporation and is also a member of the Council on Foreign Relations.[53]

What exactly is the Rand Corporation?

Chalmers Johnson, a former distinguished political science professor at the University of California, Berkeley, as well as University of California, San Diego, has referred to the Rand Corporation as "America's University of Imperialism." In an April 30, 2008 article he wrote:

The RAND Corporation of Santa Monica, California, was set up immediately after World War II by the U.S. Army Air Corps (soon to become the U.S. Air Force). The Air Force generals who had the idea were trying to perpetuate the wartime relationship that had developed between the scientific and intellectual communities and the American military, as exemplified by the Manhattan Project to develop and build the atomic bomb.

Soon enough, however, RAND became a key institutional building block of the Cold War American empire. As the premier think tank for the U.S.'s role as hegemon of the Western world, RAND was instrumental in giving that empire the militaristic cast it retains to this day and in hugely enlarging official demands for atomic bombs, nuclear submarines, intercontinental ballistic missiles, and long-range bombers. Without RAND, our military-industrial complex, as well as our democracy, would look much different.[54]

Why would an executive whose biggest successes lay in achievements like acquiring Michael Jackson's music and making Spiderman films, get asked to join the Board of Overseers of the RAND Corporation?

Surely, rock and roll music and superhero movies are a world away from atomic bombs and intercontinental ballistic missiles?

Or are they all projections of American power and influence?

I want to give you a perspective an insider gave me about the links between intelligence agencies and American businesses. This insider said that whenever an American company reaches a certain level of size and influence, they WILL be contacted by somebody in the intelligence agencies.

What shape will this relationship take?

It depends on the business and the needs of the intelligence agency at that time.

This insider said it's most accurate to compare the intelligence agencies to some twenty-two-year-old blonde bombshell, looking for a sugar daddy, always promising more than is actually delivered. In other words, they're looking for a lot of free stuff, but instead of drinks, fancy dinners, or exotic vacations, they want access to information, or for the corporation to hand over free samples of its products for use by the agency.

Put yourself in the shoes of a corporate executive, whose company just crossed fifty million dollars in annual sales.

Your secretary says there's a man from the government who wants to speak to you, but won't provide much more information. You take the meeting; he flashes a card from one of our country's eighteen different acknowledged intelligence agencies and says there's an important matter he needs to "discuss" with you.

Throughout the talk the agent is friendly, maybe he lets drop a few facts he knows about you, or even lets you ask him a question about "spy stuff" you always wanted to know, and to your surprise, he even answers it.

You feel you've crossed over the line and you're one of the important people "in the know."

Your mind is a storm of conflicting thoughts.

The first is the possible threat to your company: "If I turn this guy down, how might he hurt this organization I've spent years building?"

The second is the possible benefit to your company: "He seems like a good guy, a real patriot. And he's let drop once or twice that if I help him, he might be able to pass along some information that might be helpful to my company or point us in directions likely to be financially successful."

The meeting ends, everything has been friendly, and as the agent walks out the door, he says he certainly hopes the two of you can work together for the benefit of the country, as well as each other.

What do you do?

I think the executive takes that deal nine times out of ten.

There's a tremendous potential upside if you agree, and no downside. In case of any problems at your company, you feel like you've got an ace in the hole, an intelligence agency which owes you a favor.

How does an executive not take that deal?

It is an irresistible honeypot.

Let's discuss Michael Lynton's membership in the Council on Foreign Relations (CFR). This is the CFR's own description of itself from their webpage:

> The Council on Foreign Relations (CFR) is an independent, nonpartisan membership organization, think tank, and publisher dedicated to being a resource for its members, government officials, business executives, journalists, educators and students, civic and religious leaders, and other interested citizens in order to help them better understand the world and the foreign policy choices facing the United States and other countries. Founded in 1921, CFR takes no institutional positions on matters of policy.[55]

Maybe every word of that description is true.

Maybe it's not.

Let's go to the Frequently Asked Questions section of their website for further helpful information:

How is CFR managed? Who is in charge?

> CFR is incorporated under New York State law. Its Board of Directors provides overall direction, and Richard N. Haass, CFR's president and a former senior government official, leads daily operations. David M. Rubenstein, co-founder and co-chief executive officer of the Carlyle Group, is the chairman. Blair Effron, cofounder of Centerview Partners, and Jami Miscik, chief executive officer and vice chairman of Kissinger Associates, are vice chairman.[56]

Haass was not just any former senior government official. From 1989 to 1993 he was special assistant to President George H.W. Bush and senior director for Near East and South Asian affairs on the staff of the National Security Council.[57] (Author's note – In order to serve on the National Security Council, you are read into our country's most sensitive intelligence information and sign security oaths to never reveal that information.)

In the George W. Bush administration, Haas was director of policy planning for the Department of State from January 2001 to June of 2003, as well as being a principal advisor to Secretary of State Colin Powell, (who was famously duped into believing by the intelligence agencies that Iraq possessed weapons of mass destruction) and also served as U.S. Coordinator for Policy Towards the Future of Afghanistan.[58] David M. Rubenstein and Blair Effron are clearly big money guys, but then the next name is Jami Miscik, CEO of the Kissinger group, founded by former Secretary of State under Richard Nixon, Henry Kissinger.

Henry Kissinger is known as a leading proponent of globalism and is one of the founders of the Trilateral Commission, and its most recent incarnation, the World Economic Forum under Klaus

Schwab, which meets yearly in Davos, Switzerland. In fact, the Frequently Asked Questions addresses this issue:

Is CFR Part of the U.S. Government, the United Nations, or Organizations such as the Trilateral Commission?

No. CFR is an independent, nongovernmental, nonprofit and non-partisan organization. Learn more here. The following studies explain CFR's history.[59]

The section then directs the reader to a series of books about the CFR.

Yes, you should believe the CFR is an independent organization, despite being led by a man who likely has the highest security clearances possible from the United States government from his time as a member of the National Security Council and U.S. Coordinator for policy Towards the Future of Afghanistan, some really rich Wall Street guys who benefit when American products are sold overseas, and the CEO of Henry Kissinger's lobbying group.

How dumb do they think we are?

Do you start to wonder if some of the criticisms of our adversaries about the corruption of our institutions, might contain at least a kernel of truth?

Let's spend a little time talking about Amy Pascal. This is from a timeline put together by *Variety* in 2007 as Amy was quickly becoming the most powerful woman in Hollywood:

1958 – Amy Pascal was born March 25 in Los Angeles to Tony Pascal, an economist at RAND Corp., and Barbara, a bookstore owner.

1973 – Attends Crossroads School for Arts and Sciences in Santa Monica and works as a bookkeeper at the school's library.

1976 – Graduates from Crossroads and segues to UCLA.

1980 – After graduating from UCLA with a B.A. in international relations, Pascal works as a secretary for BBC producer Tony Garnett at Kestrel Films and moves herself into a development position by hiring UCLA students to do the grunt work.[60]

Amy's father was an economist at the RAND Corporation when she was born. You might say Amy was born into the RAND family. Her attendance at the Crossroads school suggests she had an interest in the arts from an early age, but then when she went to UCLA, she studied international relations.

However, instead of going into the diplomatic corps and promoting the interests of her country abroad, she got a job in the movie business. There are some other interesting developments in Amy's personal life.

1997 – Marries Bernie Weinraub, a former political correspondent and longtime Hollywood reporter for the *New York Times* on August 9.

1999 – Women in Hollywood honors Pascal along with Meg Ryan, Anjelica Huston and Susan Sarandon.

2000 – Produces "Charlie's Angels," a film she says is about "girl empowerment."

Acknowledging that his marriage to Pascal presents a conflict of interest, Weinraub asks to be taken off the movie beat and is given the title of senior West Coast cultural correspondent, responsible for more general entertainment coverage.[61]

Choosing a spouse always involves many considerations, and although one might cite their common interest in film, the fact remains that Weinraub's initial work for the *New York Times* was as a foreign correspondent, based in Saigon, London, Belfast, Nairobi, and New Delhi. One might joke that for most Americans, Hollywood qualifies as an exotic foreign capital, although that luster has certainly dimmed over the past few years.

Besides the academic jumping around, from foreign relations in college, to film as a career, then marrying a former foreign correspondent for the *New York Times*, does Amy have any other intriguing connections?

We have her father as an analyst for the RAND Corporation at the time of her birth as well as during her childhood, as an adult she served on the Board of Directors of the RAND Corporation[62], and helped produce the documentary "Ideas in Action – 60 Years of RAND," for the company's 60th anniversary in 2007. A press release from the RAND Corporation highlighted this partnership. From the press release:

"Ideas in Action – 60 Years of RAND" was the brainchild of Amy Pascal, Sony Pictures, and several other RAND trustees underwrote the costs. Pascal helped us select the filmmaker and Sony Pictures made space and equipment available for the production.

Filmmaker Richard Robbins has done most of his work for Peter Jennings Productions and ABC News. He produced and directed "I Have a Dream," the documentary about Martin Luther King, Jr., that aired on ABC in August 2003, the 40th Anniversary of the March on Washington.

Robbins and his team filmed 59 hours of interviews with 74 individuals associated with RAND – mostly current and former employees. Obviously, he could only include a small fraction of that material in the final cut. The film is narrated by Tobey Maguire.[63]

Sony Pictures and Amy Pascal not only bent over backwards to assist this documentary for the RAND Corporation, but the project was apparently her "brainchild," as if the company was part of her family.

Not only does Sony lend equipment and space to the RAND Corporation, it gets Tobey Maguire, one of the hottest actors of the day from his role as Spiderman, to narrate the film.

The government hires RAND for many projects (the infamous "Pentagon Papers case, being just one example), and RAND works with Amy and Sony Pictures on certain projects, such as this laudatory documentary.

How much of a leap in logic is to ask the question, does the United States intelligence community work with Hollywood studios, like Sony Pictures, to further their policy objectives?

However, the person who might have been most responsible for the government's fixation on North Korea is Bruce Bennett, an analyst recommended by the RAND Corporation to Sony Pictures as *The Interview* was in production.

Who is Bruce Bennett?

He is currently an Adjunct International Defense Researcher and Professor at the Pardee RAND Graduate School, located in Santa Monica, CA.

He received a B.S. in Economics from the California Institute of Technology in 1973 and his Ph.D. in Policy Analysis from the Pardee RAND Graduate School in 1979. In his career he's been a professor at the National Defense University in Washington, D.C., a professor at the University of California, Los Angeles, and a Senior Defense Analyst for the RAND corporation. His resume for the RAND Corporation describes his research in these words:

Dr. Bennett is an Adjunct International Defense Researcher who is an expert in North Asian Military issues, having visited the region over 120 times and written much about Korean military issues (see his webpage cited above). His research addresses the North Korean military threats, understanding and shaping the ongoing Korean crises, North Korean denuclearization (especially if negotiation fails), future US and ROK military force operations and requirements, preparing for and dealing with a North Korean collapse, and/or Korean unification, the Korean military balance, and managing third party intervention in Korea. He has also worked in the Persian/Arab Gulf region.

Isn't it comforting to know that Bennett also worked on planning for the Persian Gulf region, since our two wars in that area turned out to be complete failures?

Bennett was brought into planning for *The Interview* by Sony Entertainment CEO, Michael Lynton, who as we have mentioned, served on the Board of Directors of the RAND Corporation, as well as being a close confidante of then President of the United States, Barack Obama.

Bennett's basic theme for years has been that the North Korean regime is on the verge of collapse because the country's military and technical elite have given up on Kim Jong-un and his family.

Let's look at some of RAND consultant, Bruce Bennett's advice to Sony head Michael Lynton, which he delivered in an email on July 15, 2014 (more than five months before the alleged "hack"), ratcheting up tension with North Korea:

Michael:

I thought you would want to see the article below. Radio Free Chosun is a South Korean radio station that seeks change in North Korea. The DailyNK newspaper is a pretty good source of news on North Korea.

Thanks,
Bruce.[64]

The most conservative description of this exchange is that there's a North Korean hawk (Bennett), employed by the country's most well-known defense linked company (RAND corporation), advising a studio head (Michael Lynton) on what he should do about a provocative film with the potential to affect international relations.

The title of the article is "North Korea Should Stop Helping "The Interview"" and Bennett adds "There is a lot of interest in the information and opinion that is broadcast by shortwave radio stations targeting North Korea."[65] Let's look at the opening of the opinion piece Bennett sent to Lynton in July of 2014:

North Korean ambassador to UN Ja Song Nam recently sent a letter of protest to UN Secretary General Ban Ki Moon regarding the new Hollywood comedy film, "The Interview", claiming it promotes terrorism against North Korea. The letter includes a statement from the North Korean Ministry of Foreign Affairs requesting that a formal memorandum be sent to the UN General Assembly and UN Security Council.

Calling on senior officials to get involved in this case only lays North Korea open to further ridicule. Could they possibly think that this type of behavior would improve the image of Kim Jong-un? Many films poking fun at political leaders have been made down the years, and yet none has elicited such a protest. This is of course because most of the world recognizes that film content is subject to creative license and freedom of expression.[66]

Is this the reality of the situation?

Artists of the west were commenting on an international situation in the guise of a comedy film and found themselves under threat by a foreign dictator?

It's a compelling narrative and it might be true.

But would we be so sanguine if the situation was reversed, and a foreign adversary was promoting a comedy about the assassination of an American political leader, and there was at least some evidence it was being promoted by military and intelligence interests?

In recent years Bennett has testified before Congress, suggesting that the U.S. Air Force might fly over North Korean missile bases and drop leaflets inviting the North Korean soldiers to defect. He also suggests using the South Korean rock group, K-Pop, as a cultural weapon, or perhaps DVDs smuggled into North Korea, depicting how much better life is in South Korea.

The purpose of the operation, Bennett said in a recent Congressional hearing, is to convince the North Korean people that their "paranoid" leader is not a "god," and to plant the idea in Kim's mind that his country is unstable.

Bennett believes "If that's in his mind, it will affect his behavior."

It sounds suspiciously like the plot of a certain Hollywood movie.

Has the United States had surveillance capability over North Korea's internet use since 2010?

An article from *The New York Times* in January of 2015, shortly after the Sony hack, claims that's exactly what we did.

> The trail that led American officials to blame North Korea for the destructive cyberattack on Sony Pictures Entertainment in November winds back to 2010, when the National Security Agency scrambled to break into the computer systems of a country once considered one of the most impenetrable targets on Earth.

> Spurred by growing concerns about North Korea's maturing capabilities, the American spy agency drilled into the Chinese networks that connect North Korea to the outside world, picked through connections in Malaysia favored by

North Korean hackers and penetrated directly into the North with the help of South Korea and other American allies, according to former United States and foreign officials, computer experts later briefed on the operations and a newly disclosed N.S.A document.[67]

If this is true, one would have to say, "Good job, American intelligence agencies!" But then it raises some troubling questions.

If our intelligence agencies had access to the North Korean network for four years before the Sony hack, how did we let it happen?

If this was an attack by North Korea, it had to be planned for quite some time.

As will be discussed later, the evidence provided by the U.S. government did not convince many outside cybersecurity efforts, or even the writer and co-star of the film, Seth Rogen. The *New York Times* article continued:

> A classified security agency program expanded into an ambitious effort, officials said, to place malware that could track the internal workings of many of the computers and networks used by the North's hackers, a force that South Korea's military recently said numbers roughly 6,000 people. Most are commanded by the country's main intelligence service, called the Reconnaissance General Bureau, and Bureau 121, its secretive hacking unit, with a large outpost in China.

> The evidence gathered by the "early warning radar" of software painstakingly hidden to monitor North Korea's activities proved critical in persuading President Obama to accuse the government of Kim Jong-Un of ordering the Sony attack, according to the officials and experts, who spoke on the condition of anonymity about the classified N.S.A. operation.[68]

Any fair-minded investigator would have several suspicions about the accuracy of the information in the *New York Times* article.

Does it make sense that an intelligence agency would publicly admit it placed malware on the computer network of a foreign government?

However, one might say this was an instance in which disclosure was warranted.

I agree that is a possibility, but why didn't the NSA go all the way and let us see the evidence?

The only scenario which makes sense to me is that the NSA wanted to disclose this information to the public, while at the same time appearing not to disclose it. Why are we forced to depend on "officials and experts, who spoke on the condition of anonymity about the classified operation?"

Any person who has even a passing familiarity with cyber-security knows it's relatively easy to "spoof" an account and pretend to be somebody else.

That's one of the basic operating tenets of hacking.

You attempt to hide your identity through any number of strategies, hijacking the server or account of an innocent party, then convincing the target you're a friend rather than a foe. I have a friend whose account was hacked and every few weeks I still get an email from her saying something like, "I think you'll recognize these girls."

Of course, the first time I fell for it and clicked on the link.

I had never seen those girls, especially not in those intriguing positions.

And if I had, I'm certain if I would have remembered them.

I do not click on those links anymore.

It's worth at least raising the possibility that if the NSA had access to the North Korean systems, it would be relatively easy for them (or others if they were also in the network) to stage an attack on Sony and leave a trail pointing to the North Koreans. (I don't think the evidence points in that direction of our own intelligence agencies, but in the shadowy world of espionage they must remain on the list of suspects.)

In early November of 2014, the Director of National Intelligence, James Clapper, arrived in North Korea on an unprecedented mission. As detailed by ABC News:

> When Director of National Intelligence James Clapper arrived secretly in North Korea this week he had no guarantees that he would be able to secure the release of Kenneth Bae and Matthew Todd Miller.

> In fact, all Clapper had when he arrived in Pyongyang was a brief letter of introduction from President Obama indicating he was his envoy seeking their release.

> According to senior administration officials the U.S. and North Korea had been in discussions for weeks about the possibility of a visit to the reclusive country by a high-ranking U.S. official.[69]

Sounds exciting, doesn't it? Just like your proper spy story. The breathless ABC account continued:

> Clapper cleared his schedule so he could undertake the risky trip. His cancellation of a pre-scheduled appearance at a New York think tank [author's note – the Council of Foreign Relations] drew little attention. By then, Clapper was already enroute to North Korea aboard a U.S. military aircraft.

> The officials said upon his arrival, Clapper presented the North Koreans with a brief written message from Obama indicating that Clapper was his personal envoy to bring the two Americans home.

> The officials said the short letter did not contain an apology "in any way, shape, or form."

Clapper did not meet with North Korean leader Kim Jong-un, instead his discussions were with North Korean security officials.[70]

All of this seems very unusual. Clapper goes to North Korea with basically nothing, except for the promise that President Obama would consider it helpful for the North Korean leader to release the two Americans.

And what do we know of these two Americans and why did they travel to North Korea?

Kenneth Bae had been held since November of 2012. This is how Mr. Bae's work was described in a *New York Times* article published around the release of a book he wrote in 2016 about the experience.

A naturalized American originally from South Korea, Mr. Bae was arrested in the North Korean city of Rason while leading an officially permitted tour from China, where two years earlier he had started a travel business that specialized in North Korea.

His underlying motive in that business was missionary work, which is illegal in North Korea. The North Korean authorities discovered his real purpose by examining files in a computer hard drive that Mr. Bae says he had inadvertently left in his luggage.[71]

Bae cannot be seen as an innocent victim of North Korea. He went into the country with the intent to break their laws.

We may applaud or condemn his actions, but that is the truth.

How would we treat an American, who is ostensibly living in Mexico, leading tours of wealthy Mexicans to the United States, only to have it be revealed he was secretly promoting Chinese style communism in America?

And it was a curious imprisonment, suggesting the North Koreans may not be as cruel as they have been painted.

Kenneth Bae says his North Korean captors interrogated him up to 15 hours a day for the first four weeks of his incarceration and yelled with impatience until he wrote a confession to their liking. But they would later allow Mr. Bae to read his Bible and permit him to pray.

They told Mr. Bae that nobody from America cared enough to negotiate his freedom and that he would most likely spend his entire 15-year sentence of hard labor in North Korea's penal system, where he toiled on a soybean farm and lost more than 30 pounds. But they let Mr. Bae read hundreds of letters emailed from the United States by his family and friends.[72]

A communist regime allowed Bae to read his Bible, pray, and read letters from home? Isn't it possible that we might have a dialogue with such people to determine if we can find a way out of our difficulties? If we're being honest, do you think Bae could have kept his activities in China secret from their intelligence services, or that our own intelligence services had no knowledge of his actions?

If I was a suspicious sort of person, I'd suspect Bae was working for our intelligence services.

And what of Matthew Todd Miller, detained on April 10, 2014? This is the bizarre behavior in which he engaged:

Miller, 24, entered April 10 with a tourist visa but tore up his documents upon arrival at the airport and shouted that he wanted to seek asylum, which North Korea says was a "rash behavior." Miller is accused of a "gross violation of its legal order."[73]

Maybe he's just a crazy person, but an American crazy person and we're obligated to seek his release, even from his own stupidity.

Some of the Westerners detained by North Korean surely must have had the North Korean officials scratching their heads in confusion was Arturo Pierre Martinez. Martinez illegally crossed into North Korea from southern China by crossing a river. He was detained on November 10, 2014, a few weeks before the Sony hack became public.

Martinez spent only twenty-one days in detention, before the North Koreans decided to have him speak at a press conference at the People's Palace of Culture before deporting him.

At first, he acted like a perfect North Korean puppet.

Martinez began by apologizing to the North Koreans for illegally entering the country, then pivoted into a hard-left critique of American imperialism, taking shots at the American justice system, the privatization of prisons in the U.S., and the growing disparity of wealth in America.

But then he switched topics, calling out the United States for having its own fleet of UFOs, technology incorporating X-ray and nanotechnology implanted in Americans to control their thoughts and make them hear voices, as well as having given cancer to five South American heads of state.

After that brief digression, Martinez returned to praising the accomplishments of North Korea, discussing the CIA's acknowledged torture program, then asking for asylum in Venezuela.

Was Arturo Pierre Martinez a U.S. intelligence asset, designed to cause chaos, or just a crazy person? It can be difficult to determine the difference, and one must also be open to the possibility that both might be true. Regardless of intent, it would certainly put the North Korean officials on edge about what the United States might be planning.

In 2013 there was perhaps the most intriguing story of a westerner held hostage by North Korea, that of Merrill Newman, who was originally identified by the media as an eighty-five-year-old Korean War Veteran. For the forty-two days he was held in captivity, the Western media couldn't make sense of this story.

Why would North Korea hold this harmless, elderly man?

However, during the Korean War, Newman was a member of the United Nations Partisan Infantry Korea (UNPIK), a top-secret precursor of today's U.S. special operations forces that combined South Korean and American forces. They ran several partisan groups behind enemy lines, including one known as the "White Tigers," a name which would eventually be used by South Korea's own counterterrorism unit. Newman's assignment was to advise South Korean operatives behind enemy lines in North Korea, around Mount Kuwol, just south of the capital city of Pyongyang. These guerillas, long known in South Korea, are known as the Kuwol Comrades, and their fame was celebrated in a popular movie called "Blood-Soaked Mount Kuwol."

Both UNPIK and the CIA ran numerous missions into the North, and these efforts lasted beyond the war. Hundreds of CIA-trained South Korean agents were parachuted into the North and almost all of them were killed.

The North Koreans reserved enormous hatred for these agents and those who assisted them. During the war, 85% of the country's buildings were destroyed by U.S. bombing and more than a million and a half North Koreans died. After the war there was a series of purges in North Korea, and while in the West we usually look at these actions of authoritarian regimes as unnecessary, there is little doubt that paranoia among the leadership of these countries was real.

The unanswered question regarding Merrill Newman was whether he was simply an old man who wanted to revisit the area around Mount Kuwol, where so many of the friends of his youth had fought and died, or whether he was on one last mission for the intelligence agencies. Newman was held for forty-two days, and released after confessing to his crimes during the 1950-1953 Korean War and apologizing for his actions.

In order to understand North Korea, it is important to understand their history, as well as their perceptions of modern-day events, and their possible link to past actions by the United States and other western powers.

It seems to me that any halfway intelligent person could fig-ure out a way to lower tensions through dialogue, as demonstrated from this account given by James Clapper and detailed in a January 15, 2015 article in the *Daily Mail.*

> Director of National Intelligence James Clapper gave a rivet-ing account of the visit at a New York conference on cyberse-curity, just days after the government imposed new sanctions on North Korea in retaliation for the late November attack.

> He said that on November 7, the first night of the mission to free two Americans, he dined with General Kim. 'in charge of the Reconnaissance Bureau, the RGB, who's the organi-zation responsible for overseeing the attack against Sony ... '

> Clapper called the elaborate, 12 course repast 'one of the best Korean meals I've ever had' but said the four-star gen-eral spent most of the time berating him about American aggression 'and what terrible people we were ... '

> 'They really do believe they are under siege from all direc-tions and painting us as an enemy that is about to invade their country every day is one of the chief propaganda ele-ments that's held North Korea together.'[74]

Let's play the *Are You Smarter than a 5th Grader?* version of inter-national diplomacy. You're confronting a nuclear armed nation and come to realize they have a completely unrealistic view of the situation, namely, that you are about to attack their nation.

What do you do?

Sit quietly and take the abuse because you fear they might take you hostage? (This might be a smart move in the short term, but not in the long term.)

Threaten them with military force or additional crushing sanctions?

Or do you acknowledge their fears, then try to convince them that such fears have no basis in reality?

In that short excerpt from the article don't you see exactly how to deal with the North Koreans? Since we weren't planning to invade the country (maybe just messing with the mind of the dictator and hoping he made a mistake which might lead to him being killed by his generals), we could demonstrate we had no plans for invasion.

Is it asking for too much intelligence from the Director of National Intelligence to suggest that he lean over and quietly whisper in the ear of General Kim, "Both of us have some crazy people in our countries. I mean, this Kenneth Bae guy, trying to convert your country to Christianity, we totally understand why that would make you mad. And Matthew Todd Miller, ripping up his passport and declaring he wants asylum in your country? That's nuts on so many levels we probably couldn't even count them.

I think we can agree Arturo Pierre Martinez is a loony for claiming the US has its own UFO fleet, and as for Merrill Newman, he genuinely was just an old man wanting to revisit the battlegrounds of his youth."

Let's get the crazy people behind us, and then you and I can figure some things out for the benefit of both of us. How does that sound to you?"

Let's consider another possibility. Since we claimed to care about the North Korean people, maybe hunger in the country wouldn't be so bad if we dropped the sanctions. Let's assume for a moment that the isolation and sanctions strategy was developed with the best of intentions to bring about democracy in the country.

However, it clearly hasn't worked.

There's another problem with believing James Clapper.

He's probably America's most notorious liar.

Roughly a year and a half before Clapper's trip to North Korea, he was in front of the Senate being asked by Senator Ron Wyden, whether the NSA conducts surveillance on Americans. The is how the exchange was framed by National Public Radio in July of 2013:

> After telling Congress that the National Security Agency does not collect data on millions of Americans, National Intelligence Director James Clapper has issued an apology, telling Senate Intelligence Committee Chairwoman Dianne Feinstein that his statement was "clearly erroneous."
>
> Secret documents leaked by former NSA contract worker Edward Snowden have shown that the agency has been collecting metadata from phone records on millions of Americans. The documents also indicated an ability to conduct surveillance on Americans' internet activities.
>
> When Clapper was asked by Sen. Ron Wyden in March if the NSA collects "any type of data at all on millions, or hundreds of millions of Americans," Clapper answered, "No sir," before adding, "Not wittingly."[75]

Our government depends on a system of checks and balances. When the government allocates money, even to the intelligence agencies, they are supposed to be able to question the heads of these agencies and get honest answers. If these officials do not tell the truth, the entire system of trust upon which our government depends, collapses.

There are consequences to lies, which in this instance, it appears Clapper's enormous lie to the Senate was the final straw convincing NSA contractor, Edward Snowden to reveal secret documents.

> Snowden has said that Clapper's statement on the NSA's abilities and practices played a role in motivating him to reveal the classified information. Here's what he said, as the Two-Way reported last month:

"It was seeing a continuing litany of lies from senior officials to Congress – and therefore the American people – and the realization that Congress, specifically the Gang of Eight, wholly supported the lies that compelled me to act. Seeing someone in the position of James Clapper – the Director of National Intelligence – baldly lying to the public without repercussion is the evidence of a subverted democracy. The consent of the governed is not consent if it is not informed."[76]

Some people consider Snowden a traitor, and others a patriot. I'll let you come to your own conclusions. However, I consider those who fight against monstrous lies told by either government bureaucrats or powerful entities to be heroes.

Despite one's specific views on Snowden, I think the average person would agree with his claim that if one is not first informed, there can be no informed consent.

The self-confessed liar, James Clapper, remained as the Director of National Intelligence, when the Sony hack took place and he would guide the government's presentation of the evidence.

This becomes a central dilemma of our story.

Who do you trust more?

A North Korean dictator, a bunch of Hollywood executives, or a group of American liars?

CHAPTER FOUR
EVERYBODY IN THIS STORY
COULD BE A LIAR

A big budget Hollywood movie, particularly with stars as well-known as James Franco and Seth Rogen, attracts attention, even before its theatrical release. Add to the mix a plot centering around a CIA/journalist operation to assassinate a foreign leader and it would be surprising if it didn't generate some controversy.

In June of 2014, things started to heat up as reported by ABC News in an article entitled *Could Seth Rogen and James Franco's New Film Start a War?* From that article:

> Seth Rogen and James Franco are going for laughs with their new film, "The Interview," about a TV journalist and his producer recruited by the CIA to try to kill Kim Jong-un, but they may get a lot more than that.

> The North Korean government is calling the film an "act of war" and has promised a "merciless" retaliation against the United States if the film is released. In a statement by North Korea's Foreign Ministry, a spokesman said "The Interview" is the work of "gangster filmmaker[s]" that is triggering "a gust of hatred and rage," according to the Associated Press.

> Rogen responded with his typical humor. "People don't usually want to kill me for one of my movies until after they've paid 12 bucks for it. Hiyoooo!: he wrote Wednesday on Twitter.

An unofficial spokesman for the communist nation's supreme leader told the Daily Telegraph last week that the film represented the "desperation of the U.S. government and American society," but that Kim Jong-un still planned to watch it.

This prompted a tweet from Rogen: "I hope he likes it."[77]

What might we think about a Chinese comedy about a bunch of bumbling Asian journalists who tried to assassinate President Joe Biden? (Okay, I know some of my readers would gladly pay admission, but the good part of you should be offended.) We would probably think of it as a provocation and denounce it throughout the Western world. The media would rightly proclaim it to be exciting the crazies in our society to engage in an act of political violence.

And how did Seth Rogen come up with the idea of a movie depicting the assassination of the North Korean leader?

Rogen, 32, who co-wrote and co-directed the movie, told ABC News' "Nightline" that the idea came from "the thought that these big journalists are face-to-face with the world's worst people and it kind of became a running conversational joke: 'Why don't they kill them?'"[78]

When Rogen explains the genesis of the movie in this fashion it has the ring of truth, the sort of thing you'd expect comedians to think about. Probably more than any other group in society, comedians have often been the first to bring new ideas into the public consciousness. However, what must also be acknowledged is that comedians like Rogen exist in a corporate Hollywood, which might be just as subject to outside influence as any other industry.

And yet, the coauthor of the screenplay, Daniel Sterling, in an interview with *Esquire* magazine, tells an interesting story of how the original script, with a fictional Asian dictator, turned into something much more provocative.

During the development of the movie, Kim Jong-il died, and when the movie was greenlit, we had our first meeting with the Sony executives who were overseeing the project. We were in a trailer on the set of *Neighbors*, and they suggested that I ought to go off and write a draft with the name Kim Jong-un and I was like, "Wow, really?" and they were like, "Yeah, just give it a try and see how it feels." As soon as they said it, I knew we were going to like this a million times better because it was going to feel realer and more provocative. Seth has spoken recently in the press about some stuff in the back and forth with Sony when they ultimately asked us not to do it, and Seth pretty much said, "Nope, we are doing it." And Sony supported us because they've been pretty brave throughout this whole thing.[79]

Rogen might have developed the idea in a script, but what powerful forces might have had a hand in greenlighting it, or steering its course as a potential international flashpoint with North Korea?

Are we to believe that a movie studio was brave about the possibility of taking on an Asian dictator? Or could Michael Lynton, who sits on the board of directors of the RAND Corporation, have passed that idea along to one of his executives?

Which possibility sounds like the bigger Hollywood fantasy?

In addition to a North Korean dictator, Hollywood executives, and lying members of our own intelligence community, the final group with whom we need to be concerned are cyber-hackers.

Cyber-hackers are in a class of liars as far above the other three groups as a Superbowl champion is from your local high school football team.

These are just a few of the tricks which hackers will use.

They'll pretend to be somebody else.

They'll pretend to be in a different location.

If they hack into a computer system using a virus, they'll steal some parts of the computer code from another hacker, so that another hacker will be blamed.

A hacker can plant a virus into a system, allowing it to remain for weeks, months, or even years, until the order is given to extract information or wreak havoc on the system.

Cyber-criminals are not like other criminals.

They tend to have high intelligence, are usually not known to law enforcement, and are masters at covering their tracks.

Hackers want the authorities to follow the wrong suspect.

It allows them to get away.

In fact, I am willing to concede the possibility that this fourth group of liars, the cyber-hackers, may have been so good at concealing their true identities, that they may have genuinely deceived the North Korean dictator, the Hollywood executives, and our own intelligence agencies.

Let's review the timeline of what happened with the Sony hack, an event which may have brought us closer to nuclear war than any event since the Cuban Missile Crisis of 1962.

<u>Day 1 – Monday, November 24, 2014</u> – A group calling itself the "Guardians of Peace" announces they have stolen data from the Sony servers, an amount which will later be estimated to be 100 terabytes of information. To put this into perspective, the entire printed collection of the U.S. Library of Congress would require only 10 terabytes of data.

The image of a skull with long skeletal fingers flashes on the screen of every employee's computer screen with the words:

Hacked by the #GOP

Warning: We've already warned you, and this is just the beginning.

We continue till our request be met.

We've obtained all your internal data including your secrets and top secrets.

If you don't obey us, we'll release data shown below to the world[80]

The phones and email service of Sony are paralyzed, as are all computers.

Day Two – Tuesday, November 25, 2014 – The Sony computers remain shut down in Southern California, as well as New York City. News of the hack begins to leak out.

Jean Guerin, the spokesperson for Sony Pictures Entertainment admits, "We are investigating an IT matter." Multiple news organizations report that the studio has suffered a hack, but the breadth and depth of the breach is unrealized outside of the company. Wee Teck loo, head of consumer electronics research at Euromonitor, tell the BBC that the hack is likely to be less damaging than a previous attack on Sony's PlayStation three years earlier. "This time around, I don't believe there will be massive damage, save for Sony's ego, even if the hack is real."

Day Three – Wednesday, November 26, 2014 – On the day before Thanksgiving, Sony employees are still working without computers, email and voicemail.

Day Four – Thursday November 27, 2014 – Sony does not feel very thankful this Thanksgiving. Five Sony films are dumped onto online file-sharing hubs, giving people the opportunity to download and view these films without paying for them.

The five films were *Fury,* with Brad Pitt, a World War II story, *Annie,* based on the Broadway play of the same name, *Mr. Turner,* by Academy Award winning director Mike Leigh, *Still Alice,* for which Julianne Moore will be nominated for an Oscar for Best Actress, and *To Write Love on Her Arms,* a story of teen drug addiction and mental health problems.

Only *Fury* had been previously released, and this act of piracy has direct financial consequences to Sony. On the first two days

Fury is dumped onto the internet it is downloaded by more than 888,000 users. With the average movie ticket price in 2014 being a little over $8 dollars, it represents a direct loss to Sony of more than $7 million dollars.

One might question whether a closed off communist state like North Korea would come up with such an excellent strategy to harm a movie studio.

Maybe.

But then it seems these communist hackers would have to understand the widespread technology to download a movie, the public sentiment as to whether this actually constituted theft, and despite those questions, whether the public would embrace such a move. Personally, it seems to me the sophistication of this stage of the attack is more consistent with the hackers being from the West, rather than a closed off society like North Korea.

Day 5 – Friday, November 25, 2014 – The first reports appear which suggest North Korea was behind the attack, in retaliation for *The Interview*. A North Korean government-controlled website called "Uriminzokkiri" (roughly translated as "among our nation") says that the film is an "evil act of provocation" which deserves "stern punishment."

Day 6 – Saturday, November 29, 2014 – Sony's computers, voice-mail, and email, remain down. A source familiar with the matter tells Reuters that Sony has not yet uncovered any link to North Korea.

Day 7 – Sunday, November 30, 2014 – More speculation and reports that North Korea is behind the attack.

Day 8, Monday, December 1, 2014 – The pre-bonus salaries of the top seventeen Sony executives are leaked, as well as the salaries of more than 6,000 current and former Sony employees. Leading the pack at $3 million dollars a year before bonuses are Michael Lynton and Amy Pascal, while the three lowest paid executives, Tom Bernard, Michael Barker, and Michael Pavic, each receive a million dollars.

Sony hires the cyber-security firm SealMandiant, to help investigate the attack.

The FBI confirms that it has launched its own investigation. FBI spokeswoman Laura Eimiller says that "The FBI is working with our interagency partners to investigate the recently reported cyber intrusion at Sony Pictures Entertainment. The targeting of public and private sector computer networks remains a significant threat, and the FBI will continue to identify, pursue, and defeat individuals and groups who pose a threat in cyberspace."[81]

Day 9 – Tuesday, December 2, 2014 – Sony chiefs, Michael Lynton and Amy Pascal issue a company-wide alert to their employees about the attack.

> "It is now apparent that a large amount of confidential Sony Pictures Entertainment data has been stolen by the cyber attackers, including personnel information and business documents. This is the result of a brazen attack on our company, our employees and our business partners. This theft of Sony materials and the release of employee and other information are malicious criminal acts, and we are working closely with law enforcement…
>
> While we are not yet sure of the full scope of information that they attackers have or might release, we unfortunately have to ask you to assume that information about you in the possession of the company might be in their possession. While we would hope that common decency might prevent disclosure, we of course cannot assume that…
>
> We can't overemphasize our appreciation to all of you for your extraordinary hard work, commitment and resolve."

Kevin Roose, an employee of the small cable network, Fusion, pulled out some interesting facts about the top salaried executives, namely that they are 88% white and 94% male. It is also revealed that for *The Interview*, Seth Rogen was paid $8.4 million and James Franco $6.5 million.

<u>Day 10 – Wednesday, December 3, 2014</u> – A large cache of data which contains PDF files showing the passports and visas of stars such as Angelina Jolie and Jonah Hill are dumped onto the internet. Film budgets and confidential contracts, and the usernames and passwords of Sony executives are also included in the dump.

However, most of the day's news commentary focused on complaints from Sony's own employees covered in a Gawker article entitled *Sony Hack Reveals 25 Page List of Reasons It Sucks to Work at Sony*. Among the comments from Sony employees:

> There is a general "blah-ness" to the films we produce. Although we manage to produce an innovative film once in a while, *Social Network, Moneyball, The Girl with the Dragon Tattoo*, we continue to be saddled with the mundane, formulaic Adam Sandler movies. Let's raise the bar a little on the films we produce and inspire employees that they are working on the next Social Network. That said, there's a strange dichotomy of encouraging us to be fiscally responsible, but then upper management allows certain talent and filmmakers to bleed us dry with their outlandish requests for private jets, wardrobe and grooming stylists – and are surprised when they are asked to work more than 5 hours to promote their film.[82]

When one reads such a well-reasoned critique by this employee, one believes there actually are people in the movie business who want to create works of art which engage the public, as well as satisfy the company's bottom line.

Maybe this employee should have been making three million dollars a year, rather than Michael Lynton and Amy Pascal.

> Perhaps it's a generational thing, but I've been disappointed with the content of some of the films we've been producing lately. I don't think people who know me would consider me a prude, but the boorish, least common denominator slate strikes me as a waste of resources and reputation.

"I think the mirror should be tilted slightly upward when it's reflecting life – toward the cheerful, the tender, the compassionate, the brave, the funny, the encouraging, all those things – and not tilted down to the gutter part of the time, into the troubled vistas of conflict." (Greer Garson 1990) I think that quote could be adapted to apply to the base elements of some of the films we produce.[83]

This employee expresses a classical view of the purpose of art, that it's meant to show us how to live the good life and be a positive force in the world. Is it a better use of our brief time on this planet to focus on what is going wrong, or what is going right? But perhaps the Sony executives should have been most focused on this comment.

I work in IT [information technology] and while I feel we have a very strong CIO [Chief Information Officer] (strongest in 9 years that I have been here at SPE) that is doing a good job. The next level of management below the CIO needs some work. They don't even seem to get along.[84]

As Mr. Grey and Eric, the experts from Norse Security, had suspected on their visit to Sony in August of 2014, security at the studio seemed to have some gaping holes.

The information technology department at Sony was beset by strife.

Were there long-festering grudges?

Could these grudges have ripened into a plan for vengeance?

The technology department of any company in the modern age is probably the greatest area of vulnerability. They already know how to enter the system. You don't want them angry, because they are the members of your company most capable of inflicting great damage.

Sony released a statement saying that "The investigation continues into this very sophisticated cyberattack."

In what would be an escalation in the campaign against North Korea, Ed Lee, the managing editor of *Re/Code*, released a statement, pointing the finger of blame at Kim Jong-un. The statement read:

> Sony and outside security consultants are actively exploring the theory that the hack may have been carried out by third parties operating out of China on North Korea's behalf. The sources stress that a link to North Korea hasn't been confirmed, but hasn't been ruled out, either.

> Similarly devastating attacks have been blamed on North Korea in the past. Last year, North Korea was said to have been behind an attack against two South Korean TV broadcast networks as well as its financial system. Employees of the two TV networks were left with blank computer screens. The attack also paralyzed South Korea's network of ATM machines, preventing people from withdrawing money from their bank accounts.

The narrative is beginning to come together. The blame is put on a North Korean hacking unit which is operating out of China, for their mutual benefit.

It is factually accurate that North Korea has a hacking unit stationed just over the border in China.

From that point, the facts become less clear. It is true that South Korea suffered a major hack of its media and financial institutions (the operation was dubbed "Dark Seoul" by Western intelligence).

But the "Dark Seoul" hack was never conclusively linked to North Korea. (We will delve into the "Dark Seoul" attack in a later chapter.)

In addition to Sony, the hack claims another victim, Deloitte and Touche, the giant consulting and auditing firm, when the hackers dump the salaries of 30,000 of its employees into Pastebin, an anonymous posting website.

<u>Day 11 – Thursday, December 4, 2014</u> – The Associated Press reports that they've found "striking similarities between the code used in the hack of Sony Pictures Entertainment and attacks blamed on North Korea which targeted South Korean companies and government agencies last year."[85] In a more expansive explanation the article said:

> Analysts said they were able to examine code that was shared online after the FBI sent a flash alert to businesses this week, warning about a new threat from "destructive malware." While the FBI alert did not mention Sony Pictures by name, researchers said the alert listed Internet Protocol addresses that led them to samples of malware and references to Sony's internal network and passwords.

> "We've seen it and it has a number of similarities to the attack code used in March 2013 during "Dark Seoul," said Tom Kellerman, chief cybersecurity officer for Trend micro, a Japanese security company with operations in the United States…

> Kellerman stopped short of saying the attack that crippled Sony's internal computer systems last week was definitely the work of North Korea. But he said, "There are strong indications of North Korean involvement. All roads lead to Rome here."[86]

Let's be skeptical here for just a moment. The FBI sent a "flash-alert to businesses" warning of destructive malware, along with some samples of the code, but didn't say it was from the Sony hack?

Maybe they just wanted to protect Sony's privacy.

However, if that was the intention, why did they allow "references to Sony's internal network and passwords?"

Was the FBI counting on some independent cybersecurity experts to chime in with, "Hey, this has some similarities to the code used by the cyberhackers who went after some South Korean television stations and banks!" Is this leading a horse to water and hoping after it takes a drink it says, "Tastes like North Korea!"

The Associated Press article continued with concerns about how cyberattacks were being used by lawless foreign nations.

> There have been previous cyberattacks that were blamed on national governments. Bruce Schneier, a well-known cybersecurity researcher and chief technology officer at Co# Systems in Cambridge, Massachusetts, cited the so-called Stuxnet virus, which the New York Times has reported was developed by the United States and Israel to disrupt Iran's nuclear capabilities.[87]

The reporters probably strayed a little off message with that last paragraph. I'm sure the American cyber-intelligence spooks didn't want the public to be reminded of our own remarkable capabilities in the digital realm.

But sometimes facts are just facts.

While the article interviewed several cyber-experts who thought the evidence pointed towards North Korea, the final word was from a group with a different take.

> Experts at another security firm, AlienVault of San Mateo, California, reported similar findings, including evidence of Korean-language tools in the Sony malware. But the hackers could have used those tools to throw investigators off track, said AlienVault lab director Jamie Blasco. "In this world you can fake everything, so it's really difficult to say" where the code originated.

> Blasco said one thing is certain: "From the samples we obtained, we can say the attackers knew the internal network of Sony." He said the malware contained coded names of Sony servers, usernames and passwords.[88]

Even as the crisis was unfolding, another narrative was developing.

The guilty party did not seem to be North Korea, but an insider, angry at Sony.

Day 12 – Friday, December 5, 2014 – The Guardians of Peace sent another threat to Sony employees. They wrote:

> Many things beyond imagination will happen at many places of the world. Our agents find themselves act in necessary places. Please sign your name to object the false of the company at the email address below if you don't want to suffer damage. If you don't, not only you but your family will be in danger.[89]

This is either a terrifying threat from a nuclear armed power, or a hilariously inappropriate and racist imitation of an Asian leader trying to speak English.

I'll let you decide.

Day 13 – Saturday, December 6, 2014 – Actor James Franco guest hosts *Saturday Night Live* and in his monologue makes fun of the hack and its effect on him. He said:

> Something pretty crazy happened this week. I have this movie called *The Interview* coming out at Sony and this week Sony Studios got all their computers hacked. This is true. These hackers have leaked real personal information about everybody that works at Sony. Social security numbers, emails, and I know eventually they're going to start leaking out stuff about me. So before you hear it from someone else, I thought it would be better if you hear it from me. Soon you'll know that my email is CuterThanDaveFranco@aol.com. My password is LittleJamesyCutiePie – and this is all just a real violation of my personal life.[90]

When you find yourself in a terrible situation, sometimes the best thing you can do is make fun of the situation. One can't really criticize Franco for taking this approach.

Many of us might do the same thing.

On this same day, Kevin Mandia, the top executive at FireEye's, a cyber-security company hired by Sony, sent an email to Michael Lynton, in which he wrote, "The scope of this attack differs from any we have responded to in the past, as its purpose was to both destroy property and release confidential information to the public...the bottom line is that this was an unparalleled attack and well-planned crime, carried out by an organized group, for which neither SPE nor other companies could have been fully prepared."[91]

It's pretty convenient when the company you hire finds you innocent of any negligence and that email finds its way into a story published the very same day. However, the CNBC story which covered the findings of Kevin Mandia, absolving Sony of liability, also presented a contradictory view of Sony's responsibility.

> Daniel Clemens, chief executive of boutique cybersecurity firm Packetinjas, said that while the attack was unprecedented in impact, "There are many things Sony could have done to prepare and defend against this attack."

> He added that if the government launches probes into the breach, they are likely to find that Sony did not have all necessary safeguards in place to fend off and uncover hackers.[92]

Where does the truth lie, and who is more likely to tell it? Is it more likely the company hired by Sony will tell the truth, or a rival cybersecurity firm, looking for clients in the wake of the Sony debacle?

However, amidst the joking and the finger-pointing, one serious fact remained.

For the more than fifteen thousand Sony employees and contractors who had their private information made public, they had to deal with the fact that criminals could now open bank accounts, credit cards, and claim tax refunds in their names. "For the rest of their lives, they have to worry about identity theft," said Todd Feinman of Identity Finder, LLC, a data protection company that combed through the data. "Credit monitoring doesn't help these people. This data is now permanently in the public domain."[93]

And even though at this time North Korea had been named as the prime suspect, U.S. intelligence hadn't weighed in with their final conclusion, Sony's lax digital security was becoming clear to many in the cybersecurity industry.

> The vast majority of the files weren't even password-protected. And in several instances, huge lists of SSNs were in the background of a spreadsheet that didn't need them there anyway.

> So why did Sony Pictures keep 601 different files lying around with a total of 1.1 million SSNs?

> This kind of practice broke a basic rule about sensitive data: Keep it in one place and protect it.

> In fact, Sony broke a lot of commonsense rules. Workers also kept password lists, which gives hackers access to even more data going forward.[94]

Even the naivest user of technology understands the necessity for a password, even if your kids make fun of you for using 1-2-3-4-5-6 on your iPhone.

And letting employees keep password lists?

What might happen, if you let employees keep password lists... then fire a couple hundred of them? Do you expect there might be a few "disgruntled" members of the group?

Even just two weeks shy of the hack, outside experts were finding a great deal wrong with what Sony had done in failing to protect its data.

> Sony could have spent just $5 million to lock down its entire computer network, according to Phil Dunkelberger of Nok

Nok Labs, which makes authentication technology that protects data.

Outside hackers would have been stopped if Sony had employed routine security measures, including encrypting its servers and forcing its employees to use several layers of secret keys.

Even if the files were being stolen by an insider, Sony could have used widely available corporate software that monitors employees – and warns the company if someone downloads unusually large amounts of data.[95]

One might say these comments represent Monday morning quarterbacking. And yet a large corporation like Sony should have had some elementary protections of its digital network. This is important for our story, because the lack of such safeguards substantially lowers the skill necessary to engineer such a hack.

In other words, if stealing the data from Sony was as easy as taking candy from a baby, you don't need to be a top cyber-mastermind to pull it off.

Day 14, Sunday, December 7, 2014 – North Korea denies involvement in the hack while at the same time praising it as a "righteous act" and suggesting it may have been done by "supporters and sympathizers" of North Korea.[96]

Day 15, Monday, December 8, 2014 – The Guardians of Peace post a letter on the file-sharing site, Git-Hub, telling Sony not to show *The Interview*, but also noting that the previous letter, allegedly from the Guardians of Peace, was not from them. The letter read:

We are the GOP working all over the world.
We know nothing about the threatening email received by Sony staffers, but you should wisely judge by yourself why such things are happening and who is responsible.

Message to SONY

We have already given our clear demand to the manage-
ment team of SONY, however, they have refused to accept.
It seems that you think everything will be well, if you find
out the attacker, while no reacting to our demand.
We are sending you our warning again.
Do carry out our demand if you want to escape us.
And, Stop immediately showing the movie of terrorism
which can break the regional peace and cause the War!
You, SONY & FBI, cannot find us.
We are perfect as much.
The destiny of SONY is totally up to the wise reaction and
measure of SONY.[97]

What's the proper response when a group of cyberterrorists
tells you that there's another group of cyberterrorists, impersonat-
ing them?

You just can't trust anybody these days.

Later that night the cyberhackers revealed the most damaging
information yet, the list of aliases celebrities use to protect themselves while working on Sony projects.

Tom Hanks goes under the name "Harry Lauder" or "Johnny
Madrid."

Jessica Alba prefers "Cash Money."

Ice Cube likes to be listed as "Darius Stone" or "O'Shea Jackson,"
the name of his character in the movie, *XXX: State of the Union*, and
part of his actual last name.

The comedian Rob Schneider goes by "Nazzo Good."

Would the terror never end?

Day 16 – Tuesday – December 9, 2014 – The hackers dumped
all of studio co-head Amy Pascal's emails onto the internet, along
with those of the President of Sony Entertainment Television, Steve
Mosko. The files were large, each containing multi gigabytes of information, with thousands of emails, as well as contact information for

executives at other companies. The Guardians of Peace took credit for the dump, and media vultures quickly picked through the information looking for salacious or incriminating tidbits.

Of course, they found a few gems.

And yet, it wouldn't be fair to look at these emails without acknowledging a few facts. Amy Pascal had a sterling reputation in Hollywood as being a calm, unflappable woman, not driven to craziness by the chaos so often generated by creative types.

But she was only human.

There had to be some place she blew off steam about what she saw. I would argue, that like a good piece of literature, these emails depict a more rounded picture of an actual human being dealing with the high-pressure job of running a major studio. We all need to let our hair down with somebody. Maybe she should have done it with her husband, but she chose to do it with her fellow executives.

In a March 2014 thread between Amy Pascal, Michael Lynton, and Screen Gems President Clint Culpepper, they complained about comedian Kevin Hart wanting additional money to pitch their new movie to his 14.4 million followers on Twitter, as well as his other social media platforms.[98] As later reported in *The Wrap*, a Hollywood trade publication:

> While Hart's team said he would happily do the normal publicity rounds like junkets and photo calls, the emails hinted that he wanted additional money to pitch the movie on social media. "I'm not saying he's a whore, but he's a whore," Culpepper wrote.

After the leak, Hart wrote a lengthy response on Instagram.

"Knowing your self-worth is extremely important to people… I worked hard to get where I am today. I look at myself as a brand and because of that I will never allow myself to be taking advantage (sic) of. I own my brand… I make smart decisions for my brand… I protect my brand… which is why I'm able to brush ignorance off of

my shoulder and continue to move forward. I refuse to be broken people... with that being said its now time for me to get back to building this empire that I've always dreamed of.[99]

Let's look at this dispute objectively. Sony spends millions of dollars making a Kevin Hart movie. In addition to paying the actor a salary, they pay him for press availability and publicity, which generally means photo shoots, meeting with reporters in person, and doing radio interviews.

Then along comes social media.

Should this be simply an addition to the normal publicity process, or is this significant additional work?

Kevin Hart has a good point as well. Social media is something new and maybe there needs to be an additional charge for it.

Does it really matter what people say behind closed doors or in their private communications?

If we heard all of Kevin Hart's private comments about Sony, would there be anything of interest?

I suspect Hart probably said some pretty harsh things about Sony over the years he's been working with them. In a story with so many potential liars, we should do our best to be honest about ourselves, as well as others.

Day 17 – Wednesday, December 10, 2014 – More email revelations come to light, this time speculation by Amy Pascal and Scott Rudin in a series of emails about President Obama's favorite movies and the difficulties of working with temperamental stars like Angelina Jolie.

Does it make you feel better or worse to know that even Hollywood liberals weren't above making jokes about President Obama? Is there anything more American than making jokes at the expense of our elected leaders?

Super-producer Scott Rudin and Sony big shot Amy Pascal traded the malevolent missives as she was heading to an Obama fund-raiser at Dreamworks chief Jeffrey Katzenberg's house in November 2013.

"What should I ask the president at this stupid Jeffrey breakfast?" Pascal wrote, according to Buzzfeed.

"Would he like to finance some movies," replied Rudin, the Oscar-winning producer of "No Country for Old Men."

"I doubt it," Pascal, the co-chair of Sony Pictures Entertainment, replied. "Should I ask him if he liked DJANGO?"

That was a reference to Quentin Tarantino's bloody slave revenge flick "Django Unchained."

"12 YEARS," Rudin fired back, referring to the slave movie that nabbed the Best Picture Oscar last year.

Rudin and Pascal continued exchanging emails in the same lame vein, trading titles of popular movies starring black actors like "The Butler" and "Think Like a Man."[100]

The reason one has private conversations out of earshot of others is so that one can make private jokes, understanding that their very inappropriateness is what makes them funny. And that the jokes are not serious.

Let's talk about the racist, Amy Pascal.

She was going to an Obama fundraiser and handing him money. A 2011 article detailed the close relationship between Sony and President Obama.

When President Barack Obama swoops into Sony's Culver City lot Thursday afternoon, he'll be arriving on safe ground ...

Sony Pictures Chairman and CEO Michael Lynton was an early Obama booster thanks to his wife Jamie's Chicago connections. Team Lynton hosted a fundraiser for Obama in 2004 when he was running for Senate.

According to public filings, Lynton donated the maximum $4,600 during Obama's 2008 presidential race. As a reward for his early support, Lynton was part of the Hollywood contingent invited to the president's first State Dinner for India's Prime Minister Manmohan Singh.

Also, digging into her pocketbook: Lynton's co-chairman Amy Pascal. The studio chief gave $4600 during the president's 2008 race.[101]

This article probably only scratches the surface of the support given by Sony, Michael Lynton, and Amy Pascal. $4600 doesn't get you an invitation to a White House state dinner. The game is then to figure out how much money Sony and their executives gave to Obama political action committees, or the democratic party. There are many ways to funnel money to a political candidate, like getting a bunch of your rich friends to give money as well.

Was Rudin incorrect in assuming the Obamas might have some interest in movies? Right after leaving office in 2017, the Obamas signed two massive deals designed to keep them in front of the public. As reported in *Newsweek*:

After completing their two terms as president and first lady, Barack and Michelle Obama have signed up for some pretty lucrative projects.

The first, announced in February 2017, was a joint deal worth an estimated $65 million to publish their memoirs. Michelle Obama's *Becoming* was released last November and became an instant-best-seller; Barack Obama's was reportedly due for release this fall but has been pushed back to 2020.

While memoirs from past presidents are nothing new, the forward-thinking Obamas also struck an exclusive deal with Netflix to produce their own movies, series and documentaries to continue the philanthropic and social change work they championed while in office.[102]

Barack and Michelle Obama each wrote their own book and got $65 million for the effort.

Then there's the Netflix deal.

How much is that worth? Well, they won't tell us. The article compares other creators for Netflix, one who made $150 million dollars over five years and another who made $300 million dollars over the same amount of time.[103]

It's difficult to believe the claim there is genuine racism against President Obama from members of the creative community, when even from a conservative perspective, it seems they've handed him well over a hundred million dollars.

Another issue raised by the emails was the difficulty surrounding the actress Angelina Jolie, a favorite of the tabloids for her marriages to Billy Bob Thornton and Brad Pitt. Scott Rudin wrote of the troubled attempt to do a movie about Cleopatra, starring Jolie. Rudin wrote:

> I've told you exactly how I want to do this material. It's the ONLY way I want to do this material. I'm not remotely interested in presiding over a $180m ego bath that we both know will be the career-defining debacle for us both. I'm not destroying my career over a minimally talented spoiled brat who thought nothing of shoving this off her plate for eighteen months so she could go direct a movie. I have no desire to be making a movie with her, or anybody, that she runs and that we don't. She's a camp event and a celebrity and that's all and the last thing anybody needs is to make a giant bomb with her that any fool could see coming.[104]

It probably won't come as any surprise to learn that the Cleopatra movie with Angelina Jolie never got made.

Apparently, sometimes even Hollywood can avoid a disaster.

Day 18 – Thursday, December 11, 2014 – *The Interview* premieres amid tight security at the 1600 seat theater, located in the Ace Hotel in downtown Los Angeles. The venue is classic old-time Hollywood, a movie palace from the 1920s, with a massive three-story grand lobby, and built by Mary Pickford and Charlie Chaplin. There were three police cars stationed outside the theater and a small, invited list of guests. As reported in *Variety*:

> The audience cheered as Rogen and co-director Evan Goldberg took the stage to intro the comedy with a heartfelt shout-out to studio president Amy Pascal.
>
> "Before we start, we just want to thank Amy Pascal for having the balls to make this movie!" Rogen said to a near standing ovation. Before the screening started, Pascal was greeted continuously with hugs from well-wishers including Caines [Sony executive], producers Matt Tolmach, Tom Rothman and Donald De Line.
>
> Charles Chun, who plays General Jong in the film, said afterwards that he had no doubt about the origin of the hack.
>
> "I think we know who did this," he said. "And if they can do this to a big corporation like Sony, what does that mean for everyone else?"[105]

The narrative had been set by the media, a few private cyber-security companies with questionable links to the government, was now blessed by Hollywood. To the casual observer it might seem as if a thorough investigation was proceeding. All that remained was that final proclamation by the United States government.

I mean, if you can't trust President Barack Obama, who can you trust?

This next episode is not part of the official timeline of the Sony hack.

About two weeks after the news of the hack broke, Mickey Shapiro got a late-night call from Amy Pascal. "You never get these calls during regular business hours," Mickey recalled. "It's always nights or weekends when they call."[106]

Amy was very upset over the hack and the release of some of her emails. She may have been contacting Mickey as much for his problem-solving skills as the fact she trusted him as the leader of the Ohr HaTorah congregation. She was very distressed and after a few minutes of conversation he said, "Listen, I can bring my guys over to your house and see if they can help."

"Would you do that?" she asked.

They made arrangements to meet.

Mickey got off the phone and called Mr. Grey and they made plans to fly down the next afternoon with Eric, who'd been investigating the hack and had already developed his own theory.

Mickey recalls the door to her beautiful Pacific Palisades home was answered by Amy's husband, Bernie Weintraub, the former foreign correspondent for the *New York Times*. Mickey was well-acquainted with Bernie as well from the congregation. Amy quickly joined them. "She was very, very agitated. Like she was having an anxiety attack. She literally couldn't sit still. She was very panicked."

Amy explained her emails had been hacked, they put her in a bad light, and for a woman with a reputation for being one of the calmest people in the movie business, it was a nightmare come true. The reputation she'd earned over decades of hard work was quickly being unraveled before her eyes.

Eric flipped open his laptop, opened the files, and calmly began talking about what he believed had happened. Even though Mickey had seen Eric work many times before, he always found Eric's skills to be jaw-dropping, like watching Michael Jordan play basketball. As a later article detailed the Norse conclusions:

> Norse, the cybersecurity firm that first identified a potential insider in the massive November hack of Sony Pictures, believes it's uncovered evidence on six individuals primarily involved in the attack, including one former Sony employee with "extensive knowledge of the company's network and operations."
>
> Senior vice president at Norse Kurt Stammberger told the Security Ledger late Sunday the company had identified six people "with direct involvement in the hack," two of whom were based in the U.S. along with one in Canada, Singapore and Thailand.
>
> The list also includes a former decade-long Sony veteran who "worked in a technical role" and was laid off in May. Norse previously identified the ex-employee as "Lena," and said she claimed to have connections to the "Guardians of Peace" hacker group that took credit for the attack against Sony, which has so far resulted in leaked employee information, executives' emails, unreleased films and the limiting of "The Interview" theatrical release in response to a terrorist threat.[107]

Finally, there was a narrative which made sense, backed by some actual evidence. The perpetrators had names and a digital footprint which could be followed. Mickey could tell by the quiet way in which Amy listened to Eric's presentation it was making an enormous impact on her. As Eric explained to her, the hackers wanted to embarrass Sony Japan, as punishment for the layoffs they'd instituted against Sony Pictures.

According to Stammberger, Norse, which is not involved in the official investigation, began its own independent examination under the premise that the attack would have been best executed from the inside – an assumption numerous cybersecurity experts have put forth since the FBI formally accused Pyongyang.

Using Sony human resources documents leaked in the hack itself, researchers looked back through employees with the background and motivation that would likely preclude such an attack. One with a "very technical background" included on a list of layoffs from earlier this spring stood out, and a follow up investigation of the individual's online communications revealed disgruntled posts on social media referencing the layoffs.

After examining intercepted communications of other individuals engaged in contact with hacker and hacktivist groups in Europe and Asia (where the Sony hack was routed through), Norse connected one of those individuals with the Sony employee on a server that featured the earliest-known version of the malware used against Sony.[108]

Mickey could feel Amy's interest in Eric's presentation, then her growing horror at what had likely taken place. This wasn't a problem which emanated from the dictator of North Korea, but from the executives of Sony Japan and their brutal layoffs.

If true, it was all a masterful diversion, worthy of the very best hackers.

"Lena and the Sony Five" had concealed their activities at the cost of inflaming international relations to the point that people were openly talking about the threat of nuclear war. Eric had located the server on the dark web which contained all the information stolen in the Sony hack. And the server wasn't located in

North Korea, China, or even Russia, but in Canada. Eric believed he might be able to destroy the site, sparing Amy and Sony further embarrassment, but being unable to do much about the information which had already been released.

"Oh my God, I have to call Michael," said Amy standing up from the chair in which she'd been sitting.

The group listened to Amy talk on the phone with Michael Lynton about what she'd just learned.

Their message had been heard at the very highest levels of Sony Pictures.

But was it the message Michael Lynton wanted to hear, even after the group he'd hired, CrowdStrike, had assured him the attack had come from North Korea?

Despite the findings of Norse, Kim Jung-un, the villain of the film, was quickly becoming a villain in real life, who had struck at the heart of Hollywood.

But was this the truth?

Or was it a lie?

And if it was a lie, who was responsible for it?

The RAND Corporation, with its murky ties to U.S. intelligence, on whose board Michael Lynton and Amy Pascal sat? It's easy to imagine a sinister plan hatched by our government to provoke the North Korean leader, possibly causing him to make a fatal mistake.

Could it lie with Sony executives, anxious to capitalize on this hack, as a way to explain their flagging fortunes to their Japanese owners? Might there be a convenient way out of their financial difficulties if there was a generous insurance payout of a cyber-security policy, or perhaps assistance by the U.S. government?

Might hackers have pulled off the ultimate coup, a hack which caught the attention of the entire world, and successfully pointed the finger of blame at an innocent actor? Surely, they'd be patting themselves on the back, high fiving each other and proclaiming themselves the best hacking group in the world.

Could the intelligence analysts for our own government have been blinded by their own bias that the guilty party must be North Korea? It's common for analysts to be warned to avoid "target fixation" the situation in which pilots are warned to look out for one problem, say a stray aircraft, and miss the fact they're heading straight towards a mountain.

There are many possible scenarios for what happened, and I'm humble enough to admit I'm not sure which one is true.

But there was one group that quickly assessed the information, providing critical information to the government, and would eventually be asked to present their findings to a quickly convened meeting of top generals and leading political figures in a secure "Situation Room" at the Pentagon with the Undersecretary of Defense.

CHAPTER FIVE

HOW THE BLOODHOUND OF NORSE CAUGHT THE SCENT

Although Mr. Grey and Eric thought they'd given a good pre-sentation in August of 2014 to Sony about what their company, Norse Corporation, could do to protect the Sony computer net-work, the call from Amy Pascal that they were hired never came.

Mickey saw Amy at the congregation a few times, had small talk, and she thanked him for bringing his team in, but no deci-sion was forthcoming. Mickey knew in the entertainment business there was usually a more pressing matter one needed to deal with IMMEDIATELY. Then when she had the luxury of a little more time she'd look closely at the proposal and decide.

Mickey would then call Mr. Grey at the corporate headquar-ters in Foster City, located in the San Francisco Bay Area, and let him know there still wasn't an answer. It was a common occurrence in business that you'd give a presentation to a company, then wait weeks or months for a definitive yes or no. That was the game, you played the odds, and besides, they had a number of other clients to worry about.

Mr. Grey and Eric were in Lake Tahoe on November 24, 2014, at Eric's large vacation home in Tahoe City. He was planning to stay there with his family until the first of the year. Eric had set up a workstation in the home, so he could do his work for Norse, then in the afternoon he might go trout fishing, or just walk by himself along the lake. There were extra rooms for other Norse executives, and the Thanksgiving to New Year time was something of a movable feast, with different people

As part of Norse's mission to be the leading company in cybersecurity they performed analyses of any significant hacks, using their globally deployed system of sensors to determine what had happened and if possible, provide real time analysis. Sometimes they could present the information to a company within a matter of days. That was often the best way to nab a client. Norse could be like the knight riding in on a white horse telling the king where his kidnapped princess was being held.

Mr. Grey knew immediately that plans had changed for the ski week that had been planned. Eric would go into bloodhound mode, lost for hours if not days, before he would come up for air and share what he'd learned. He decided to leave Eric to himself in the cabin and go out and enjoy the snow.

Within a day, Eric had come up with three suspects, all women, at Sony who fit the profile he had developed.

After further investigation, Eric settled on one of the women, she was an IT administrator with Sony for ten years, had recently been fired, belonged to a hacker collective, and her boyfriend belonged to the notorious hacker group, Lizard Squad, out of Canada. In what may have been an intentional taunt, two members of Lizard Squad gave an interview to William Turton of *The Daily Dot*, in December of 2014, regarding their alleged hack of the Sony Playstation in 2012.

The information was already well-known to Eric and informed his opinion of the likely perpetrator. From the opening of the article:

Vinnie Omari [a pseudonym] was still a bit drunk when he initiated what could be the biggest distributed denial-of-service attack in history. He woke up around 1 pm on Christmas Day, he told me, reeling from a long night getting "shitfaced" to celebrate his 22nd birthday. He quickly ate Christmas dinner and sat down at his computer. It was going to be a long day: Omari and his friends were about to ruin the holiday for console gamers the world over by taking down Xbox Live and Playstation Network services.

The attacks worked. It was a complete worldwide outrage. No one was able to connect to the online services on an Xbox One and Playstation 4. Omari's group, working under the name Lizard Squad, quickly gained international media attention, as well as plenty of angry messages from kids who couldn't play with their new Christmas gifts.[109]

Some argue a criminal doesn't return to the scene of the crime, but that's not true. More often than not, there's a narcissism to the criminal mind, seeing the crime as the highlight of their life, and like the high school quarterback who won the big game, wanting to revisit the scene of their greatest glory. In this interview, Lizard Squad was taunting what they'd done in 2012 to Sony. Was it a dangle, a confession that they'd done the same thing in 2014?

According to Lizard Squad, their attacks against Microsoft and Sony maxed out at 1.2 terabits per second. If true – we were unable to verify – that's about three times largerthan the previous record, an attack aimed at Cloudflare's content delivery in February, which exceeded 400 gigabits per second, according to Ars Technica. Microsoft and Sony have yet to release any details about the size of the hack…

Lizard Squad quickly rose to fame after claiming responsibility for attacks on Blizzard and Playstation Network earlier this year, as well as grounding Sony Online Entertainment President John Smedly's flight after issuing a bomb threat. Lizard Squad also took responsibility for taking down North Korea's internet earlier this week and targeting the Vatican a few months ago. The group has been teasing plans to target PSN and Xbox Live for months.

The hackers said they wanted to exploit the "incompetence" of Microsoft and Sony.[110]

Is it a stretch to say that Lizard Squad was one of the most capable hacker groups in the entire world, with the ability to extract large amounts of information at lightning speed, and a well-documented hatred of Sony?

When you add to the picture their admission of taking down North Korea's internet (at the same time the Sony hack was playing out in the news), it's not difficult to come up with a scenario.

First, Lizard Squad takes down Sony, laying the trail that it's North Korea.

Second, North Korea is on a state of high alert because they've been falsely accused by the United States.

Third, Lizard Squad takes down North Korea's internet, making them think the United States is attacking them.

It's a miracle we didn't get to stage four, where we launched a preemptive military attack on their missile bases, or North Korea fired their nuclear missiles at us.

Vinnie Omari and Ryan Cleary (pseudonyms) continued to talk about the 2012 Christmas hack of the Sony Playstation.

"Microsoft and Sony are fucking retarded, literally monkeys behind computers," Omari said. "They would have better luck if they actually hired someone who knew what they were doing. Like, if they went around prisons and hired people who were convicted for stuff like this, they would have a better chance at preventing attacks."

"If I was working [at Microsoft or Sony] and had a big enough budget, I could totally stop these attacks," Cleary claimed. "I'd buy more bandwidth, some specific equipment, and configure it. It's just about programming skill. With an attack of this scale, it could go up to the millions. But that's really no problem for Sony or Microsoft."[111]

The contempt these hackers had for Sony was just overwhelming. How could the federal authorities have avoided taking a serious look at Lizard Squad as the culprits, rather than North Korea? One begins to question whether it was an honest mistake, "target fixation" by the US intelligence analysts or something more sinister? And how did Lizard Squad explain their remarkable exploits, such as infiltrating the Vatican or shutting down North Korea's internet? They detailed their capabilities (although we must be skeptical that they lie about everything) and yet much of what the claim rings true.

What made Lizard Squad so successful? Without specifying how exactly, Cleary claimed that the group has direct access to the infrastructure of these networks, putting little between the hacks and their targets. "We've just got a bunch of people with really particular skill sets, and we've been working to get access to some of the core routing equipment of the internet," Cleary explained, excitement in his voice. "We've got some devices that are connected to undersea cables that facilitate the Internet connects between the United States and Europe. We have access to some of the devices that are in the middle of the ocean that have something like 100-gigabit-per-second Internet connections. Not even the Russian government is doing attacks our size – they were only managing 100 gigabits per second against some Estonian websites."[112]

They certainly seem to be a terrifying cyber-hacking group.
But as I've said, this arena is filled with liars. We must be aware of what is claimed, and yet remain skeptical at the same time.

As Eric scanned through the information which had been dumped on the internet, a particular email from the hackers caught his attention. As related in a later article:

> The email was titled "Notice to Sony Pictures Entertainment" and was sent at 9:44 am PST on November 21, [three days before the threatening skeletal message appeared on the Sony computer screens] from a Gmail account registered in the name "Frank David." It was addressed to five top Sony executives.

> The IP address of the sender wasn't visible because Gmail's Web interface appears to have been used to compose the note, but there was one striking detail.

> It was not signed in the name of "Guardians of Peace," the name used by hackers who claimed responsibility for the attack but was signed "From God'sApstls." That text appeared in a different font, as if it had been cut and pasted into the message.

> The God'sApstls name was found inside the malware that attacked Sony, said Symantec.[113]

When Eric discovered this information, he was dumbstruck. Would a bunch of North Korean hackers nickname themselves "God's Apostles?"

Probably not unless they wanted to get shot.

In fairness, it could have been something of a North Korean trick. But if so, why didn't they go all the way with it? What better way to throw the intelligence agencies off the track than make it sound like it's coming from some right-wing Christian group? As Eric read the actual message from the hackers, his suspicions only grew.

We've got great damage by Sony Pictures," the message began, "The compensation for it, monetary compensation we want."

"Pay the damage, or Sony Pictures will be bombarded as a whole. You know us very well. We never wait long. You'd better behave wisely," it read.[114]

Why would a new North Korean hacker group, the so-called "Guardians of Peace", claim that the Sony leadership knew them "very well?"

From where?

As Eric poured over the dumped data with his analytic tools, it became clear that while the first public notice of the hack had come on November 24, 2014, the actual hack had taken place on July 15, 2014, which meant the cyber-thieves had been lying in wait for months before releasing the information.

Eric was the first to find the malware code used to accomplish the hack and confirmed that the original malware had been composed in Korean and Chinese texts. But the actual malware used in the Sony hack was mostly in English. This was a common hacker tactic of taking an old code and repurposing it to avoid detection.

Eric's initial suspicion of a former Sony IT administrator of Asian descent, who had worked for Sony for ten years, had been recently fired, was part of a hacker collective, and whose boyfriend was a member of Lizard Squad in Canada, was looking even stronger.

The other tip-off to Eric was the way the hackers moved through the system. Once the initial hack had been accomplished, it took the hackers approximately three days to download their materials. Eric saw the hackers knew exactly where to go to find the incriminating information and didn't seem to make many wrong turns in their search for data. Eric was also able to get the list of the passwords used by the hackers to gain access to the system, discover that this former fired IT employee had those passwords in her possession, and was even able to pinpoint the machine from which she logged in to initiate the hack.

From their previous experience, Eric and Mr. Grey understood that despite the claims of a vast North Korean hacker army, their skills were not that good. They also discovered that in November of 2014 North Korean hackers had gotten into the Sony computer network, but by that time all of the information had been exported several months earlier.

It was akin to robbers showing up at a house that had already been robbed.

When Eric completed his analysis, he turned all of his information, including the malware code he had analyzed, over to the FBI, and waited for the burgeoning international crisis to cool.

It only got hotter.

Let's talk about how a narrative is created.

Within a few weeks of the Sony hack, Eric and Norse Corporation had turned over to the FBI, not only their analysis of the Sony attack, but also the source code which was used in the hack.

If the initial suspicion of North Korea as being responsible for the hack had been genuine, then this was the time to set the record straight and assert it was most likely the hacker group known as Lizard Squad, along with a disgruntled former Sony employee.

But that's not what happened.

Instead, there was a continuing campaign of escalation by the United States against North Korea, culminating in a declaration by U.S. President Barack Obama, that Kim Jong-un was responsible. This is how it played out in the press, starting with a *Business Insider* article from December 15, 2014, by Michael B. Kelley and Armin Rosen. It had the subtle title of "The US Needs to Stop Pretending the Sony Hack is Anything Less than an Act of War."

Dave Aitel, a former NSA research scientist and CEO of the cybersecurity firm Immunity, argues that while the attack "doesn't meet the threshold for a response by our military," it should still be viewed as an act of war.

"We need to change the way we think about cyberattacks," Aitel told Business Insider in an email. A non-kinetic attack (i.e., destructive malware, destructive computer network attack) that causes just as much damage as a kinetic attack (i.e., a missile or bomb) should be viewed at the same level of urgency and need for US government/military response."

Aitel, one of the preeminent experts on cybersecurity, said "there should at least be firm diplomatic repercussions for these types of attacks. After all, what would we have done if they'd blown up the buildings at Sony Pictures but not caused any casualties? That is the context these attacks need to be put in."[115]

In the drug world the dealers need to launder their money. But in the battle for the public's attention, the information gets laundered through journalists. Thus, we have the spectacle of a former NSA researcher telling us how we need to view the Sony hack, and most importantly, how we should respond.

Aitel goes even further by giving advice on how American businesses should respond in the wake of these alleged cyberattacks by a foreign power.

One way to bolster US cyber defenses, according to Aitel, would be for the government to provide companies "with the option to have their web hosting and security provided by the federal government itself."

And even though turning over the "IT keys" to the government would be an unpopular idea – especially after the revelations by Edward Snowden – Aitel calls it "the most effective model the cybersecurity industry would have to protect against state-sponsored attacks like the one that hit Sony or the millions of cyber-espionage attacks that occur yearly against other key US entities."

That's because a critical attack on a US-based company would be treated, legally and politically, as an attack on the US itself.[116]

What better way for the United States to obtain complete control over American industry than taking over their computer networks in the name of freedom?

However, the very next day, December 18, 2014, a decision was made which shocked artists around the world, including comments from President Obama.

Cinemas in the US canceled screenings of the film, about a plot to kill North Korea's leader, prompting Sony to shelve it altogether.

But there has been dismay in Hollywood, with Ben Stiller calling the move "a threat to freedom of expression."

Hackers had issued a warning to cinemagoers who planned to watch the movie.

President Obama recommended that "people go to the movies," but stressed that the hack was "very serious."

Speaking to US television network ABC, he added: "We'll be vigilant – if we see something that we think is serious and credible, then we'll alert the public."[117]

And one has to be sympathetic to Sony's decision, made because theater owners declined to show it because of the threat of violence made by the Guardians of Peace. Yes, the Guardians of Peace were threatening to kill people. The group had written:

"Remember the 11th of September 2001. We recommend you to keep yourself distant from the places at that time…Whatever comes in the coming days is called (sic) [caused?] by the greed of Sony Pictures Entertainment."[118]

Did one really want to be killed going to the movies?

I mean, there's free speech, and then there's dying for a Seth Rogen movie.

Another article released the same day suggested this was a "Comedy of Terrors" but in four specific acts. Act One was the penetration of the Sony network, act two was the release of the embarrassing emails, act three was when people started talking about freedom of speech, and act four was when the cyberattack was declared an act of war, along with a possible nuclear exchange.[119]

The following day, December 19, the BBC put out a more skeptical piece on the hack, pointing out the holes in the theory that the hack was initiated by North Korea.

First, the FBI says its analysis spotted distinct similarities between the type of malware used on the Sony Pictures hack and code used in an attack on South Korea last year.

Suspicious, yes, but well short of being a smoking gun. When any malware is discovered, it is shared around many experts for analysis – any attacker could simply reversion the code for their own use, like a cover version of a song.

This has happened in the past – most notably with Stuxnet, a cyber-attack malware believed to have been developed by the US, which was later repurposed by (it is believed) the Russians.[120]

Why was the FBI citing evidence which wasn't very strong? It's almost as if they wanted it to be North Korea, either by accident or design. Perhaps it was a problem of "target fixation," but one must wonder if there was some darker plan.

Another piece of evidence that the FBI cited was IP addresses which had been used by North Korea in the past. However, that presents problems of attribution as we know US intelligence had been in the North Korean network since at least 2010, and Lizard Squad claimed to have been messing around in the North Korean network as well. Either the US, or Lizard Squad could have easily taken control of certain IP addresses and used them to fool investigators as to their true identity.

But what the FBI is very careful not to say is whether it thinks the attack was controlled from within North Korea itself – although in a press conference President Barack Obama did say there was no indication of another nation state being part of the hacking.

This is an important detail to pick apart.

Experts think it's unlikely, if indeed it was North Korea, that the country would have acted alone. Unnamed US officials quoted by Reuters said the US was considering that people operating out of China, with its considerable cyber-attack capability, may have been involved.[121]

At the beginning of an international investigation, it's important for political figures to maintain neutrality. But they were certainly pointing some fingers. But the China factor is something which would complicate the matter. If North Korea had hacked into Sony, it would have required China's permission.

The question then is whether China would put its relationship with the United States at risk to please North Korea. I can't say I have a window into that relationship, but I can't believe China would make such an ill-considered move.

And the article made the point how accusing North Korea was a good move for Sony, and possibly the United States.

Moving onto next year, the attack being attributed to a nation state rather than an independent hacking group is the one glimmer of good news for Sony.

There had been serious and mounting rumblings from both former employees and security analysts saying Sony did not take corporate security seriously enough – but words like "unprecedented" will bolster Sony's defense that no amount of security would have prevented what happened.

"We have to wait and see what evidence they present later on but often nation states are the easier to blame," said Marc Rogers, a security researcher for Cloudflare, who is skeptical about the extent of North Korea's involvement.

"If it's a nation state people shrug their shoulders and say they couldn't have stopped it. It lets a lot of people off the hook."[122]

The picture was starting to look very similar to many members of the cybersecurity community. There were definite reasons to put North Korea on the initial list of suspects, but the closer one looked at the evidence, the less likely it appeared.

Mr. Rogers is one of several security experts to question the use of *The Interview* as the obvious motive for the hack. It was not until the media made the link, Mr. Rogers notes, that the hackers started mentioning the film.

Up until that point, it was all about taking on the company, with language that hinted more at a grudge than a political statement.

"When you look at the malware it includes bits and pieces from Sony's internal network and the whole thing feels more like someone who had an issue with Sony," Mr. Rogers said.[123]

It begins to take on the appearance that North Korea was a convenient suspect, either because it fit a preapproved narrative, or it simply clicked in the mind of government investigators as being the most likely answer. Perhaps the investigators began to suffer from "target fixation" on North Korea rather than any nefarious intent behind a larger agenda. It's probably the only innocent way to explain how government investigators apparently overlooked the fact that part of the malware code included "bits and pieces from Sony's internal network."

However, more cynical observers correctly note that analysts are supposed to take into consideration their own potential biases. Failing to see your own bias sets one up for failure, which in this instance could be a miscalculation that leads to war.

Some suggest that billing North Korea as a cyber villain is a convenient foe for the US. Respected technology magazine *Wired* went as far as drawing a comparison between North Korea's cyber "capability" and Saddam Hussein's "weapons of mass destruction."

As we head into 2015, at least one senior US politician is calling for North Korea to be re-designated a state sponsor of terrorism.

And with the government declaring it a matter of national security, the next thing is for the US to consider its response.

President Obama said: "We will respond proportionally, and we will respond in a place and time and manner that we choose."[124]

Does the United States ever benefit from having a "convenient foe?" Some might point to President Lyndon Johnson's use of the phony Tonkin Gulf Incident to justify the escalation of the Vietnam War, or President George W. Bush's claim of "weapons of mass destruction," claimed to be held by Saddam Hussein as justification for the second Iraq War.

These well-documented historical facts have caused others to question the official narrative underlying other foreign interventions by the United States.

Are the lies behind Vietnam and the Second Iraq War an exception to the general rule of honesty from our government, or are they business as usual?

Although the FBI released a statement blaming North Korea for the hack on December 19, 2014[125], a few weeks later, FBI Director James Comey decided to weigh in on the controversy.

> FBI Director James Comey says hackers who attacked Sony last month were sloppy, posting directly from a server used exclusively by North Korea.
>
> Comey Wednesday urged the intelligence community to declassify information that proves the hackers used servers directly linked to the government in Pyongyang...
>
> Comey made the comment Wednesday at a cyber security conference in New York. U.S. Director of National Intelligence James Clapper, who also spoke at the conference, called the cyber-attack the most serious ever against U.S. interests. He warned Pyongyang will continue online attacks against American interests unless Washington "pushes back."[126]

It wasn't enough for the FBI to release a statement assigning blame to North Korea, but they needed the Director to come out and highlight it. (It's almost like J. Edgar Hoover coming out and saying we need to take on the mafia! Oh, wait, he NEVER did that in the decades he was in power.) Therefore, the public was being told they needed to take this information VERY SERIOUSLY.

And if that wasn't enough to get the public's attention, there was James Clapper ("Do we spy on Americans...uh .. not wittingly?"), Director of National Intelligence to reinforce the message.

On one side, there was James Comey, Director of the FBI, James Clapper, Director of National Intelligence, and President Obama, all saying the Sony hack was the work of North Korea.

On the other was Eric and a good chunk of the cybersecurity industry calling into question that very assumption.

In the public arena, the dump of the Sony emails was raising many troubling issues, not only of corporate power, but of bravery and cowardice among the artistic world, and free speech itself.

<u>Day 25 – Thursday, December 18, 2014</u> – White House Press Secretary tells reporters the Sony cyberattack, and the ensuing threats need a tempered response. "I can tell you that, consistent with the president's previous statements about how we will protect against, monitor, and respond to cyber incidents, this is something that's being treated as a serious national security issue," he said.

A heated exchange broke out in the media between Sony and the giant search engine, Google, over something called "Project Goliath." A few years earlier there had been a campaign to stop the online piracy of movies, leading to the introduction of a bill called the "Stop Online Piracy Act" or SOPA. The legislation would have allowed movie studios to shut down websites which were distributing stolen entertainment content. The big tech companies, led by Google, claimed that would give too much power to the Hollywood studios, and the proposed act was defeated. It appeared to be the opinion of the studios that the reason the legislation failed was because big tech had utilized a corrupt cabal of lobbyists and blatant payoff of politicians to achieve this result. An article from *The Verge* explained the approach:

> In dozens of recently leaked emails from the Sony hack, lawyers from the MPAA and six major studios talk about "Goliath" as their most powerful and relevant adversary in the fight against online piracy. They speak of "the problems created by Goliath," and worry "what Goliath could do if it went on the attack." Together they mount a multi-year effort to "respond to/rebut Goliath's public advocacy" and "amplify negative Goliath news." And while it's hard to say for sure, significant evidence suggests that the studio efforts may be directed against Google.[127]

It's a curious battle we see playing out in the leaked Sony emails. One might believe the big tech companies and Hollywood share a common ideological framework and are united in promoting that worldview.

But when it came down to the financial bottom line, many in Hollywood viewed big tech as online buccaneers, indifferent to the fact that their content was being stolen and placed before the public for free.

The on-line file sharing of Brad Pitt's movie, *Fury*, as well as the other films stolen from Sony during the hack, are examples of this dynamic. The article was sympathetic towards the position of Sony and the other studios against the indifference of the big tech companies to the question of on-line piracy.

> Still, the emails reveal a remarkable hostility towards Goliath, [Google?] and a persistent desire to stop copyright infringing traffic as it moves across the web, a position that puts it in stark conflict with many of the guiding principles of the web. That, in turn, has created a serious conflict with many of the companies that have grown powerful on the web, a fight that without an ambitious action like Project

Goliath, the industry seems primed to lose. As one counsel noted in March, "There is much to commend an expanded Goliath strategy – the status quo has not exactly been favorable for us and, absent our doing something, it doesn't promise to get better anytime soon."[128]

What happens when two industries who may be ideologically in tune with each other, and yet one seems willing to steal from the other? When reviewing Sony's efforts, the conclusion appears to be that the industry getting raided will fight back.

By the same token, what does it say about big tech, that even though they may be ideologically sympathetic to Hollywood, they will look the other way when others are stealing from Hollywood?

One is tempted to use that old adage, "there's no honor among thieves" to explain how Big Tech and Hollywood treat each other in the marketplace.

For the moment, let's leave aside the fact that big tech is showing themselves as indifferent to the fact that their platforms are being used to take the property of another industry. That's assuming big tech wanted to act as a responsible member of society.

But Hollywood can't even count on their fellow liberals in big tech to stop the theft of their property.

With friends like that, who needs enemies?

While the Hollywood studios seemed to have no problem banding together to fight an outside force, what if a situation arose in which a single studio found itself in the hot seat?

The leak of Sony data presented a remarkable opportunity for the rest of Hollywood to turn on them, and thus lessen the competition.

Surprisingly, one of the few in Hollywood to stand up to the ridicule against Sony was the actor, George Clooney. While Clooney appears convinced it was North Korea, apparently because President Nixon once used the term "Guardians of Peace" when he visited China,[129] (not the strongest piece of evidence in my mind) he took a rare, principled stand about the greater issues of artistic freedom and hacking. This is how he framed the importance of this issue:

> We have a new paradigm, a new reality, and we're going to have to come to real terms with it all the way down the line. This was a dumb comedy that was about to come out. With the First Amendment, you're never protecting Jefferson; it's usually protecting some guy who's burning a flag or doing something stupid. This is a silly comedy, but the truth is, what it now says about us is a whole lot. We have a responsibility to stand up against this. That's not just Sony, but all of us, including my good friends in the press who have the responsibility to be asking themselves: What was important? What was the important story to be covering here? The hacking is terrible because of the damage they did to all those people. Their medical records, that is a horrible thing, their social security numbers. Then, to turn around and threaten to blow people up and kill people, and just by that threat alone we change what we do for a living, that's the actual definition of terrorism.[130]

There's a lot which is commendable in Clooney's stand. Hacking is terrible, as is the release of people's individual data. Even worse was the threat of violence against movie theaters. However, I think even Clooney would agree that all of those concerns pale before the question of blaming the wrong group, or starting a nuclear war.

In the article Clooney does an admirable job of showing how Amy Pascal's joke about President Obama's movie tastes made her persona non grata among the Hollywood elite. His opinion was that if you opened up the email of all the studio executives, you would find similarly unflattering things. Clooney tried to put together a letter of support for Sony in the crisis, but he couldn't get anybody in Hollywood to sign it. The ending of the statement read:

… This is not just an attack on Sony. It involves every studio, every network, every business, and every individual in this country. That is why we fully support Sony's decision not to submit to these hackers' demands. We know that to give in to these criminals now will open the door for any group that would threaten freedom of expression, privacy, and personal liberty. We hope that these hackers are brought to justice, but until they are, we all stand together.[131]

It was a relatively mild statement, basically saying Hollywood shouldn't submit to a ransom, and shouldn't let hackers change the way people see movies. When asked about how many people he tried to get to sign the statement, Clooney replied:

It was a fairly large number. Having put together telethons where you have to get all the networks on board to do the telethon at the same time, the truth is once you get one or two, then everybody gets on board. It is a natural progression. So here, you get the first couple of people to sign it…well, nobody wanted to be the first to sign on. Now, this isn't finger-pointing on that. This is just where we are right now, how scared this industry has been made. Quite honestly, this would happen in any industry. I don't know what the answer is, but what happened here is part of a much larger deal. A huge deal. And people are still talking about dumb emails. Understand what is going on right now, because the world just changed on your watch, and you weren't even paying attention.[132]

When one considers the situation in which Clooney found himself, a great deal of what happens in the world becomes clear. The simple fact is most so-called leaders lack courage. Clooney gave Hollywood the opportunity to make a simple statement, information from a hack should not be used to criticize or embarrass people.

I want it understood that I have a different opinion.

I believe rich and powerful corporations should not be able to hide their private communications. As a public-school teacher, I assume all of my work emails could be viewed by anybody in authority. Should I assume that my principals have privacy for their work emails when I don't? I assume the employees of most corporations also assume that their work emails are not private. Why should the leaders of powerful corporations be able to live under a different standard than their employees?

The public is best protected when our leaders in business and politics must tell us what they say and do in private.

And yet, Clooney has made a strong argument, stated it publicly, and acted upon it.

That is the way people are supposed to act in a democracy.

<u>Day 26 – Friday, December 19, 2014</u> - Reports surface early in the day that the hackers contacted Sony, telling them that the decision to pull *The Interview* from theaters was a "very wise decision." The email went on to imply that as long as the movie was kept out of theaters and elsewhere, the attacks would end.

During his annual year-end press conference, the first question President Obama got was about Sony deciding not to release *The Interview* in movie theaters. Obama bluntly said Sony "made a mistake" in caving to the demands of the North Korean hackers. He said the United States "will respond proportionally" to the attack "at a place and time we choose." Obama went onto say:

> We cannot have a society in which some dictator someplace can start imposing censorship in the United States. Because if somebody is able to intimidate folks out of releasing a satirical movie, imagine what they start doing when they see a documentary they don't like, or a news report they don't like – or even worse, imagine if producers and distributors

and others start engaging in self-censorship because they don't want to offend the sensibilities of somebody whose sensibilities probably need to be offended. That's not who we are. That's not what America is about.[133]

It's a fine sentiment if the underlying allegation was true, but as we have pointed out in this book, North Korea was unlikely to have been behind the attack.

What are we looking at then?

A cynical attempt to manipulate the country and the world against North Korea, potentially provoking a nuclear exchange?

And the entire apparatus of the United States government, overt and covert appeared on cue to support President Obama.

The FBI released a statement which read: "As a result of our investigation, and in close collaboration with other U.S. Government departments and agencies, the FBI now has enough information to conclude that the North Korean government is responsible for these actions. North Korea's actions were intended to inflict significant harm on a U.S. business and suppress the right of American citizens to express themselves."[134]

Bruce Bennett, the expert from the RAND corporation brought in to "consult" on the movie goes public with the opinion he expressed privately to Sony, that the release of *The Interview* would have damaged Kim Jong-un internally.[135]

Everything seemed to be working out so well in the plan to blame North Korea, except for one small detail.

President Obama had just thrown his buddies at Sony under the bus with the claim Sony should have continued with the planned release of *The Interview*.

Sony Pictures CEO, Michael Lynton, responded swiftly in an appearance on CNN. In the interview he said, "We did not cave. We did not back down," placing blame on the exhibitors who refused to show the film over potential violence against their patrons. On the same day Sony later released a statement which reads:

"The decision not to move forward with the December 25 theatrical release of *The Interview* was made as a result of the majority of the nation's theater owners choosing not to screen the film. This was their decision. Let us be clear – the only decision that we have made with respect to release of the film was not to release on Christmas Day in theaters, after the theater owners declined to show it. Without theaters, we could not release it in the theaters on Christmas Day. We had no choice."[136]

All in all, it was a good news day for the U.S, campaign against North Korea. For those who might question whether there was a strong relationship between President Obama and Sony studios, you had an apparent spat between the two. Nobody is questioning the public appearance of the RAND corporation in this story, and the media doesn't seem to be interested in it, either.

Day 27 – Saturday, December 20, 2014 – North Korea proposes to the United States they join forces in a joint inquiry with the United States. In addition to denying the claim they were behind the attack and warn of "serious consequences" if the United States retaliates.

The United States does not respond to North Korea's offer of a joint inquiry, and instead says North Korea must admit "culpability" in the hack.

Day 28 – Sunday, December 21, 2014 – North Korea claims the U.S. government was behind the making of *The Interview* and says that if the United States responds against North Korea they will attack "the White House, Pentagon, and the whole U.S. mainland, that cesspool of terrorism."[137]

As Americans were finishing up their Christmas shopping in 2014, they also had to worry about the possibility of a surprise North Korean nuclear attack.

Was this just the outcome the experts at the RAND corporation had been planning?

Because when a person has been frightened by the possibility their city and everybody they love may be vaporized in a mushroom cloud, they aren't thinking rationally.

They simply want the threat to go away and feel safe.

Chapter Six

Wikileaks Spills the Beans on Sony and RAND Corporation

How might the world look with radical transparency?

On April 16, 2015, the website, Wikileaks, run by journalist and political prisoner, Julian Assange, published the "Sony Archives" of leaked information from the November 2014 hack of Sony Pictures Entertainment with a wonderfully helpful list of topics and an excellent search engine. This is how the Wikileaks press release on Sony opened:

Today, 16 April 2015, Wikileaks publishes an analysis and search system for The Sony Archives: 30,287 documents from Sony Pictures Entertainment (SPE) and 173,132 emails, to and from more than 2,200 SPE email addresses. SPE is a US subsidiary of the Japanese multinational technology and media corporation Sony, handling their film and TV production and distribution operations. It is a multi-billion-dollar US business running many popular networks, TV shows and film franchises such as *Spider-Man, Men in Black,* and *Resident Evil.*

In November 2014 the White House alleged that North Korea's intelligence services had obtained and distributed a version of the archive in revenge for SPE's pending release of *The Interview,* a film depicting a future overthrow of the North Korean government and the assassination of its leader, Kim Jong-un. Whilst some stories came out at the time, the original archives, which were not searchable, were removed before the public and journalists were able to do more than scratch the surface.

Now published in a fully searchable format The Sony Archives offer a rare insight into the inner workings of a large, secretive multinational corporation. The work publicly known from Sony is to produce entertainment; however, The Sony Archives show that behind the scenes this is an influential corporation, with ties to the White House (there are almost 100 US government email addresses in the archive), with an ability to impact laws and policies, and with connections to the US military-industrial complex.

Wiki-Leaks editor in chief Julian Assange said: "This archive shows the inner workings of an influential multinational corporation. It is newsworthy and at the center of a geo-political conflict. It belongs in the public domain. WikiLeaks will ensure it stays there."[138]

Have I mentioned how much I love Julian Assange? Yes, he sits in prison now for doing journalism, but all of us must pick up the torch.

Let's see if we can put Bruce Bennett and Michael Lynton into perspective. This relationship was proposed by Michael Rich, at the time the President and CEO of the RAND Corporation. The email, dated June 18, 2014, at 5:52 pm, reads:

Bruce:

I have recommended that trustee Michael Lynton, CEO of Sony Entertainment get in touch with you for some quick assistance. If you give me a call on my mobile number, xxx. xxx.xxxx, anytime – I can fill you in. If you prefer I call you, just send a good number to use (I've left a voicemail on your office number, too.)

I've copied Michael on this email so he and you can communicate with each other directly.

Many thanks,
Michael.[139]

What do we know about Michael Rich, who at the time was the President and CEO of the RAND Corporation. I went to his webpage at RAND for information. This is how RAND described him in 2023:

> Michael D. Rich is president emeritus at the RAND Corporation, a nonprofit, nonpartisan research organization that helps improve policy and decision-making through research and analysis. For nearly 50 years, he helped RAND become a leading source of expertise, analysis, and evidence-based ideas in an increasingly complex and polarized policymaking environment.
>
> During his tenure as president and CEO from 2011 to 2022, Rich focused on extending the impact of RAND's work. He challenged the organization to broaden its legacy of innovation and help decisionmakers stay ahead of the curve on the issues that matter most.[140]

It's beyond doubt Michael Rich was the consummate insider at RAND during this period, and here he was putting a RAND expert, Bruce Bennett, together with a member of RAND's board of directors, Michael Lynton. Michael Rich's biography on the RAND website details some of his work history, suggesting strong and long-lasting ties to the military and intelligence communities.

HE [Michael Rich] served in a variety of senior leadership positions at RAND and was instrumental in the creation of the RAND National Defense Research Institute, a federally funded research and development center that provides research and analysis to the Office of the Secretary of Defense, the Joint Staff, the Unified Commands, the Navy, the Marine Corps, the defense agencies and the Intelligence Community.[141]

I'm a little puzzled how RAND can claim to be "non-partisan" while at the same time having a "federally funded research and development center that provides research and analysis to the Office of the Secretary of Defense, the Joint Staff, the Unified Commands, the Navy, the Marine Corps, the defense agencies and the Intelligence Community."

To me it sounds like RAND is claiming, "Yeah, we work with the military/intelligence communities, but we're not PART of them."

Is RAND simply laundering the views of the intelligence community into Sony Pictures and their movies? Or is it more accurate to view the intelligence community, the RAND Corporation, and Sony as fellow players on Team America?

Or is there some third option I haven't yet considered?

Within a few days, Bennett and Lynton were in constant communication. From RAND's North Korean specialist, Bruce Bennet, to Sony CEO, Michael Lynton, dated June 20, 2014, or a little more than five months before the hack broke into the news.

Michael:

Just so you get a sense of this Kim Myong Choi, below is an article he wrote shortly after the North Korean 2nd nuclear weapon test. It is reminiscent of the Kim Jong-un rant on using nuclear weapons in the film. The part in the middle in red provides a particular indication of his thinking.

Thanks,
Bruce.[142]

The opening of the letter is friendly, indicating that by this time these two already had a well-established relationship. What is curious about the article he includes is that it was written in 2009, five years before the current situation. The history related in the article would probably hold some surprises for American audiences, as it paints the North Korean regime as a rational actor.

> The nuclear game plan is designed firstly to militarily prevent the US from throwing a monkey wrench into the plans of the Kim Jong-il administration from economic prosperity by 2012 – the centenary of the birth of founding father Kim Il-sung, a bid to complete its membership of the three elite clubs of nuclear, space and economic powers.

> Its second aim is to win the hearts and minds of the 70 million Korean people, North, South and abroad, and leave little doubt that Kim Jong-il has what it takes to neutralize and phase out the American presence in Korea. This will hasten the divided parts of ancestral Korean land – bequeathed by Dankun 5,000 years ago and Jumon 2,000 years ago – coming together under a confederal umbrella as a reunified state.

> It is designed to impress upon the Korean population that Kim Jong-il is a Korean David heroically standing up to the American Goliath, that he can lead the epic effort to settle long-smoldering moral scores with the US over a more than 100-year-old grudge match that dates as far back as the 1905 Taft-Katsura Agreement and the 1866 invasion of Korea by the USS General Sherman.

> Third, Kim-Jong-il has described the shift to plan B as a stern notice for the governments of the US and its junior allies that they cannot get away with their hostile behavior any longer, unless they are prepared to leave their booming

economies consumed in a great conflagration of retaliatory thermonuclear attacks.

The game plan assumes that the US is unlikely to shake off its aggressive behavior until it is wiped off the planet. The Barack Obama administration has not taken much time to reveal its true colors, which are no different from the George W. Bush administration. There have been four compelling signs:

First, the March 9-20 Key Resolve (Team Spirit) joint war games between the US and South Korea.

Second, the US-led United Nation Security Council's (UNSC) Condemnation of an innocuous April 5 satellite launch.

Third, the rehashing of counterfeit money charges that the US failed to produce compelling evidence to support. As Newsweek wrote in its June 8 issue, "The Treasury Department couldn't find a single shred of hard evidence pointing to North Korean production of counterfeit money."

Fourth, the presence of Bush holdovers in the Obama administration, such as Stuart Levy, the architect of Bush-era financial sanctions intended to criminalize the DPRK.[143]

This is a relatively long passage, but I kept it together because it is a complete argument. Bruce Bennett is quoting a proponent of an aggressive policy against North Korea, but Kim Myong Chol has some intellectual honesty by recounting some US/Korean history of which American audiences were probably unfamiliar.

Most Americans are probably scratching their heads about the "1866 invasion of Korea by the USS General Sherman." They never read about that in any history book.

Well, it was part of the campaign by Western powers to open up Asia to trade.

From 1839 to 1842, Britain fought a war with China so that the British could sell opium in China.

In 1853, Commodore Matthew Perry led four US warships into Tokyo Bay to force the Japanese to open up trade with the west.

Korea maintained its isolation from the Western powers longer than China and Japan, until 1866 when an American armed merchant ship, the USS General Sherman, took a load of cargo to Korea, armed with its 12-pound cannons.[144]

Despite repeated warnings they could not trade, the Americans continued, were attacked by the Koreans, and almost all the crew members were killed. Their fate remained a mystery to the west for years.

The Koreans denied responsibility for these acts, but under pressure from the United States and France the truth came out, and Korea was opened to trade with the Western powers in 1876 under threat of military action, as had happened to both China and Japan.

The Korean view of the United States looks a little different, now, doesn't it?

How would we have felt if a fleet from Japan showed up in San Francisco in 1865, and demanded we trade with them?

Or maybe the African nation of Angola showed up in Miami in 1870 and demanded we had to buy their elephant tusks?

The land of Korea has long been occupied, and they want the occupiers gone, whether it's the Chinese, the Japanese, or the Americans.

It's instructive to note that according to the article, the North Korean leaders are only interested in the use of their weapons in retaliation to a strike by the United States. North Korea does not seem to have any dreams of conquest, only of being left alone in their own land.

The article was written shortly after President Obama took office, and the North Koreans were waiting for some positive sign from the new American President. The signs they did see were all negative.

First, we continued to conduct joint military drills with the South Korean military.

Second, the UN Security Council criticized North Korea for a peaceful satellite launch.

Third, the US accused North Korea of counterfeiting money, despite producing no evidence.

Fourth, the holdover from the Bush administration of many officials with anti-North Korean sentiments.

North Korea seems to have some historical grounds for criticizing the United States and other western powers. The history is one of imperialism from the west towards Asia.

The article begins by stating the North Koreans are engaging in this behavior because they are fearful of a United States attack, and only intend to use such weapons if such an attack occurs.

Why then, does the author then veer into alarmist territory about what North Korea might possibly do?

The game plan for nuclear war specifies four types of thermonuclear assault: (1) the bombing of operating nuclear power stations; (2) detonations of a hydrogen bomb in seas off the US, Japan and South Korea; (4) detonations of H-bombs in space far above their heartlands; and thermonuclear attacks on their urban centers.

The first attack involves converting operating nuclear power plants on the coastline of three countries into makeshift multi-megaton H-bombs.[145]

The *New York Times* on January 24, 1994, quoted Paul Leventhal, president of the Nuclear Control Institute, warning that North Korea could easily launch de-facto hydrogen bomb attacks on South Korea.

"North Korean retaliation to bombing could result in vastly more fallout in the South than in the North ... North Korean retaliatory bombing could bring Chernobyls multiplied.

If bombed, one average operating nuclear power station is estimated to spew out as much deadly fallout as 150-180 H-bombs. Bombing one nuclear power plant would render the Japanese archipelago and South Korea uninhabitable. Doing the same to the US may require bombing one plant on its west coast and another on its east coast.[146]

This scenario only takes place if the United States acts against North Korea. Why is this terrifying possibility any different than what we already face in a nuclear exchange with China or Russia? Are we to believe that only the North Koreans have figured this out? Additionally, have we not also figured out how to inflict maximum damage on our adversaries with nuclear weapons?

As North Korea clearly seems to be subservient to China, how could this take place without China agreeing to this action? If we genuinely wanted peace on the Korean peninsula, it seems we would need to acknowledge past historical injustices, as well as recent actions, such as claiming North Korea was involved in counterfeiting, as a prelude to a more positive relationship.

Or does the current military-industrial complex, of which the RAND Corporation and Sony belong, benefit from these existing tensions?

The article continued and it became clear that Bruce Bennet was simply using Kim Myong-chol's article to launder previous RAND studies to Sony CEO, Michael Lynton.

The detonation of sea-borne or undersea H-bombs planted on the three countries' continental shelves will trigger nuclear tsunamis with devastating consequences.

A 2006 RAND study of a ship-based 10-kiloton nuclear blast on the port of Los Angeles had some harrowing conclusions:

"Within the first 72 hours, the attack would devastate a vast portion of the Los Angeles metropolitan area. Because ground-burst explosions generate particularly large amounts of highly radioactive debris, fallout from the blast would cause much of the destruction. In some of the most dramatic possible outcomes:

Sixty thousand people might die instantly from the blast itself or quickly thereafter from radiation poisoning.

One hundred and fifty thousand might be more exposed to hazardous levels of radioactive water and sediment from the port, requiring emergency medical treatment...

RAND projects that the economic costs would exceed $1 trillion.[147]

Let's simply look at the facts of this exchange.
I am making no assumptions.
This is simply an accurate rendering of this email exchange.
Bruce Bennett, an analyst for the RAND Corporation, is communicating with Sony CEO, Michael Lynton, a member of the Board of Trustees of the RAND Corporation in June of 2014, about an allegedly independent opinion piece, written by Kim Myong-chol in June of 2009, and in the article this supposedly independent expert is citing a 2006 RAND Corporation study.
Does it seem like the RAND Corporation is crafting a certain long-term narrative about North Korea?
The article continued with the final two ways North Korea might cripple the United States.

The third possible attack, a high-altitude detonation of hydrogen bombs that would create a powerful electromagnetic pulse (EMP), would disrupt the communications and electrical infrastructure of the US, the whole of Japan, and South Korea.

Many of the essential systems needed to survive would be knocked out, as computers are instantly rendered malfunctioning or unusable. Military and communications systems such as radars, antennas, and missiles, government offices, would be put out of use, as would energy sources such as nuclear power stations and transport and communications systems including airports, airplanes, railways, cars, and cell phones...

The last and fourth attack would be to order into action a global nuclear strike force of dozens of MIRVed ICBMs – each bearing a thermonuclear warhead on a prefixed target.[148]

There is little doubt that these are terrifying possibilities to consider. But what's left out of this conversation is that the United States has thousands of nuclear bombs, as well as intercontinental ballistic missiles. Did the author consider how other countries might be terrified by the size of our nuclear and ballistic missile arsenal?

The next paragraph would probably be stunning to most Americans, as it asserts this nuclear program has been going on for decades at a very high level, long before Presidents George W. Bush or Barack Obama decided to go poking the hermit kingdom.

The Yongbyon nuclear site has always been a decoy to attract American attention and bring it into negotiations on a peace treaty to formally end the Korean War. Since as far back as the mid-1980s, North Korea has assembled 100-300 nuclear warheads in an ultra-clandestine nuclear weapons program. The warheads can be mounted on medium-range missiles designed to be nuclear capable.[149]

When reviewing this email, it can feel as if one has entered an upside-down world, in which those things you most fervently believed turn out to be completely wrong. In their own words, this RAND connected expert tell us that the Yongbyon site was constructed with the intention of bringing the Americans to the negotiating table to sign an agreement ending the Korean War of 1950-1953. In addition, we're told that this nuclear program has existed since the mid-1980s, a time frame of just a little over four decades.

So much for the "madman" theory of North Korea.

Why were we saber-rattling in North Korea when there were other countries around the globe with similarly bad human rights records? Were RAND and Sony pushing for a war, or did they only want to drive up the profits of the military-industrial complex?

An email in response from Shiro Kambe, an Executive Vice-President at Sony in Japan revealed corporate concerns over whether North Korea was prosecuting two American tourists over *The Interview*, and how that might impact then Sony Chairman Kazuo Hirai, as he prepared to travel to Sun Valley, Idaho for a corporate retreat. in Kambe's email he excerpted this passage from a *New York Times* article:

> North Korea's decision to put two detained American tourists on trial for unexplained hostile acts may have nothing to do with what they did, and instead could reflect the isolated nation's frustration that is it no longer viewed as a front-burner issue for the United States, experts on North Korean behavior said on Tuesday.
>
> Some even suggested the decision, announced on Monday, to prosecute the two Americans, Matthew T. Miller, 24, and Jeffrey E. Fowle, 56, might be one of North Korea's "decisive and merciless countermeasures" threatened last week over the release

of "The Interview," a Hollywood sendup about a fictitious plot to assassinate the North Korean leader, Kim Jong-un.[150]

One might look at this "suggestion" from "experts on North Korean behavior" as the beginning of an attempt to link North Korea to any problems associated with *The Interview.*

Shiro's email to Nicole Seligman and Charles Sipkins of Sony read, "We understand that several US media recently reported about North Korea's decision to put two detained American tourists on trial. Are these changing the tension of the US media or government on the movie?"[151]

The response from Charles Sipkins of Sony Pictures to Shiro Kambe of Sony Japan on July 2, 2014 read:

Shiro,

Last week, there was great interest from the media in "The Interview" from U.S.-based media. As you know, we chose not to comment. There has actually been a decrease in inquiries over the last several days despite the news of the trial and the news tonight of the Japanese government lifting sanctions. Our strategy remains the same in that we will not be commenting on the movie.

I will defer to Michael and Nicole regarding your question about government interest/tension related to the movie.

In the interim, I will prepare and send through Nicole and Michael a brief Q&A so Kaz is prepared for Sun Valley next week. I will make sure you receive it by the end of day tomorrow.

Charlie[152]

This email clearly states that Michael Lynton and Nicole Seligman were the point people for Sony's dealing with the

United States government about any problems *The Interview* might cause.

Unlike in *The Interview*, where the CIA shows up on the Dave and Aaron's doorstep the morning after the meeting with Kim Jong-un was announced, this email suggests Sony's ties to the government were of long standing.

As for the last part of the email, it must be noted that several considerations were at play, not the least of which was the need to placate Sony Pictures Japanese owners. On the one hand, Japan was easing sanctions against North Korea,[153] and yet on the other hand, it was allowing production of a movie about assassinating the leader of North Korea. In speaking about how Sony Chairman, Kazuo Hirai was going to be in Sun Valley, Idaho the following week, Kambe wrote:

> While he has no intention to proactively engage in the dialogue with the press, he thinks it may be difficult for him to completely avoid having any interaction with the reporters who are visiting there and would like to have the basic Q&A to deal with the on the spot attack by the press. Typical questions could be: (i) How does he think about the movie and North Korea's response? (ii) Has he seen the movie? (iii) Does Sony still plan to release the movie as announced? Please work out the draft Q&A. He knows our basic strategy is to have him and Sony Corp. keep the distance from the movie as much as we can, but likes to have the basic Q&A just in case. Can you work something in line with the above?[154]

One gets the idea that the Sony executives in Japan might have been questioning the behavior and judgment of their American studio, not only with their continuing financial difficulties, but also the choice of such provocative material as *The Interview*, especially given Japan's brutal history on the Korean peninsula.

But whatever may have been the thinking of Sony executives in Japan, Bruce Bennett of the RAND Corporation kept hyping the film, as detailed in this email to Lynton from July 17, 2014 with the subject line reading "The Latest Wrinkle on The Interview."

Michael:

Here is the latest from my colleague, Ambassador King. [President Obama's Special Envoy for North Korean Human Rights Issues – November 2009 – January 2017.] Note that Alastair Gale is actually the Wall Street Journal's Seoul Bureau chief (I know because he recently asked me to do an OpEd for WSJ), despite the "AP" byline …

I had not talked to Alastair about the movie.

I think interest in the film is also growing in South Korea: in addition to Alastair, the staff of a National Assemblyman contacted me about it, anxious to figure out how they could get a preview copy. I am being very careful in talking about what I know [author's note – Bennett had already seen the movie], focusing on the trailer and directing such inquiries to Sony Pictures.

Thanks,
Bruce.[155]

Let's talk about the cozy little world inhabited by Bruce Bennett. He's a longtime consultant for RAND, and Ambassador Robert King, President Obama's Special Envoy for North Korean Human Rights, and just happens to send Bennett an article written by Bennett's friend, Alastair Gale (who may or may not be double-dipping by working for both the Wall Street Journal and the Associated Press), and who recently asked Bennett to write an OpEd in the Wall Street Journal.

Could we assume Ambassador King knew Bennett was working for Sony Pictures at the time, or was it just dumb luck? Here's the brief exchange between President Obama's Special Envoy for North

Korean Human Rights, and the RAND consultant who was secretly advising Sony Pictures CEO and RAND director, Michael Lynton.

> Bruce,
>
> Hope you are still enjoying a pleasant time on the Cape. Since you may be less in touch on North Korea, thought you might want to see the latest on DPRK's response to "The Interview."
>
> Bob[156]

The "Cape" presumably refers to Cape Cod, the summer playground for the wealthy and powerful of the East Coast. Ambassador King didn't have to worry about Bennett keeping up on North Korea during his warm weather sojourn on the Atlantic. But it's instructive to read the first few paragraphs from Alastair Gale.

> How much free publicity can North Korea give to an upcoming movie about a plot to assassinate its leader?
>
> Pyongyang's latest escalation of its PR campaign against "The Interview", a comedy caper due to be released in the U.S. in the fall, is a letter to the office of U.S. President Barack Obama, according to Voice of America.
>
> In it, North Korea again complains that the movie is an insult to its leader, Kim Jong-un, VOA reports, citing unnamed sources. In the film, a U.S. TV crew secures an interview with Mr. Kim and is hired by the CIA to assassinate him. (it's not clear yet if they succeed.)[157]

Again and again, we get the same message drilled into our heads.

The CIA will hire and train journalists to assassinate a foreign leader.

And it's presented to us as a comedy.

Just don't look too closely at the fingerprints of the RAND Corporation, from the executive leadership at Sony, to the Sony consultant brought in by RAND, to the interlocking series of relationships between members of the government, a supposedly independent think tank, and a freewheeling Hollywood studio losing hundreds of millions of dollars for its Japanese owners.

It's a setup guaranteed to result in chaos.

But does this chaos provide an opportunity for other actors to take the stage, grasp the wayward strings, and get the puppets to put to dance a different jig?

How deeply was President Obama, or the White House, involved with altering plans for *The Interview*, in August of 2014?

I remind you of the official position of the Obama Administration, as voiced by National Security Council spokesman, Patrick Ventrell on July 17, 2014 that "The views [in the movie] are obviously those of the filmmaker and the producer of the film but we don't have any role in that. They are free to do whatever they want to do artistically."[158]

But August of 2014 was a busy month for Sony and the Obama White House.

On August 13, 2014, Valerie Jarret, the senior adviser to President Obama, and assistant to the president for Public Engagement and Intergovernmental Affairs, sent the following email to Sony Pictures CEO, Michael Lynton:

Michael-

The President would like to invite you and Jamie to dinner tomorrow. I am copying Kristen who will follow up.

VJ[159]

(Jarrett had made a mistake and the dinner with Obama and Michael Lynton was scheduled for two days away, Friday, August 15, 2014.)

It is difficult to find any information about what Michael Lynton and President Obama said to each other at that dinner, but in light of the evolving North Korean situation, it is difficult to believe they did not share at least a few thoughts about the film.

Because prior to the dinner with Obama, Sony Pictures had made two significant decisions about *The Interview.*

The first decision, announced on August 7, 2014, was to move the release for *The Interview* from October 10, 2014 to December 25, 2014. As detailed in *Variety*:

> "The Interview" will go head-to-head with five other wide releases in its Christmas slot, including "Paddington," "Into the Woods" and the awards contenders "Big Eyes" and "Unbroken." It will compete for comedy audiences with "Hot Tub Time Machine 2." The film has been testing well and Sony is hoping to capitalize on the younger college crowds who will be out on break for the holiday.
>
> In its vacated slot, it would have faced a number of wide releases including the family film "Alexander and the Terrible. No Good, Very Bad Day" and the Robert Downey Jr. drama "The Judge."[160]

Release dates for movies can be changed for a variety of reasons. The initial reason given was that they wanted young people out on Christmas break from school to go out and see the movie.

That's an entirely reasonable explanation.

However, on August 13, two days before Michael Lynton and Barack Obama would be meeting for dinner, an article in the *Hollywood Reporter* disclosed significant changes being made to *The Interview* which might have prompted the changed release date.

Sony Pictures is pulling out all the stops to keep its Seth Rogen-James Franco North Korea-set comedy *The Interview* from igniting a tinderbox.

Sources say the studio is digitally altering thousands of buttons worn by characters in the film – which on Aug. 8 was pushed from October to a prime Dec. 25 release – because they depict the actual hardware worn by the North Korean military to honor the country's leader Kim-Jong-un, 31 and his late father, Kim Jong-il (showcasing military decorations would be considered blasphemous to the nuclear-armed nation) ...

... Sources say the studio is considering cutting a scene in which the face of Kim Jong-un (played by Randall Park) is melted off graphically in slow motion. Although studio sources insist that Sony Japan isn't exerting pressure, the move comes in the wake of provocative comments from Pyongyang that the film's concept "shows the desperation of the U.S. government and American society."[161]

I'll have to disagree with the writer for *The Hollywood Reporter,* that Sony was "pulling out all the stops" to keep its film from causing problems.

Changing buttons and deciding whether you want a villain's face to melt can hardly be described as "pulling out all the stops."

And yet I find myself curious about the "button" issue.

Who made the decision to change the buttons?

If somebody replies, "Well, the article says why. Sony realized it would be 'blasphemous' to the North Koreans to depict an actual part of their military uniforms."

I'd nod my head in agreement with you, but then ask, "And depicting the assassination of their leader by a CIA-trained hit squad isn't blasphemous?"

Let me speculate for a moment.

The only thing that makes sense for me is that somebody in this venture was trying to lower the temperature of a quickly bubbling problem.

I don't know if that person was at Sony Pictures.

I don't know if it came from executives at Sony Japan.

I don't know if it came from the RAND Corporation.

I don't know if it came from the Obama White House and somebody with a rare amount of common sense.

My suspicion is it was somebody in the United States government passing the request to Sony Pictures as a prelude to having a less dangerous relationship with North Korea.

The article claims the decision came from inside the legal department at Sony Pictures and the concern over "clearance issues" but even inside Sony there appeared to be confusion, as documented in this email exchange between Leah Weil (General Counsel of Sony Pictures) and Aimee Wolfson (Director of Intellectual Property and Deputy General Counsel at Sony Pictures), on August 13, 2014. Weil wrote:

> It's a stupid statement, but I don't think it's a blame thing. I think they are trying to convey that we are making changes independent/having nothing to do with the Korean position – so face scene b/c it might not be funny, etc.[162]

Wolfson wrote back:

> Well the highlighted sentence certainly stuck in my throat. Publicly blaming legal? Couldn't we just own the idea that we are trying to be nice and not offend unnecessarily?[163]

Can somebody please explain the thought process of these legal eagles to me? *Yes, we're still going to depict the assassination of your leader with a CIA trained hit squad of journalists, but your people won't think it's real because the buttons are obviously not accurate?*

A *New York Times* opinion article circulated among Sony executives Stephen Basil Jones, Nigel Clark and Steven Odell, in an email on July 8, 2014, gives some background as to why the North Korean leadership took *The Interview* so seriously.[164]

It seems absurd for the leader of a nuclear state to be so incensed over an anarchic comedy by the guys who brought you "This is the End" and "Pineapple Express." But movies have held inordinate importance in North Korean politics, beginning even before the country's founding in 1948. One of the earliest actions by Kim Il-sung, called Great Leader, was to create a Soviet supported national film studio, where he gave filmmakers and crews preferential food rations and housing. His son, Kim Jong-il, was a film buff who owned one of the largest private film collections in the world and whose first position of power was in running the regime's propaganda apparatus, including its film studios. For over 20 years he micromanaged every new North Korean film production, as writer, producer, executive and critic; to his people he is still known today first and foremost – thanks to propaganda rather than any real talent or skill – as the greatest creative genius in North Korea's history.[165]

It's kind of like that old joke in Hollywood that you can be the most powerful man in the world, but what you really want is to be a film director. Kim Jong-il was a film director, then became the most powerful man in North Korea, and yet it seemed he forever longed to be back on a film set. One wonders how Kim Jong-il might have managed as a film director in Hollywood.

The grandfather, Kim Il-sung saw the value of propaganda and set up a movie studio, the father Kim Jong-il became a movie director, and Kim Jong-un found himself the subject of a major Hollywood film.

But who is Kim Jong-un, the man behind the dictator?

The *New York Times* tried to answer that question.

As a character type, Kim Jong-un may be difficult to place: educated in Switzerland, he is a basketball fan and alleged computer nerd; his wife is Pyongyang's equivalent of Kate Middleton, and there are hopes he may yet open up the Hermit Kingdom – but oops, there he goes again, testing ballistic missiles, executing his own uncle, and letting his press agents call his South Korean counterpart a "filthy comfort woman."

One thing is clear: Mr. Kim deals in perception, not reality. His father and grandfather tried to assert that North Korea was the more legitimate and successful of the two Koreas. That battle was lost a long time ago. Now the grandson and his theater state must act as if his country has any reason to exist, and so his first job is to sustain that illusion.[166]

The *New York Times* had its narrative and was selling it to the country. Kim Jong-un dealt in "perception, not reality", he "must act as if his country has a reason to exist" and "his first job is to sustain that illusion."

That is the armchair psychologists' explanation for why he was so deeply troubled by *The Interview* and directed his hacker army to break into Sony Pictures Entertainment and release their data.

In the view of the *New York Times*, the North Korean regime releases propaganda, while in the United States we pursue art (even of the lowbrow variety), free from any government influence.

Right?

However, the Sony emails released by Wikileaks portray a Washington and Hollywood elite swooning over each other like a pair of star-crossed lovers, who can only be together for brief periods of time, before being separated by a cruel and remorseless fate.

This is an email from Sony Pictures CEO Michael Lynton to Senior Obama Advisor, Valerie Jarrett on July 15, 2014 at 2:06 pm:

Valerie:

Hope all is well with. I know the President is in town next week and it would be great to get together if you are with him and have a minute. Otherwise, I will see you on the Vineyard [Martha's Vineyard]. We get there August 2 and are here through the 14th. Dance party is on the 11th. Invitation to come. Looking forward to seeing you.

Warmly,
Michael.[167]

Within a minute, at 2:07 pm, Jarrett quickly wrote him back.

Yes, I will definitely be with him next week. Will circle back when I know our schedule.[168]

This email establishes two timeframes for Michael Lynton, to directly interact with President Obama, (in Hollywood on July 23, 2014, or at Martha's Vineyard from August 2-14) and if not the President, his most senior advisor, Valerie Jarrett.

This timeframe is critical as it is prior to the decision to move the release date of *The Interview* from October 10, 2014, to December 25, 2014, as well as digitally altering thousands of North Korean buttons in the film, as well as cut the scene of Kim Jong-un's face melting off during his assassination by a team of CIA-trained journalists.

It's circumstantial evidence to be certain, and yet there aren't many CEOs who have the opportunity to visit with a President of the United States twice within a month.

In the late afternoon of July 23, 2014, just before the event, Lynton sent a quick email to Jarrett, which read:

Looking forward to seeing you tonight. Malcolm Gladwell is going to join us who is staying at our house and who I think you will really like. Quick question, I am in Hancock Park at an event before our dinner and I just saw that you and the

President will be there. Any chance I could catch a ride with you back to the hotel as traffic may be tough. Obviously, this would not work if you were going back with the President! Just a thought.[169]

For those not familiar with Malcolm Gladwell, he's one of the country's leading non-fiction writers, the author of five New York Times bestsellers, and has been included in *TIME*'s 100 Most Influential People list.[170]

This is what life is like among the rich and famous.

You're a famous author, you get to stay at the home of a Hollywood studio CEO when you're in town, and you just might be able to hop a ride with the President's senior advisor before a dinner with the President. They're all part of the same club, and as George Carlin used to say, you're not in it. Jarrett wrote back to Lynton:

Say I am going back with him and cannot add to the manifest this late. Hopefully we will be well ahead of you so traffic won't be so bad. Really looking forward to it. I have not met Malcolm, but the President speaks very highly of him. I wish he could join us, but he is swamped. Marty Nesbitt and Eric Whitaker are two of the President's best friends. I think you will enjoy them too.[171]

As the head of a Hollywood studio, you might not be able to catch a ride with the President's senior advisor, but you will be introduced to the President's two best friends.

And apparently, it was a lovely evening, because Jarrett wrote Lynton back on August 1, 2014:

Hi Michael –

Two things: Could you invite Eric Whitaker to the dance party? Could you send me Malcolm's email?

VJ[172]

One can conclude that *New York Times* bestselling author Malcolm Gladwell was well-taken care of by the Obama White House and that Presidential best friend, Eric Whitaker, thoroughly enjoyed himself at the Michael Lynton dance party on Martha's Vineyard.

Probably the clearest example of Sony Pictures attempting to curry favor with the Obama Administration was the effort by Michael Lynton to hire retiring White House Press Secretary Jay Carney to the media team for Sony.

Of course, it started with an email from Valerie Jarrett to both Jay Carney and Michael Lynton, with the subject line "Connecting Two of my Favorite People."

Jay:

Michael called me today about a position that may be of interest to you, so you two can now communicate directly.

All the best,
VJ[173]

Lynton quickly responded and was apparently not above a little subterfuge. He claimed the position was not with Sony, but that was an incomplete answer. Lynton would dangle two positions before Carney, one of them with Sony. Lynton wrote:

Thanks Valerie! Jay, I am a big fan from a distance. I live in Los Angeles and am the CEO of Sony Entertainment. I would love to talk to you about an opportunity, not with Sony, and if you have a moment, I can describe it on the phone. I look forward to talking.[174]

It was Carney's last day working at the White House, so he was busy, but they made plans to talk the following Monday. After the conversation, Carney sent an email to Lynton.

Michael:

Thank you very much for connecting with me today. Both possibilities interest me. Tomorrow will be hard for me to do a video chat – I'll be moving around town all day. But Wednesday would work.

As for my California trip, I'm available Thursday evening, if you could come up to SF for dinner. Otherwise, my day Friday is booked. I'm supposed to have dinner with Michael Lewis on Friday in Berkeley, but I could see if he could move that to another day — if Friday would work for you and Evan. Otherwise, I could be available Saturday in SF for Evan. Or I could see if I could come down to LA Saturday morning.

Let me know what you think.

All the best,
Jay C.[175]

The Michael Lewis referenced in the email was another author, best known for his non-fiction books such as *Liar's Poker, Moneyball,* and *The Big Short. Moneyball* and *The Big Short* have both been made into movies starring the actor, Brad Pitt. Lewis and Gladwell can easily be seen as probably the two most favored writers of the Obama Administration.

However, the effort by Lynton to recruit Carney would ultimately fail, as detailed in a later *Politico* article published after the Sony hack.

In August, Lynton wrote an email to writer Walter Isaacson, saying, "I had lunch with Jay Carney who said wonderful things about you. Would love to have him for the big comms job at Sony if he asks about me."

Carney expressed interest in the position but reluctance about leaving Washington. He also told Lynton he'd have to convince his wife Claire Shipman, an ABC News correspondent, about leaving Washington …

The last correspondence between Carney and Lynton is from September, at which point Carney had joined CNN as a contributor. It's not clear where the discussions went after that point.

In February, Carney was hired by Amazon as senior vice president for Worldwide Corporate Affairs. [176]

Might an alien from outer space, observing how the American power structure works, conclude it's a small group of insiders who simply move between different centers of power?

As a studio chief, Michael Lynton had easy access to President Obama, his most senior advisor, Valerie Jarrett, as well as the most popular writers in the country, including Malcolm Gladwell, Michael Lewis, and Walter Isaacson. If Lynton couldn't catch President Obama while he was in Los Angeles soliciting money, there's always the chance they could catch up with each other in August at Martha's Vineyard.

Perhaps there will even be dancing.

And if you're White House Press Secretary Jay Carney, you can expect positive coverage from ABC News because your wife works there as a correspondent. And when you leave the White House you'll be pursued for a job by the head of Sony Pictures, and while you may not take that job, you can do a stint as a CNN contributor, before going to work for Amazon, one of the most successful companies on the planet.

Does anybody wonder whether a similar yellow brick road would be laid before the feet of the Press Secretary for a Republican administration?

I'll give the final word in this chapter to Julian Assange, from his press release of April 16, 2014:

The connections and alignments between Sony Pictures Entertainment and the US Democratic Party are detailed through these archives, including SPE's CEO Lynton attending dinner with President Obama at Martha's Vineyard and Sony employees being part of fundraising dinners for the Democratic Party. There are emails setting up a collective (https://wikileaks.org/sony/emails/emailid/135225) within the corporation to get around the 5,000 USD limit on corporate campaign donations to give 50,000 USD to get the Democratic New York Governor Andrew Cuomo elected as "Thanks to Governor Cuomo, we have a great production incentive environment in NY and a strong piracy advocate that's actually done more than talk about our problems. (https://wikileaks.org/sony/emails/emailid/49813)"

Sony Pictures Entertainment CEO Michael Lynton is on the board of trustees of RAND Corporation, an organization specializing in research and development for the United States Military and Intelligence sector. The Sony Archives show the flow of contacts and information between these two major industries, whether it is RAND wanting to invite George Clooney and Kevin Spacey to events, or Lynton offering contact to Valerie Jarrett (a close advisor to Obama) or RAND desiring a partnership with IMAX for digital archiving. With this close tie to the military-industrial complex it is no surprise that Sony reached out to RAND for advice regarding its North Korea film *The Interview*. RAND provided an analyst specialized in North Korea and suggested Sony reach out to the State Department and the NSA (https://wikileaks.org/sony/emails/emailid/12866) regarding North Korea's complaints about the film.[177]

Sony Pictures wanted to have a strong relationship with President Barack Obama, and more generally the Democratic Party, including Governor Cuomo in New York, who at the time was considered a likely eventual candidate for the Presidency. The evidence suggests they were even willing to bend election finance laws in order to achieve this objective.

It's odd that both Michael Lynton and Amy Pascal sat on the Board of Trustees for the RAND Corporation, designed as they are to serve the military and intelligence services of the United States.

What is the argument for a Hollywood studio being linked to a military and intelligence contractor, interested in the continuing profits of the defense industry and continuing American dominance in the world?

I can't think of one, unless it's to serve as the de facto propaganda wing of our military and intelligence communities.

In North Korea, we're told that Kim Jong-un's grandfather "gave filmmakers and crews preferential food rations and housing."[178]

It's difficult to see how the process is much different in the United States.

In America the food rations are far better, the mad paychecks these guys get take care of any housing issues, and their wives might even get to dance with the President during their summer vacation on Martha's Vineyard.

By simply bending the knee to the ruler, one gets access to the most accomplished writers and actors, the best intelligence from the nation's leading military think tank, and a phone call to the right person might net you a high-profile job at one of the wealthiest companies on the planet.

One might say in both instances those who curry favor with the leader are just rats in a maze, finding their way to the cheese, but in America the portion sizes are much larger.

CHAPTER SEVEN
AND JUST WHEN ALL
SEEMED DARKEST ...

Day 29 – Monday, December 22, 2014 - On Monday morning, State Department Deputy Spokesperson, Marie Harf, thirty-two years old, straight blonde hair to her shoulders, and glasses, took the podium at the Loy Henderson Room at the State Department (the main briefing room was undergoing renovations) to update the world on the ongoing dispute with North Korea.[179]

Unidentified reporter: Can I ask you about North Korea?

Marie Harf: Yes.

Unidentified reporter: I think over the weekend, they have threatened thousands of times greater punishment on the U.S. if there's any sort of move against them for the Sony attack, including attacks on the White House and Pentagon. I was wondering if I could get a response to that?

And also, if you can comment on reports, they [North Korea] have lost internet access and may be under attack?

Marie Harf: Well, on the first question, obviously, we take very seriously any threats to U.S. citizens, to U.S. companies, regardless of what that threat looks like. We're obviously aware of these recent reports. At this time, we have no specific credible threat information that lends credence to these reports.

But obviously, law enforcement, homeland security officials continue to monitor the situation and would closely follow any leads they may get, providing appropriate guidance to any one individual or entities that may be at risk. We do urge North Korea to exercise restraint, to refrain from further threatening actions at this time. Obviously, we talked about this a lot in the last few days, but that's what we're focused on right now.

In terms of your second question, as the president said, we are considering a range of options in response. We aren't going to discuss, you know, publicly, operational details about the possible response options or comment on those kinds of reports in any way, except to say that as we implement our responses, some will be seen, some may not be seen.

So, I can't confirm those reports, but in general, that's what the president has spoken to.[180]

Let's translate Marie Harf's comments into something we can all understand. The United States urged restraint and didn't want North Korea to keep making threats to attack the White House, Pentagon, or the American homeland.

As far as whether the U.S. had shown restraint, or whether they'd taken down North Korea's internet, Harf offered a "no comment."

Here's what you should actually hear. "Hell, yeah, we took down their internet! Yee haw! Praise the Lord and pass the ammunition!" The briefing continued:

Unidentified reporter: A follow up on North Korea. Also, over the weekend, the government [of North Korea] urged the United States to apologize for linking it to the Sony attacks. Any reaction to that call?

Marie Harf: Well, as the FBI and the president and everyone who's now made clear, we are confident the North Korean government is responsible for this destructive attack. We stand by this conclusion.

The government of North Korea has a long history of denying responsibility for destructive and provocative actions, and if they want to help here, they can admit their culpability and compensate Sony for the damages that they caused. Do you want to follow up?

Unidentified reporter: Yeah. You're calling on the North Korean government to compensate Sony?

Marie Harf: Well, over the weekend, they said a number of things, including what Pam referenced, but also talking about a joint investigation. And yes, if they want to help here, then they can admit their culpability and compensate Sony for the damages this attack caused.

Unidentified reporter: Okay. And you also said that the North Koreans have a long history of covering up—

Marie Harf: Of denying responsibility—

Unidentified reporter: Denying responsibility—

Marie Harf: —for destructive and provocative actions. That's obviously now cyber-related. Other actions as well.

Unidentified reporter: How would you rank the USA record on that?

Marie Harf: I don't think there's any comparison at all.

Unidentified reporter: Has not the United States government denied responsibility for things they ultimately admitted to?

Marie Harf: I don't think there's any comparison to anything the U.S. government does and anything the North Korean government does, period. If you have a more specific question, I'm happy to entertain that, but a broad comparison is just not warranted.

Unidentified reporter: Well, I mean for years and years you denied it. There was a denial of any role in the coup in Iran in 1953, for example. So, I'm just saying—

Marie Harf: An episode about which we've been very open and public and discussed—

Unidentified reporter: Recently. But it took about 40 years for that to happen.

Marie Harf: We are – look, I will put our record of discussing our history and our past up against any other country on the planet, particularly North Korea.[181]

You know you're having a bad day when you're trying to call somebody a liar, they ask about your lies, you ask for an example, then they provide an example in which you overthrew a country (not just hacked a company) and lied about it for forty years.

It should be more difficult to fool people in a democracy, but that requires paying attention. The reporters in the room can do their best, but it requires the greater media to point out the obvious inconsistencies.

Unidentified reporter: Can you talk about your consultations with the Six Party Talks about the hacking incident?

Marie Harf: What consultations specifically? The secretary spoke with his Chinese counterpart over the weekend, I believe, on December 21st to talk about a range of issues, including the recent cyber-attacks on Sony Pictures. We have discussed this issue with China specifically, in order to share information, express our concerns about the attack, and ask for its cooperation. That's a conversation that will be ongoing.

Unidentified reporter: Has the history between the U.S. and China on cybersecurity, like considering that the U.S. indicted five Chinese hackers this year, has that met any contentious discussions with China?

Marie Harf: First, the president said we have no evidence that any other government was involved here, and that includes the Chinese government. But look, we share a concern about cyber incidents. We raise them with China when we have a concern, but this is an area where, again, the secretary and others have asked for China's cooperation.

Obviously, despite our differences, I would say on this or other issues, we have affirmed that malicious cyber activity like this attack can pose a risk to international peace and security. So, we'll keep having the conversation with them.

Unidentified reporter: Do you have any thoughts about the fact that Chinese servers may have been used in this attack?

Marie Harf: I know there's an investigation on-going. I don't have any confirmation on those kinds of details. I know there's a lot of rumors out there. But again, no information, no evidence that any other government was involved here at this time.[182]

Chinese servers were used in the attack?

That can only mean two possible things. First, China was aiding North Korea's attack, which necessitates us doing to China what we did to North Korea, such as possibly disabling their internet.

Or that means somebody else took control of the Chinese servers as a way to make others believe it was North Korea.

The fact that we didn't attack China, or absolve North Korea of responsibility, makes little sense.

On this day, North Korea bowed out of a United Nations Security Council meeting which was to discuss North Korea's human rights record.

Day 30 – Tuesday, December 23, 2014 – As if we were at the climax of a film, where all seemed hopeless for our heroes, Sony announced *The Interview* would have a limited release on Christmas Day at any theaters that wanted to show the film.

A press release from Sony read:

"We have never given up on releasing *The Interview* and we're excited our movie will be in a number of theaters on Christmas Day," said Michael Lynton, Chairman and CEO of Sony Entertainment. "At the same time, we are continuing our efforts to secure more platforms and more theaters so that this movie reaches the largest possible audience."

"I want to thank our talent on The Interview and our employees, who have worked tirelessly through the many challenges we have all faced over the last month. While we hope this is only the first step of the film's release, we are proud to make it available to the public and to have stood up to those who attempted to suppress free speech."[183]

Doesn't it make you proud to be an American when Hollywood stands up so strongly for freedom of speech? I might be a little more inclined to join in the celebration but for the fact the CEO of that studio was on the Board of Trustees for the RAND Corporation. Or, if the work of art I was celebrating didn't involve the CIA recruiting journalists to assassinate a foreign leader.

But maybe those are just my problems.

Seth Rogen joined in the celebration, tweeting out, "The people have spoken! Freedom has prevailed! Sony didn't give up! *The Interview* will be shown at theaters willing to play it on Xmas Day!"[184]

The leading theater in this country for this effort was the Alamo Drafthouse in Austin, Texas, followed by the "Art House Convergence," a group of about 250 screens.[185]

And President Obama was a big fan of this decision as well, with the White House releasing the following statement:

> The president applauds Sony's decision to authorize screenings of the film. As the president made clear, we're a country that believes in free speech and the right of artistic expression. The decision made by Sony and participating theaters allows people to make their own choices about the film and we welcome that outcome.[186]

Isn't it great when you can become a rebel by getting the President of the United States and the military/industrial complex to cheer your efforts?

Day 31 – Wednesday, December 24, 2014 – Sony made *The Interview* available for rent online for $5.99 from YouTube Movies, Google Play, Microsoft's Xbox Video and a dedicated site run by the studio.

Day 32 – Thursday, December 25, 2014 – *The Interview* opened on Christmas day, there were no acts of violence, and the film made a million dollars from theaters on the day of release.[187] This did not include money made from online rentals and purchases, as the film was the number one rental on both YouTube and Google Play, with 110,000 upvotes on the YouTube platform, with 20,000 downvotes.[188]

One might say it was a Hollywood ending, North Korea free and liberated, Kim Jong-un dead, the North Koreans realizing their dictator was not a god who didn't have a butthole, Aaron and Dave were back home safely in America, the CIA was happy that they didn't screw up this assassination plot, and Sook, the former North Korean propaganda minister was presiding over the first free elections in North Korea, which of course made her the newly elected president of the country.

But was it good for Sony?

It's a complicated question.

The budget for the film was reported to be $44 million dollars. With a typical film, marketing costs usually equal or exceed the marketing budget. On January 20, 2015, it was reported *The Interview* had made about $6 million from theaters, but $40 million from video on demand sales like YouTube and Google Play.[189]

To most observers, it seemed *The Interview* was going to be somewhere between a thirty-to-forty-million-dollar loss for Sony Pictures, a company which couldn't keep losing money in such a dramatic fashion.

However, for those who wanted to keep heightening tensions with North Korea, the situation couldn't have been any better.

Saber-rattling with foreign adversaries, had traditionally been an activity often associated with the political right (George W. Bush falsely accusing Iraq of possessing weapons of mass destruction and initiating a catastrophic invasion which resulted in the death of more than a million Iraqis, or the supplying of arms to Central American rebels during the 1980s under the Reagan Administration). These types of efforts were now strongly linked to the progressive left, with Hollywood and President Obama captaining the ship, (maybe with the RAND Corporation as first mate) which like the *USS General Sherman*, might steam right into North Korea and demand terms.

Nothing like replacing gunboat diplomacy with a little cyber-terrorism (taking down the North Korean internet for example) and media hysteria, right?

On January 2, 2015, Obama imposed additional sanctions against North Korea:

Pursuant to the International Emergency Economic Powers Act (50 U.S.C. 1701 et seq.) (IEEPA), I hereby report that I have issued an Executive Order (the "order") with respect to North Korea that expands the national emergency declared in Executive Order 13466 of June 26, 2008, expanded in scope in Executive Order 13551 of August 30, 2010, and relied upon for additional steps in Executive Order 13570 of April 18, 2011. The order takes additional steps to address North Korea's continued actions that threaten the United States and others.

In 2008, upon terminating the exercise of certain authorities under the Trading with the Enemy Act (TWEA) with respect to North Korea, the President issued Executive Order 13466 and declared a national emergency pursuant to IEEPA to deal with the unusual and extraordinary threat to the national security and foreign policy of the United States posed by the existence and risk of the proliferation of weapons-usable fissile material on the Korean Peninsula. Executive Order 13466 continued certain restrictions on North Korea and North Korean nationals that had been in place under TWEA.

In 2010, I issued Executive Order 13551. In that order I determined that the Government of North Korea's continued provocative actions destabilized the Korean peninsula and imperiled U.S. Armed Forces, allies and trading partners in the region and warranted the imposition of additional sanctions, and I expanded the national emergency declared in Executive Order 13466. In Executive Order 13551, I ordered blocked the property and interests in property of three North Korean entities and one individual listed in the Annex to that order and provided criteria under which the Secretary of the Treasury, in consultation with the Secretary of State, may designate additional persons whose property and interests in property shall be blocked.

In 2011, I issued Executive order 13570 to further address the national emergency with respect to North Korea and to strengthen the implementation of United Nations National Security Resolution 1718 and 1874. That Executive Order prohibited the direct or indirect importation of goods, services, and technology from North Korea.

I have now determined that the provocative, destabilizing, and repressive actions and policies of the Government of North Korea, including its destructive and coercive cyber-related actions during November and December 2014, actions in violation of United Nations Security Resolutions 1718, 1874, 2087, and 2094, and commission of serious human rights abuses, constitute a continuing threat to the national security, foreign policy, and economy of the United States.

The order is not targeted at the people of North Korea, but rather is aimed at the Government of North Korea and its activities that threaten the United States and others. The order leaves in place all existing sanctions imposed under Executive Orders 13466, 13551, and 13570. It provides criteria for blocking the property and interests in property of any person determined by the Secretary of the Treasury, in consultation with the Secretary of State:

- to be an agency, instrumentality, or controlled entity of North Korea or the Workers' Party of Korea;

- to be an official of the Government of North Korea;

- to be an official of the Workers' Party of Korea;

- to have materially assisted, sponsored, or provided financial, material or technological support for, or goods or services to or in support of, the Government of North Korea or any person whose property and interests in property are blocked pursuant to the order, or to be owned or controlled by, or to have acted or purported to act for or on behalf of, directly or indirectly, the Government of North Korea or any person whose property and interests in property are blocked pursuant to the order.

In addition, the order suspends entry into the United States of any alien determined to meet one or more of the above criteria.

I have delegated to the Secretary of the Treasury the authority, in consultation with the Secretary of State, to take such actions, including the promulgation of rules and regulations, and to employ all powers granted to the President by IEEPA, as may be necessary to carry out the purposes of the order. All executive agencies are directed to take all appropriate measures within their authority to carry out the provisions of the order.

I am enclosing a copy of the Executive Order I have issued.

Sincerely,

Barack Obama.[190]

It all makes for a comforting little narrative, doesn't it?

Sony makes a film that criticizes North Korea.

North Korea complains, but nothing happens.

North Korea hacks Sony and releases embarrassing emails.

The U.S. government proclaims North Korea as the culprit.

The internet in North Korea goes down. Did we do it? We won't answer the question.

Despite the threats, *The Interview* opens on Christmas Day, and although it's a dud for Sony Pictures, it's a definite win for the military/industrial complex who've now got people terrorized about North Korean nukes raining down on the West Coast. Hollywood and the liberals are now neocons, like former Vice-President, Dick Cheney, who lied us into the Iraq War. Anti-war democrats are beginning to look like an endangered species.

The Obama Administration slaps additional sanctions on North Korea.

All in all, it's a win for Team America.

But is this an accurate narrative?

Getting to the bottom of a cyber-hacking incident is incredibly difficult because the hackers tend to be highly intelligent, experts at covering their tracks, or setting a false trail for investigators to follow.

Deception is built into the very fabric of the crime.

But as Norse Corporation and Eric began their investigation, they followed the first principles of every investigator.

Start at the beginning, the initial point of contact.

It's the place where the criminals are most likely to make a mistake. It's said that no plan survives contact with the enemy, so like a fighter who trains in a certain way to take on an opponent, those first few moments in the ring are dedicated to figuring out if the plan is a solid one, or needs to be modified, or abandoned.

On November 21, 2014, three days before the attack, a group calling itself "God'sApstls" [God's Apostles], sent an email to the Sony executives in broken English. It read:

We've got great damage by Sony Pictures.

The compensation for it, monetary compensation we want.

Pay the damage, or Sony Pictures will be bombarded as a whole.

You know us very well. We never wait long.

You'd better behave wisely.

From God'sApstls[191]

The hackers used a throwaway Gmail address, similar to other addresses they would use in future communications with reporters. The phrase "God'sApstls" was also found inside the malware code which wiped many of the Sony computers clean of their data.

In the history of ransom notes, has there ever been anything less terrifying, or more designed to make the recipients believe it's a fake?

And like the Sherlock Holmes story of the dog that didn't bark, where are any demands relating to *The Interview*?

This was a demand for money, plain and simple.

And in what may have been the most accurate prediction of the day, a user on the Reddit site (/u/Fancyjackalope) who claimed to be a former employee of Sony (and in touch with current employees), predicted that North Korea would be named as the culprit. Others were less impressed with the prediction, given the public hostility of the North Korean regime to Sony Pictures.

The FBI alert, which was sent out on December 2, 2014, nine days after the breach, noted with alarm it was the first time that dangerous wiper malware had been used in an attack against the United States, representing a significant escalation of the threat a hacker group could pose to any business or government. Wiper malware is highly destructive, having the ability to wipe hard drives and even flash memory. Individual computers may be impossible to restore, their data destroyed, with the only hope of restoration being backups which are stored offsite.

And the narrative was beginning to shift, starting with a *Wall Street Journal* article on December 1, 2014, suggesting that the evidence was starting to point to North Korea. And in their defense, the "Guardians of Peace" were beginning to suggest such a possible motive. While it was difficult to know if the message was genuinely from the group, a password protected email was sent to various journalists, which read:

> Our aim is not at the film *The Interview* as Sony Pictures suggests. But it is widely reported as if our activity is related to *The Interview*. This shows how dangerous a film *The Interview* is. *The Interview* is very dangerous enough to cause a massive hack attack. Sony Pictures produced the film harming regional peace and security and violating human rights for money. The news with *The Interview* fully acquaints us with the crimes of Sony Pictures.[192]

The question is whether the "Guardians of Peace" were simply using the opportunity presented by North Korea's protests against the film as a convenient scapegoat, expecting the American government to swallow the bait. As the article reported:

> North Korea has been intensely critical of Sony Pictures' upcoming film *The Interview*, a comedy that follows a plot to assassinate the North Korean leader Kim Jong-un. Sony has already edited out some of the film's more controversial points, including a scene in which Kim Jong-un's face melts off in slow motion in tribute to *Raiders of the Lost Ark*. North Korean officials responded to news of the film by saying, "a film about the assassination of a foreign leader mirrors what the US has done in Afghanistan, Iraq, Syria and Ukraine. [Author's note – In 2014, an uprising in Ukraine which replaced the democratically-elected pro-Russian leader with a pro-US leader was widely blamed on the American CIA.[193]][194]

Does the world look a little different when one considers that since September 11, 2001, the United States has been pretty much four and zero for making any of these countries a better place to live?

That doesn't mean that those who were on the ground, attempting to accomplish an impossible task, didn't work incredibly hard, suffer, and in many cases, sacrificed their lives.

Is North Korea's criticism of the military interventions of the United States and the loss of hundreds of thousands, if not more than a million lives during that time frame, much different than a reasonably objective individual?

However, the counter narrative to the U.S. government's conclusion that North Korea was behind the hack was building among the cybersecurity community.

Dublin-based information security consultant Brian Homan, who heads Ireland's computer emergency response team, said that despite the claims of the Guardian of Peace, "at this stage it is not possible to identify and attribute who is behind these attacks." Anyone could have repurposed previously seen wiper malware for these attacks, he contends. "There are samples of wiper-type malware available online that those with the right skills and motivation could reuse or include in their own malware."

Given the Lizard Squad's past hack of the Sony Playstation, they would have to be placed on the short list of groups possible of this type of attack.

And then, as if on cue, Lizard Squad reentered the picture. As recounted in an article from *The Guardian*, on December 26, 2014:

> Millions of people could not use their games console for a second day as disruption on the Xbox Live and Sony Playstation networks continued after an apparent cyber-attack.
>
> A group calling itself Lizard Squad claimed responsibility for bringing down both networks on Christmas Eve, which could have affected 160 million gamers…

The news is damaging for Microsoft, but particularly for Sony, which suffered a high profile hack in early December by a group called Guardians of Peace. Stolen emails were leaked and published, revealing embarrassing exchanges between executives and celebrities, while stolen files and even film scripts left the company so exposed it has reportedly reverted to using fax machines and paper in its offices.[195]

Let's think about what is being alleged.

Lizard Squad attacked the Sony Playstation in Christmas of 2012.

North Korea supposedly hacked Sony Pictures in November of 2014.

Lizard Squad attacked the Sony Playstation again in Christmas of 2014.

Is it beyond the range of possibility that when there are three attacks against a company, maybe all three were done by the same group, rather than two different groups?

Once you get into a company, one would imagine it would be easier to get in the second time, and then the third time. And it makes sense that when the hacker group got in again, they'd say something like "You know us very well" in their ransom demand.

And what did Lizard Squad have to say in regard to their hack? Helpfully, a man from Finland who appeared under the name, "Ryan" a short-haired blond man who looked to be in his early twenties, gave an interview to a journalist after their 2014 Christmas hack of the Sony Playstation. As to how they did it:

> This attack was basically done by three people. We had a couple of people from outside the group helping with the attacks, helping us a little bit, but most of the traffic was coming from one or two people.[196]

It may have taken just three people to hack Sony (whether for the Playstation or Sony Pictures), but you needed a government full of idiots to turn it into an international incident and make people fear nuclear war at Christmas time. As for the question of why this relatively small group of hackers did it:

> Mostly to raise awareness. To amuse ourselves. One of the big aspects here was raising awareness regarding the low state of computer security at these companies. Because these companies make tens of millions of dollars every month from subscriber fees and that doesn't even include purchases made by their customers. They should have more than enough funding to protect against these attacks.[197]

You know the world has turned upside-down when you find yourself sympathetic to a hacker's argument. I can't find much fault with the logical argument that when a company is making tens of millions of dollars with internet traffic, they should spend a couple of those dollars on making sure the system is secure.

When "Ryan" was asked whether he felt bad about denying millions of game users the ability to play their new game, the response might as well have come from a grumpy old man, rather than a twenty-something hacker:

> I'd rather be worried if these people didn't have anything better to do than play games on their consoles on Christmas Eve and Christmas Day…I might have forced a couple kids to spend time with their families instead of playing games.[198]

It must be remembered this is a confession to a hack of the Sony Playstation in Christmas of 2014 (as well as in Christmas of 2012) and NOT Sony Pictures.

But considering this was the second time they'd hacked Sony, it seems only reasonable to ask whether they were behind the 2014 hack, shutdown, and destruction of many Sony computer systems.

But there was more than just the Christmas 2012 and Christmas 2014 attacks on the Sony Playstation to link Lizard Squad to the Sony November 2014 attack on Sony Pictures.

On August 24, 2014, just as Sony Pictures and North Korea were publicly feuding about *The Interview,* the Lizard Squad was actively harassing Sony, putting out a bomb threat against Sony Online Entertainment President John Smedley while on a cross-country commercial flight. As the UPI reported on August 25, 2014:

> The Lizard Squad appeared to take credit for this, too, tweeting that "there are lizards in Sony's datacenter" and claimed to have "planted the ISIS flag on @Sony's servers," claiming a connection to the terrorist group acting in Syria and Iraq…
>
> One passenger aboard the flight said the pilot had announced the diversion over the intercom during flight and blamed a "security breach in the cargo section." After the plane landed in Phoenix, passengers were put on buses while dogs inspected the airplane and luggage.
>
> Smedley confirmed he was on board the flight, tweeting from the tarmac. He reassured his nearly 42,000 followers that "all is well," but refused to say more.
>
> "Yes. My plane was diverted," he tweeted. "Not going to discuss more than that. Justice will find these guys."[199]

The profile begins to form of Lizard Squad. They're willing to cross many lines in order to make their point, even claiming an association with the ISIS terrorists who are beheading people in the Middle East or resurrecting the fear of air terrorism which found full bloom in the American imagination on September 11, 2001.

An ABC News article shortly after the bomb threat against Smedley sought to paint a full picture of the group. They wrote:

Lizard Squad is vocal, taunting and a bit obnoxious on Twitter, where it has taken credit for taking down a number of high-profile targets, including the Vatican's website, Sony's Playstation network, Battle.net and League of Legends...

Cole Stryker, who explored hacking culture in his book, "Hacking the Future: Privacy, Identity, and Anonymity on the Web," said Lizard Squad's style of hacking seems very similar to the "early days of LulzSec," a former hacking group.

"Very trollish, prankstery," Stryker said. "I don't believe this person genuinely wants to be involved in geopolitics. I think this person is just having a laugh."[200]

Let's put ourselves in the "trollish" and "prankstery" mind of Lizard Squad. You take down a couple gaming sites, you hack the Vatican (maybe that's why you jokingly call yourself "God's Apostles"?), and then what do you do to top yourself?

Create an international incident between North Korea and the United States, with a side-benefit of skewering Hollywood, as if you were living your own episode of the hilariously rude, animated cartoon series *South Park*?

Lizard Squad may have been riding high in November and December of 2014, as Sony dealt with the hack of their computer system and the release of *The Interview*, or even in January of 2015, as President Obama placed additional sanctions on North Korea.

But Lizard Squad would soon find itself in very serious trouble, courtesy of the Norse Corporation, and the work of Eric and Mr. Grey.

Chapter Eight
Lost in the Forest of Shadows

Perhaps more than any other criminals, hackers have the best chance of evading justice.

Locard's Principle, which lies at the very heart of forensic science, says that the perpetrator will always leave something at the crime scene, such as fingerprints, hair, DNA, and will always take something away, such as the threads from someone's shirt, mud on the shoes, or if the crime is a heinous murder, possibly the blood of his victim.

One might think that the hack of a computer system would be an exception to Locard's principle, since the criminals can be thousands of miles away, concealing their identity by using routers and networking through multiple locations.

But digital forensics can capture a large amount of information, and although it requires a great deal of analysis, the findings gleaned from the examination can be as solid as those gained through traditional forensics.

When a major cybersecurity breach takes place in the world, the cybersecurity companies go on high alert, like a bunch of bounty hunters, who at the same time, all learn of a million-dollar reward for an escaped prisoner.

In law enforcement terms they want "the collar," or the digital putting of hands on the suspect as they hand him or her over to law enforcement.

While Eric, Mr. Grey, and Norse Corporation took some of the heaviest fire for their claim that North Korea was not behind the hack of Sony Pictures, there were many other individuals and corporations who made significant contributions.

The FBI's claim that North Korea was behind the attack seemed to rest on four pieces of evidence, and we will go over each one of them in detail.

The first was a linguistic analysis which came to the conclusion that those who created the code were Korean.

The second was that the data deletion malware used in the attack had similarities to an August 12, 2012 attack on the Saudi arm of the oil and gas giant, Aramco, (Nicknamed "Shamoon") which at the time was blamed on Iran.

The third piece of evidence was a comparison of the data deletion malware that was used in a series of attacks on South Korea banks and television stations, culminating in a large attack on June 25, 2013, the 63rd Anniversary of the start of the Korean War, (nicknamed "Dark Seoul") which was widely blamed on North Korea.

The fourth piece of evidence cited by the FBI was that there was significant overlap in the infrastructure used in the attack against Sony, and malicious cyber-activity which the U.S. Government had linked to North Korea.

We will look individually at each one of these claims and show the relative strength and weakness of each claim.

It's generally agreed that the attackers left less than 2,000 words of original text to analyze, whether in emails to Sony Pictures or on-line posts.[201] Many of the posts were in broken-English, suggesting somebody who was not a native speaker, or was trying to conceal their identity.

But a new field, computational linguistics, tried to answer the question of the nationality of the hackers. As the New York Times reported on December 24, 2014, just a day before the release of *The Interview*:

On Wednesday, one alternate theory emerged. Computational linguistics at Taia Global, a cybersecurity consultancy, performed a linguistic analysis of the hackers' online messages – which were all written in imperfect English – and concluded based on translation errors and phrasing, the attackers are more likely to be Russian speakers than Korean speakers.

Such linguistic analysis is hardly foolproof. But the practice, known as stylometry, has been used to contest the authors behind some of history's most disputed documents, from Shakespearean sonnets to the Federalist Papers...[202]

The analysis by Tai Global cannot be considered definitive. Other programs required at least 6,500 words of original text in order to determine possible authorship.[203]

However, the *New York Times* article noted a curious company, CrowdStrike, which was relatively anonymous in 2014.

In 2017 CrowdStrike broke into the headlines for their claim that "the Russians" and not an insider, had hacked the Democratic National Committee website, and released a number of embarrassing emails to Julian Assange and Wiki-Leaks.[204] This set the stage for what became known as "Russia-gate" and initiated the 637-day investigation by Robert Mueller of claims the Trump Campaign "colluded" with Russia.

But in 2014, CrowdStrike wasn't accusing Russians of hacking into our presidential elections. They were claiming North Korea had hacked Sony Pictures. Here's some of that back-and-forth exchange between CrowdStrike, and a former government official.

It is also worth noting that other private security researchers say their own research backs up the government's claims. [Of North Korean involvement] CrowdStrike, a California security firm that has been tracking the same group that attacked Sony since 2006, believes they are located in North

Korea and have been hacking targets in South Korea for years.

But without more proof, skeptics are unlikely to accept F.B.I. claims without demur. "In the post-Watergate post-Snowden world, the USG [United States Government] can no longer simply say 'trust us,'" Paul Rosenzweig, the Department of Homeland Security's former deputy assistant secretary for policy, wrote on the Lawfare blog Wednesday. "Not with the U.S. public and not with other countries. Though the skepticism may not be warranted, it is real."

Mr. Rosenzweig argued that the government should release more persuasive evidence.[205]

If one didn't know any better this would look like the debate one would expect to see in a free society. The government has an opinion, it's challenged by an independent source, then another "independent" source supports the government. The typical reader shrugs their shoulders and says, "Well, it sounds like the smart people are figuring it out" and moves on with life.

But is Crowd-Strike a legitimate actor, or a puppet whose strings are being pulled by others?

Many found it odd that in the alleged 2016 hack of the Democratic National Committee by Russia, the democrats did not allow their computers to be inspected by the FBI, and that the only report ever generated was performed by Crowd-Strike.[206]

Certainly, one would want the United States government to have access to the evidence of foreign interference in our election system, wouldn't they?

In a court case, a previous instance of lying by a witness on an important matter can be used by the jury to make conclusions about the general honesty and reliability of the witness.

If CrowdStrike lied about claims of Russian interference in our elections 2016, can we trust their claims of North Korean interference from 2014?

In May of 2020, the sworn testimony of CrowdStrike President Shawn Henry in regard to their analysis of the hack of the Democratic National Committee and the accusation it was done by Russian actors was released to the general public. It is both illuminating and deeply troubling. This is from an article by *Real Clear Politics* on the release of the sworn testimony.

CrowdStrike, the private cyber-security firm that first accused Russia of hacking Democratic Party emails and served as a critical source of U.S. Intelligence officials in the years-long Trump-Russia probe, acknowledged to Congress more than two years ago that it had no concrete evidence that Russian hackers stole emails from the Democratic National Committee's server.

CrowdStrike president Shawn Henry's admission under oath, in a recently declassified December 2017 interview before the House Intelligence Committee, raises new questions about whether Special Counsel Robert Mueller, intelligence officials and Democrats misled the public. The allegation that Russia stole Democratic Party emails from Hillary Clinton, John Podesta and others and then passed them to WikiLeaks helped trigger the FBI's probe into now debunked claims of a conspiracy between the Trump campaign and Russia to steal the 2016 election.[207]

How is it that this information on one of the most important questions our country faced from 2017 to 2019, whether or not the Trump campaign colluded with Russia to steal the 2016 election, was kept hidden?

The question which must be asked is who benefits from this secrecy? Was it necessary for the investigative process? Or did it help to keep alive the fiction that the then president of the United States owed his position to the influence of a foreign adversary?

One must ask how deep this rabbit hole goes. The article continued with even more troubling questions:

> The firm's work with the DNC and the FBI is also colored by partisan affiliations. Before joining CrowdStrike, Henry served as executive assistant director at the FBI under Mueller. Co-founder Dmitri Alperovitch is a vocal critic of Vladmir Putin and a senior fellow at the Atlantic Council, the pro-NATO think tank that has consistently promoted an aggressive policy toward Russia. And the newly released testimony confirms that Crowd-Strike was hired to investigate the DNC breach by Michael Sussman of Perkins Coie – the same Democratic law firm that hired Fusion GPS to produce the discredited Steele dossier, which was also treated as central evidence in the investigation. Sussman played a critical role in generating the Trump-Russia collusion allegation. Ex-British spy and dossier compiler Christopher Steele has testified in a British court that Sussman shared with him the now-debunked Alfa Bank server theory, alleging a clandestine communication channel between the bank and the Trump organization.[208]

Can CrowdStrike be considered an independent company, or is it nothing more than an extension of the FBI and other intelligence services? I do not want to make claims which go beyond the evidence.

But the questions must be asked.

I am agnostic on the question of whether the Russians hacked the Democratic National Committee, or whether North Korea hacked Sony Pictures.

However, I don't believe the evidence is strong for any of these claims, and the fact that the same actors seem to be on stage in both international dramas, raises strong suspicions in my mind that we've all been played.

Henry's released testimony does not mean that Russia did not hack the DNC. What it does make clear is that Obama administration officials, the DNC and others have misled the public by presenting as fact information they knew was uncertain. The fact that the Democratic Party employed the two private firms at heart of Russia-gate – Russian email hacking and Trump-Russia collusion – suggests that the federal investigation was compromised from the start.[209]

It's difficult to come to any other conclusion than that at best, Obama administration officials were willing to assert as true things which were unclear, or at worse, they were willing to manufacture evidence to frame a political figure and do their very best to cover their tracks.

Could it be that the cast of characters who brought us the discredited Trump-Russia collusion story are the same as those who pushed the story that the North Korea hacked Sony Pictures?

As I've said before, in the legal system, evidence of dishonesty in one instance can be used to create a presumption that the suspect may be lying in another situation.

Were the emails of the hackers originally written in Russian, Korean, or English, and then re-written to sound like they came from a foreign actor?

The answer seems to be that we do not know.

But what we do know is that the United States government accused North Korea of hacking Sony Pictures, then did not deny that the United States was behind an attack on North Korea's internet.

Once that attack was launched, how likely was the United States to admit it made a mistake?

The second piece of evidence is that the Sony hack resembled an attack (nicknamed "Shamoon") in 2012 on the Saudi Arabian oil giant, Aramco.

But what's curious about the claims in 2014 and 2015 that North Korea was involved in the 2012 hack of Aramco, is that at the time the government blamed it on Iran. As described in breathless terms by the *New York Times* in 2012:

> The hackers picked the one day of the year they knew they could inflict the most damage on the world's most valuable company, Saudi Aramco.

> On August 15, more than 55,000 Saudi Aramco employees stayed home from work to prepare for one of Islam's holiest nights of the year – Lailat al Qadr, or the Night of Power – celebrating the revelation of the Koran to Muhammad.

> That morning, at 11:08, a person with privileged access to the Saudi state-owned oil company's computers, unleashed a computer virus to initiate what is regarded as among the most destructive acts of computer sabotage on a company to date. The virus erased data on three-quarters of Aramco's corporate PCs – documents, spreadsheets, emails, files – replacing all of it with an image of a burning American flag.

> United States intelligence officials say the attack's real perpetrator was Iran, although they offered no specific evidence to support that claim. But the secretary of defense, Leon E. Panetta, in a recent speech warning of the dangers of computer attacks, cited the Aramco sabotage as "a significant escalation of the cyber threat." In the Aramco case, hackers who called themselves the "Cutting Sword of Justice" and claimed to be activists upset about Saudi policies in the Middle East took responsibility.[210]

Why might Iran be interested in hacking Saudi Arabia's most profitable company? Well, the two of them are not friendly. And possibly Iran was retaliating for the alleged American and Israeli attack on their computer program in June of that same year.

Shamoon's code included a so-called kill switch, a timer set to attack at 11:08 a.m., the exact time that Aramco's computers were wiped of memory. Shamoon's creators even gave the erasing mechanism a name: Wiper.

Computer security researchers noted that the same name, Wiper, had been given to an erasing component of Flame, a computer virus that attacked Iranian oil companies and came to light in May. Iranian oil ministry officials have claimed that the Wiper software code forced them to cut Internet connections to their oil ministry, oil rigs and the Kharg Island oil terminal, a conduit for 80 percent of Iran's oil exports.

It raised suspicions that the Aramco hacking was retaliation. The United States fired one of the first shots in the computer war and has long maintained the upper hand. The New York Times reported in June that the United States, together with Israel, was responsible for Stuxnet, the computer virus used to destroy centrifuges in an Iranian nuclear facility in 2010.[211]

But are we simply dealing with a house of mirrors, in which we see what we want to see? Because when independent researchers examined the malware code, they didn't point the finger at Iran.

After analyzing the software code from the attack, security experts say that the event involved a company insider, or insiders, with privileged access to Aramco's network. The virus could have been carried on a USB memory stick that was inserted into a PC.

Aramco's attackers posted blocks of I.P. addresses of thousands of Aramco's PCs online as proof of the attack. Researchers say that only an Aramco employee or contractor with access to the company's internal network would have been able to grab that list from a disconnected computer inside Aramco's network and put it online.[212]

However, just because there was an insider assisting the Aramco attack doesn't preclude Iranian involvement. The Iranians could have paid a Saudi traitor, just as easily as a Russian might bribe an American, or vice-versa.

In the world of intelligence there are few who can claim an unblemished record.

The complexity of assigning blame in these instances was detailed in a *Reuters* article from September of 2012:

> The hackers' apparent access to a mole, willing to take personal risks to help, is an extraordinary development in a country where open dissent is banned.

> "It was someone who had inside knowledge and inside privileges within the company," said a source familiar with the ongoing forensic examination.

> Hackers from a group called "The Cutting Sword of Justice" claimed responsibility for the attack. They say the computer virus gave them access to documents from Aramco's computers and have threatened to release secrets. No documents have so far been published. [Author's question – Did the Saudis pay a ransom?]

> Reports of similar attacks on other oil and gas firms in the Middle East, including in neighboring Qatar, suggest there may be similar activity elsewhere in the region, although the attacks have not been linked …

In a posting on an online bulletin board the day the files were wiped, the group said Saudi Aramco was the main source of income for the Saudi government, which it blamed for "crimes and atrocities" in several countries, including Syria and Bahrain.[213]

In August of 2015, more than nine months after the Sony hack, the perpetrators of the hack of Saudi Aramco, were still unidentified, according to CNN News.[214]

When one reads of the hack of Saudi Aramco, by a shadowy group calling itself "The Cutting Sword of Justice," it sounds like the same type of juvenile name as "The Guardians of Peace," who perpetrated the Sony hack.

One wonders if the same group of hackers were involved, or if some personnel were common to both groups, or were the hackers simply studying and copying the tactics of other successful hacker groups?

It seems to me that any of these options are possible.

What must also be remarked upon is how well the hackers planned their crime, at a time when defenses and monitoring of the computer network were likely to be low as people were planning a holiday.

The Sony hackers chose the Monday before Thanksgiving, knowing that many parents would need to take that week off from school as their children would be at home. While it's not evidence, let me share my suspicions as to why the hackers who got into Saudi Aramco were unlikely to be sponsored by a government.

Given the well-known hostility between Iran and Saudi Arabia, what's the best strategy, assuming the hackers were Iranian, to deal with the vast amount of data they stole from Aramco? Given what we know about the Middle East, and how often Saudi Arabia pays off its critics, I'd have to assume that the data stolen in the hack would show many interesting business practices.

What better way to decouple European governments from Saudi Arabia and want to engage with Iran, then to release such damaging information? I understand those who might claim Iran would be in a better position by hiding those secrets and using them to their advantage, but I see that as less plausible. Iran seeks legitimacy from the West, and the quickest way to do that would be to humiliate their rivals in the region and position themselves as the less corrupt alternative for Middle Eastern oil.

Was Iran also falsely accused by the United States government?

The next piece of evidence would seem to point to North Korea, especially given the animosity with which South and North Korea have harbored over the years towards each other. Not only is there the legacy of the Korean War, but the seventy years of tit for tat escalation between the two, with a demilitarized zone between them, the launching of propaganda balloons by South Korea, as well as the occasional small-arms fire from the North Korean side.

The attack, which began on March 20, 2013, was known as the "Dark Seoul" attack, and the investigation was similarly plagued by confusion about the guilty party. The attack took down several major South Korean banks, and television stations, as well as crippling thousands of computers.[215] The *New York Times* reported:

> The Korean Communications Commission said Thursday that the disruption originated at an internet provider address in China but that it was still now known who was responsible.

> Many analysts in Seoul suspect that North Korean hackers honed their skills in China and were operating there. At a hacking conference here last year, Michael Sutton, the head of threat research at Zscaler, a security company, said a handful of hackers from China "were clearly very skilled, knowledgeable and were in touch with their counterparts and familiar with the scene in North Korea."

But there has never been any evidence to back up some analysts' speculation that they were collaborating with their Chinese counterparts. "I've never seen any evidence that points to any exchanges between China and North Korea," said Adam Segal, a senior fellow who specializes in China and cyberconflict at the Council on Foreign Relations.

Wednesday's attacks, which occurred as American and South Korean military forces were conducting major exercises, were not as sophisticated as some from China that have struck United States computers, and certainly less sophisticated than the American and Israeli cyberattack on Iran's nuclear facilities. But it was far more complex than a "denial of service" attack that simply overwhelms a computer system with a flood of data.[216]

The attack originated from an internet provider address in China? That seems to indicate to me a number of possibilities.

First, the Chinese were involved in the hack, putting their relations with South Korea and the United States in jeopardy. Without more information, I'd be skeptical that China was involved in the attack.

Second, the Chinese were not involved in the hack. That would mean that somebody, either an independent group of hackers had hijacked the address, or North Korea was using it.

Given the well-known propensity of hackers to try to hide their identity, we must look with suspicion upon the fact that the internet provider address was located in China.

While the "experts" who suspected China was involved in the hack didn't want their names to be published by the *New York Times*, Adam Segal, a senior fellow at the Council on Foreign Relations, had no hesitation in attaching his name to the opinion that no evidence existed on Chinese and North Korean collaboration on hacking.

And it's a little concerning to me that even the *New York Times* inadvertently admits that the US is the world's dominant force in cyber-hacking, given their remarkable success with the Stuxnet virus they used to attack Iran's nuclear program. If the US is the world's leader in cyber-warfare, isn't it at least worth asking the question of whether the US might be fanning the fires of conflict, in order to justify the staggering amounts of money being spent by the defense industries?

And if the United States has such a dominance in the cyber domain, how can we be certain they are telling us the truth? If the situation were reversed, and a foreign adversary possessed control in the cyber and information realms, would we encourage our citizens to believe their claims?

My suspicion is we would not.

We would be properly skeptical of any nation which possessed such an imbalance of power.

If for the purposes of analysis, we simply shifted our opinions, and considered for a moment the possibility the United States might lie as we'd expect any foreign adversary to lie, how would we interpret this section of the *New York Times* account?

> The cyberattacks Wednesday come just days after North Korea blamed South Korea and the United States for attacks on some of its Web sites. The north's official Korean Central News Agency said last week that North Korea "will never remain a passive onlooker to the enemies' cyberattacks that have reached a very grave phase as part of their moves to stifle it."

> The South Korean government cautioned that it was still too early to point the finger for Wednesday's problems at the North, which has been threatening "pre-emptive nuclear attacks" and other, unspecified actions against its southern neighbor for conducting the military exercises with the United States this month and for supporting new American-led United Nations sanctions against the North.[217]

When North Korea makes an allegation that South Korea and the United States have attacked their internet, are there ever calls in the United Nations for a full investigation? I have no idea whether such allegations are valid, but according to my research, these claims have never been the subject of any reasonable inquiry.

Wouldn't it be interesting to have an objective source looking into the question of how the United States is conducting itself as the world's most powerful cyberwarfare force? Perhaps we would uncover some interesting facts in the shadows.

Is North Korea simply responding to Western provocations, or is an even more confusing game afoot? The *New York Times* article continued:

> The malware is called 'Dark Seoul' in the computer world and was first identified about a year ago. It is intended to evade some of South Korea's most popular antivirus products and to render computers unusable. In Wednesday's strikes, the attackers made no effort to disguise the malware, leading some to question whether it came from a state sponsor – which tend to be more stealthy – or whether officials or hackers in North Korea were sending a specific, clear message: that they can reach into Seoul's economic heart without blowing up South Korean warships or shelling South Korean islands.[218]

When there's little direct evidence, it can be an easy thing to fall back on one's biases. If you think North Korea is engaging in a lot of cyber-mischief (conveniently forgetting your attack on Iran's nuclear program, or North Korea's internet), it can be easy to conclude the villain is just who you imagined it would be.

This is a Monty Python skit, dressed up as intelligence.

It can't be North Korea because they're normally so stealthy!

It must be North Korea and the proof is they didn't disguise the malware! They're really sending us a message about how mad they are!

If a single piece of information can support diametrically opposed claims, it is useless as intelligence.

The only significance to the information is that the hackers didn't change the malware. You could say that points to a less sophisticated group, but it is not conclusive evidence of that assertion, either. Without any additional intelligence, you're simply throwing darts at a board to figure out who did it.

One of the best cyber-security analysts around, Marc Rogers, wrote a blog post shortly after the Sony hack, looking at the evidence in the Shamoon, Dark Seoul, and Sony attacks, and wrote the following:

> So while North Korea has certainly been hinted at for each of these two hacks [Shamoon and Dark Seoul], the evidence is flimsy and speculative at best. So, what about the similarities? Well, ignoring the IP addresses, as we will discuss these later, these are the "links".
>
> 1. Just like Shamoon, the Destover wiper drivers are commercially available EldoS RawDisk drivers.
>
> 2. Just like Shamoon, the Destover wiper drivers are maintained in the droppers' resource section.
>
> 3. Just like Shamoon, the Dark Seoul wiper event included vague, encoded pseudo-political messages used to overwrite disk data and the master boot record (MBR).
>
> 4. Just like Dark Seoul, the Destover wiper executables were compiled somewhere between 48 hours prior to the attack and the actual day of the attack. This means it is highly unlikely that the attackers spear-phished their way into large numbers of users, and highly likely that they had gained unfettered access to the entire network prior to the attack.
>
> 5. The Shamoon components were compiled in a similarly tight time frame prior to their deployment. The Compiled-On

timestamps all fall within five days of their executables detonation. Nearly all were compiled on August 10, 2012 (between
00:17:23 and 02:46:22) and set to detonate on August 15,
2012. That is a tight window to quietly deploy these bina-
ries considering that tens of thousands of machines were
destroyed with this payload.

6. In all three cases: Shamoon, Dark Seoul, and Destover, the
   groups claiming credit for their destructive impact across
   large networks had no history or real identity of their own.
   All attempted to disappear following their act, and did not
   make clear statements, but did make bizarre and round-
   about accusations of criminal conduct, and instigated their
   destructive acts immediately after a politically-charged event
   that was suggested as having been at the heart of the matter.

7. Images from the Dark Seoul 'Whois' [the alleged hacking
   group behind it] and Destover 'GOP' [Guardians of Peace]
   groups included a 'Hacked by' claim, accompanied by a
   "warning" and threats regarding stolen data. Both threatened that this was only the beginning and that the group
   will be back. It appears that original skeletal artwork was
   also included in both.[219]

Let's take a look at the reasons March Rogers doesn't believe
North Korea is responsible for the Sony hack, or the attack on Saudi
Arabia's Aramco oil company, or the attack on South Korean banks
and television stations.

The components used for the hacks were widely available.

The hackers used vague, revolutionary slogans and appeals
that they were attacking corrupt groups, but little else to suggest an
actual complaint.

Access by the hackers seemed to have been in a tight timeframe
from penetration to explosion of their digital packages, suggesting the use of an insider to gain access to the network. This is in

stark contrast to spear-phishing an employee's account, and moving through the system in that manner, a much more laborious endeavor for a hacker.

Hacker groups love notoriety, and these groups seem to engage in their destruction, then vanish, not appearing before their next attack. (Author's note – It might be reasonable to consider them a possible North Korean front group, but by that analysis there's no reason to conclude they might not also belong to other nation states, such as China, Russia, Israel, or the United States.)

In all three of these attacks, the hackers used skeleton imagery, love to post a "Hacked by" claim, and issued similar "warnings" and threats against the organizations.

It could be the same group, or different groups who are taking advantage of publicly available information to conceal their true identities. More information is needed, and the rush of the American government to point the finger at North Korea suggests a different motive rather than determining the identity of the hackers. The critique of Marc Rogers continued:

While some of these similarities strongly hint at a similar operation and a shared DNA between these pieces of malware, it is hardly a smoking gun. Furthermore, the strength of this particular line of analysis weakens when you consider just how much sharing happens in the malware world. Many of these pieces of malware use publicly available tools and libraries. Many of these pieces of malware are based on malware source code that has been sold/released/leaked and is therefore accessible and easy to use. Finally, many of these pieces of malware are available for purchase.

Indeed, the malware SaaS (software as a service) industry is booming – why write a complex piece of malware that requires specialist skills to write them when it will be deprecated as soon as the AntiVirus vendors record its signature. Malware SaaS operations sell wannabe malware hackers new, currently undetectable pieces of malware with a guarantee that, so long as the user pays a service charge, they will rebuild the malware to make it once again undetectable should it ever fall into the hands of the authorities.

While there is insufficient evidence to say that is what's going on in the cases of these three attacks and the malware at the heart of them, I see no effort to prove that isn't the case, either. Lastly, it's pretty weak in my book to claim that the newest piece of malware were 'rumored' to be the work of a nation state. Until someone comes up with solid evidence actually attributing one of these pieces of malware to North Korea, I consider the evidence to be, at best, speculation.[220]

The hacking world thrives on being able to conceal one's identity. The malware is freely distributed through the hacking community, allowing anybody to use off the shelf software or make minor changes to the code prior to use to avoid detection.

There are even companies which will sell you slightly modified malware for just such a purpose, and if it gets compromised, they'll write you some new code which will not be detectable.

The cyber landscape is best described as something of a lawless realm, with many nefarious actors, of whom North Korea, must be described as one of the least capable players. This information does not establish the innocence of North Korea, but neither does it establish their guilt.

In the opinion of Marc Rogers, and much of the cyber-security industry, the least compelling evidence put forth by the FBI to establish the guilt of North Korea for the Sony hack was the use by the hackers of common IP (internet protocol) addresses that have been used in the past by North Korea.

The IP addresses associated with the Sony hack were found in Thailand, Poland, Italy, Bolivia, Singapore, Cypress, and ... wait for it ... the United States.[221]

Isn't it interesting that none of the IP addresses were located in North Korea, or China? In fact, all of these countries are generally considered U.S. allies, so what gives?

The analyst known as "Krypt3ia" did an article entitled "Fauxtribution" on the IP addresses, and had the following to say: As for the Thai IP address, "It [Thailand] has also been seen as a very dirty player in SPAM and other nefarious activities. Not just DPRK/CN APT activities."[222] It also appeared to be originating from Thammasat University in Bangkok, the capital city of Thailand.

The second IP address provided by the FBI was from Poland. He wrote: "Poland too is known to be dirty and used for SPAM and malware C@C's as well. Many different groups are using this and it too is a proxy. So, once again, this does not prove out solidly that this is DPRK [North Korea]. It could, in fact be anyone who is in the know about it's being there and using it."[223]

The third IP address was listed as being from Italy. Krypt3ia wrote: "Once again, Italy has the same issue. It is a known dirty address/system and has been used for SPAM and Malware C@C's before. This does not mean it is in fact solely under the control of DPRK."[224]

The remaining IP addresses, from Bolivia, Singapore, Cyprus, and a communications company in New York (which the United States had not seized as of December 20, 2012), all had similar issues.[225]

As he wrapped up his article, Krypt3ia had the following to say:

At the end of the day, if these are all the IP's that the US is using as evidence that the DPRK carried out this attack, I think it is pretty weak as evidence goes. The majority of these systems are proxies and known to be such and others are weak systems that have likely been compromised for use in this attack and maybe others because hackers share a lot of these C&C boxes. They do so to muddy the waters so to speak, the more groups using them the more confusion can be sown.

The machine in NY is interesting in that it is still online. I would have thought the authorities would want to take that into evidence but there it is, still online. Maybe they are still getting round to that... Or maybe they are just happy to make the pronouncement that it was DPRK and leave it be. I personally think that all of these systems together do not lead me or anyone using logic to believe that these are known infrastructures for DPRK unit 128.

Even if the likes of Crowdstrike and others may claim that DPRK has been known to use the same tactics or things like them or any other vague adjectives about the data that they have seen in the past, none of it is anything that would be considered evidence in court. It is all considered circumstantial and that evidence is inadmissible. So, the US is going to base a theoretical response on a nation state level, as I said above, on circumstantial evidence?

Now that's statecraft... Of course, I remember a time a while back when we were all told that Iraq had massive WMD stocks and was in cahoots with Al Qaeda. In fact, it was a SLAM DUNK according to the then CIA director.[226]

This passage gets to the heart of the matter. What do we really know about the Sony hack? I'm comfortable with the idea that at the start of the investigation North Korea should have been on the list, but like many first assumptions, later investigation can prove them to be unlikely.

In this book I am looking at many possibilities.

One possibility is that we may be looking at an intelligence operation by our own government to whip up resentment against North Korea.

Another possibility is that a hacker group, like Lizard Squad, may have simply been attempting to hide their tracks, and in the process convinced our intelligence agencies North Korea was to blame.

Maybe it was an insider who gave access to the Sony network to Lizard Squad, and when our intelligence agencies figured it out, though the better play was to blame North Korea. After all, who would be crazy enough to defend Kim Jong-un?

Perhaps this was a hacking operation by Iran, Russia, or China, and these nations thought it would be great fun to have it blamed on North Korea.

Or maybe this is exactly what it looks like, North Korea trying to get back at Sony Pictures for making *The Interview*.

I am troubled by this story, as was Krypt3ia, who wrote an addendum to his article the following day.

There is a thing in intelligence called "cognitive bias" and I fear that our intelligence agencies fall prey to this a lot as it is. This is because it's such a slippery subject not only on a technical level, but also because it is so easy to obfuscate means, methods, and actions with technology today. Another aphorism in the IC [Intelligence Community] is that of being "lost in the forest of shadows" which means that when nothing is clear, it's easy to be confused. Well, this is the same thing.

Like I said on Twitter last night, I can see my way to saying that DPRK was behind this. I can use Occam's Razor to apply the logic of who had motive, look at their actions on the face of it, and say "most likely" it is them. However, would I want to go to war over it? Look at these people like

Dave Atiel screaming that we need to go to cyber war and drop logic bombs in their infrastructure over this.[227]

There is a great deal of wisdom in the above passage. Just because we weigh in on the strength of the evidence, or challenge the claims of our government, doesn't mean we know the answer. We are also in the dark, but we want to see strong, credible evidence.

But this uncertainty about North Korea's role in the Sony hack wasn't just disturbing those outside of government. It was disturbing people inside of it.

> This week I spoke with someone in the IC who does actual information warfare. In talking to him over the week I saw his frustration grow to the point he put in his papers to separate. He plans on going into teaching. Why? Because he said that all of this talk, this call to action over Sony was just so ridiculous that it would be hard for him to carry out an order of attack on this "evidence." His answer was to retire to teaching.

> That about sums it up with me too of late. I look at Twitter and the news feeds and see just marketing, hype and faux-tribution … And it will be to our collective doom.[228]

Who benefits the most from this state of affairs? A movie studio who wants to sell tickets?

A president who wants to look tough?

The intelligence agencies?

The defense contractors?

When one looks at the confusion rampant in this series of events it seems like hunters shooting at what they think is hiding in the dark. One thinks about the common complaint from actual veterans that those who most want to go to war are those who have never experienced it. These are little boys playing at war, not men who have seen battle and its costs.

Krypt3ia had to add a final addendum as of December 22, 2014:

It is all moot anyway it seems as reports are coming in that DPRK networks are down (mind you again, those networks only really cover the elite of KJU's inner circle, so meh). Meanwhile, it seems that "maybe" there has been some monkeying around with TOR by the FBI. RUMINT is at present that there are couple TOR boxes that have been seized in relation to the Sony investigation.

More when it is confirmed.

Let me leave you with a visual representation of how this all feels ... [229]

He left a YouTube clip from the Harrison Ford movie, *Patriot Games*, written by Tom Clancy. In the scene, Harrison, playing CIA analyst Jack Ryan, is brought into the situation room to watch the satellite feed of an attack on a North African terrorist training camp. The attack is at night, so both the US soldiers and the terrorists appear on infra-red as white lights against a dark background.

It has the feel of a video game, and Ryan is horrified at how the people in the room sip coffee as they watch people being killed in their tents, then the entire training camp destroyed by the US in an explosive blast as the soldiers retreat.

In *Patriot Games* there was no doubt that the camp we were attacking was filled with actual terrorists.

The United States is a superpower, perhaps unrivaled in history in its ability to project influence across the globe. But when we engage in actions unsupported by evidence, such as blaming North Korea on flimsy evidence and attacking their internet, we risk more than our influence.

Those who seek to change the world walk a very fine line. A policeman may not see the line he crosses when he becomes a criminal rather than a public servant. Restraint and hesitation to act until the facts are clear may be a much better response than a bias toward action.

Do we picture ourselves the hero, while the rest of the world reasonably sees us as the global bully?

CHAPTER NINE

A CONFESSION FROM LIZARD SQUAD?

On December 28, 2014, a few days after the successful Christmas Day release of *The Interview*, a representative from Norse gave an extensive interview to Paul Roberts of *The Security Ledger* about their findings.

> A strong counter-narrative to the official account of the hacking of Sony Pictures Entertainment has emerged in recent days, with the visage of the petulant North Korean dictator, Kim Jong-un, replaced by another, more familiar face: former Sony Pictures employees angry over their firing during a recent reorganization at the company.
>
> Researchers from the security firm Norse allege that their investigation of the hack of Sony has uncovered evidence that leads, decisively, away from North Korea as the source of the attack. Instead, the company alleges that a group of six individuals is behind the hack, at least one a former Sony Pictures employee who worked in a technical role and had extensive knowledge of the company's network and operations.[230]

It's said our brain doesn't think in facts. Instead, we need a narrative, a conceptual framework for understanding a story, then we can use the facts to fill in the needed details for a complete and logical account.

The narrative of a North Korean hack of Sony Pictures has a number of details from which one could construct a logically consistent narrative. But upon closer inspection of those details, several troubling questions arise, which makes us doubt the truth of that narrative.

As in a murder case, it's not enough to simply cast doubt on the guilt of the accused. The best defense lawyers know the jury hungers for an alternative narrative which points the finger of blame at somebody else. It doesn't sit well with the average person to say, "Well, the government didn't prove its case. Let the guy go free."

We understand the principle of the government needing to prove its case, but if we think the evidence has some problems, but the defendant seems guilty, the jury will probably vote for conviction.

Instead, we want to be able to say, "They've got the wrong man! If we convict him, the real murderer will get away with it!" The article continued:

> Speaking to *The Security Ledger,* Kurt Stammberger, a Senior Vice President at Norse, said that his company identified six individuals with direct involvement in the hack, including two based in U.S., one in Canada, one in Singapore and one in Thailand. The six include one former Sony employee, a ten-year veteran of the company who was laid off in May as part of a company-wide restructuring.

> Stammberger said that Norse's team of around nine researchers started from the premise that insiders would be the best situated to carry out an attack on the company and steal data. The company analyzed human resources documents leaked in the hack and began researching employees with a likely motive and means to carry out a hack.[231]

Most criminal investigators understand that there are some general patterns to human behavior. If a woman is murdered, the odds are she was killed by her husband or boyfriend. That's why one looks to a murder victims' close relations first, to see if there are any clues which might suggest a propensity for violence. It's not always true, but it's a good first place to start.

When one looks at an act against a specific company, it's probably a good first step to look for any disgruntled ex-employees.

That's why "Lena and the Sony Five," seemed to be such a good fit, rather than North Korean dictator, Kim Jong-un.

After researching those individuals, Norse said it identified one former employee who he described as having a "very technical background." Researchers from the company followed that individual online, noting angry posts she made on social media about the layoffs and Sony. Through access to IRC (Internet Relay Chat) forums and other sites, they were also able to capture communications with other individuals affiliated with underground hacking and hacktivist groups in Europe and Asia.

According to Stammberger, the Norse investigation was further able to connect an individual directly involved in those online conversations with the Sony employee with a server on which the earliest known version of the malware used in the attack was compiled, in July 2014.

Stammberger was careful to note that his company's findings are hardly conclusive, and may just add wrinkles to an already wrinkled picture of what happened at Sony Pictures. He said Norse employees will be briefing the FBI on Monday about their findings.[232]

This is the way an investigation is supposed to proceed. One may have an initial suspicion, then determine whether the initial clues stand up to scrutiny. The question which must be asked is whether the United States intelligence community made their conclusions too swiftly, took clandestine actions against the internet network of North Korea, then when the weaknesses in their assessment were made clear to them, found themselves unable to reverse course.

Based on all I have uncovered in my research, it seems plausible that the intelligence community may have had a bias against North Korea, a case of "target fixation" took over, and they interpreted the data which implicated North Korea as being of high reliability, and the evidence exonerating North Korea as being of low reliability.

It is also possible that at least part of the United States intelligence community WANTED it to be North Korea, and therefore skewed the analysis in that direction.

The only way I would ever know which possibility was true was if I found an email from an intelligence operative saying, "I know it was Lizard Squad along with the disgruntled ex-Sony employee, and not North Korea, but I'm going to blame Kim Jong-un anyway." I doubt any such email exists. (But I wouldn't be completely shocked if something along those lines was eventually uncovered.)

At a minimum, the latest theory suggests that official accounts of the hack from U.S. government sources are now just one among many competing theories about the source of motivation behind the attack that are circulating within security circles and in the mainstream media. This, ten days after the Obama Administration pinned the blame for the destructive attack squarely on hackers affiliated with the reclusive government of the Democratic Peoples Republic of Korea (DPRK).

The sheer amount of information leaked by the hackers has provided plenty of ammunition to fuel alternative narratives about what happened. Initial reports noted that the malware used in the attacks on Sony was created on systems that used Korean language software libraries, and shared similarities with malicious software used in destructive attacks on the Saudi oil firm Saudi Aramco.

But for every clue that seems to point to the involvement of the DPRK, there are others that point in other directions, as well. For example, recent analysis has focused on date and time stamps attached to the leaked Sony data. Researchers used those time stamps to infer the speed with which the data was transferred off Sony's network. Reports have suggested that the timestamp data points to a leak within Sony's enterprise network, for example: to a USB device or external hard drive.[233]

We are traveling through the forest of shadows, but the moon and starlight are faintly illuminating a path for us, and it's away from North Korea.

Aside from the issues we've already discussed, such as the original language in which the email was written (probably Russian and not Korean), there's the issue of how quickly the download of the Sony data was completed. To simply understand the problem, you should understand that the download of information happens at a much faster rate if you plug directly into a Sony computer with a USB drive or external hard drive. Think of it like how quickly the water comes out of your tap in the morning when you brush your teeth or shave. Now compare the rate at which water comes out of a fire hydrant.

That's analogous to how quickly one can download information over an internet line. But by plugging a USB drive or external hard drive directly to a Sony computer connected to their network, it's like having a fire hose plugged directly into a hydrant located on the street.

That doesn't preclude some North Korean agent from being able to obtain such access, but a former Sony employee is a much more likely suspect. The article continued:

Other analysts studied clues buried in statements made by the shadowy hacking crew, the Guardians of Peace or GOP, who claimed responsibility for the attacks. Email addresses and other ephemera from the GOP communications with Sony and the outside world have been read to reveal links to everything from Japanese anime and the Mighty Morphin Power Rangers television shows to U.S. domestic disputes over politics and gender equality...

But the Norse account of the hack does answer some puzzling questions about the incident that are yet unexplained, according to Mark Rasch, a former federal prosecutor and a principal at Rash Technology and Cyberlaw. Among those questions: How hackers were able to obtain near-perfect knowledge of Sony Pictures' network and, then, sneak terabytes of data off of the network without arousing notice.

"It has always been suspicious that it was North Korea," Rasch said. "Not impossible – but doubtful...It made a lot more sense that it was insiders pretending to be North Korea."[234]

As is often the case, the evidence can be interpreted in different ways. One view would be that the North Koreans were master hackers, able to deftly move through the Sony computer network with ease.

The other, more likely possibility is that the hackers were familiar with the system, or working with somebody with that knowledge. The article continued:

Stammberger notes the involvement of an insider would explain how the attackers obtained critical information about Sony's network, including the IP addresses of critical servers and valid credentials to log into them. Even in sophisticated attacks, remote actors might spend days, weeks, or months probing a network to which they have gained access to obtain that information: using compromised employee accounts to explore and find sensitive data before stealing it or causing other damage. It is during that "lateral movement," malicious actors are often spotted, Stammberger said. In the case of the Sony attack, however, the malware was compiled knowing exactly what assets to attack.

Still, there are many questions that have yet to be answered. Norse's own analysis has plenty of blank spaces. Stammberger said that a "handful" of former employees may have been involved, though only one was linked directly to the hack. That employee, at some point, joined forces with external actors and more experienced hackers with a grudge against Sony, including individuals with sites like Pirate Bay which offer Hollywood movies for download. "We see evidence for those two groups of people getting together," Stammberger told the Security Ledger.[235]

Locard's principle, that every contact leaves behind evidence, is just as true in the digital world as it is in the physical world. One simply needs to be able to follow the clues. Just as a burglar may be able to sneak into a house undetected, when the crime is uncovered, forensic investigators will likely be able to retrace the steps of the criminal. Did the criminal come in through a window? If so, was the window unlocked, or did glass have to be broken? If the burglar came in through a door, did he have a key, or was some device used to unlock it?

What was seen in the Sony hack?

The hackers knew where they needed to go. It's unlikely these were hackers without a clear understanding of the system they were entering. Like many crimes committed against businesses, there was likely an "insider," providing critical information to the hackers.

Are we to believe a disgruntled former Sony employee would have access to North Korean hackers?

Or does it seem more likely that this former Sony employee with a background in technology would know how to reach out to the group which had previously hacked Sony, and give them the keys to the kingdom?

In what may have been the greatest twist of all in this case, Lizard Squad came out and said that is exactly what happened.

Brian Fung, of *The Washington Post*, conducted an online interview with an individual identified as "Ryan Cleary*" (pseudonym), an administrator of Lizard Squad, which was published on December 29, 2014. A significant part of the article dealt with the reporter getting confirmation he was actually speaking to a member of Lizard Squad. The facts reported supported the claim Norse had been making for several weeks, The article recounted:

> But in an unusual interview Friday, a self-proclaimed member of the "cyberterrorist" group said Lizard Squad also played a role in the massive attack against Sony Pictures Entertainment. A person identifying himself as a Lizard Squad administrator said the group provided a number of Sony employee logins to Guardians of Peace, the organization that allegedly broke into Sony's network and prompted the film studio to initially withdraw "The Interview" from theaters.

> If true, it would be the first open acknowledgment by a Lizard Squad member that the group was involved in the Sony attack. The administrator also conceded that the group went too far in August, when it tweeted a bomb threat to American Airlines, prompting the mid-flight diversion of a jet carrying Sony executive John Smedley by F-16 fighters. He also shed more light on the group's membership, saying most are based in the European Union and eastern Europe and therefore aren't too worried about FBI investigations into Lizard Squad.[236]

This was a startling admission from Lizard Squad itself, that not only had they twice attacked the Sony PlayStation platform, but had also helped hack Sony Pictures, leading to the United States face-off with North Korea, and the likely American attack on North Korea's internet.

Additionally, the admission that most of their members were based either in the European Union or in Eastern Europe, may explain why the original communications seem to have been written in Russian. We know that many Russian emigres have settled in either Eastern Europe or the European Union.

Did this administrator say more than he intended? When dealing with young, idealistic men, as the Lizard Squad seems to be composed of, they often do extremely dumb things. They say the two halves of the brain don't fuse in males until the age of twenty-five, which is why the death rate of the under twenty-five male population is so high. The problem with older analysts and policymakers may be that they've forgotten the all-too common, absolute stupidity, of some members of this age group.

How else does one explain the half-hearted apology which could almost read, *I guess we went too far with the threat to blow up that plane. My bad.*

This is directly from the interview:

… So the big question surrounding this latest PlayStation Network/Xbox Live incident is, why, and why now? What do you hope to accomplish with it?

Well, one of our biggest goals is to have fun, of course. But we're also exposing massive security issues with these companies people are trusting their personal information with. The customers of these companies should be rather worried.

In this case it seems less like a leak of personal information than an attack that simply makes the services crash. What does overloading a system have to do with security flaws?

Quite a bit. It tells you how much money they've put into securing their systems. Not having people take down your business critical systems like this should be one of your top priorities. Which it clearly isn't.

So if I understand correctly, you're saying Sony and Microsoft's systems should be able to scale to handle all this incoming traffic.

Absolutely. We told them almost a month before that we'd do this. And yet we had no difficulties dropping them.

How much data, are, or were, you throwing at them per second?

About 1.2 [terabits per second].

Are you guys gamers yourselves?

Not really, no. Unless this counts as a game. I guess this is kind of a game for us.

Tell me more.

Well, it's often sort of like a game of chess. Your opponent does something to prevent your attack, and you alter your attack to get around your opponents' defenses.[237]

Does this read to you as if it's a bunch of young knuckleheaded guys, rather than some terrifying cyber-villains? They are puffing out their chests about their accomplishments, while not assessing the toll that their activities have taken.

But the question which must be asked, is how it is that a reporter for *The Washington Post* can get this information, and yet it appears to elude the grasp of our intelligence agencies which receive billions of dollars a year from American citizens?

Or is the picture as clear to the intelligence agencies as it is to *The Washington Post*, but they're doctoring, or withholding evidence, to point the finger of blame at North Korea?

The intelligence agencies are either incompetent, or they're playing a very dangerous game.

I'm not certain which scenario is more terrifying.

The Washington Post reporter asked the important questions, and got some surprising answers, consistent with the main claims of this book.

What kind of group are you, would you say? If you had to describe yourself?

Well, we've been humorously describing ourselves as a cyberterrorist group. I mean, referring to us as a hacker/ hacking group would probably be the simplest choice.

Some reports suggest you've got links to Guardians of Peace, and possibly to the Islamic State. Can you talk about that for a minute?

[Another long pause, about five minutes.]

Well, we do know some people from the GOP [Guardians of Peace]. We do not have any links to the IS [Islamic State].

But you didn't work with Guardians of Peace to breach Sony's network and gain access to the emails, etc.? In other words, you know some people but weren't involved in the Sony hack surrounding 'The Interview'?

[A seven-minute pause.]

Well, we didn't play a large part in that.

What part did you play?

We handed over some Sony employee logins to them. For the initial hack.[238]

Now, in addition to the evidence uncovered by Norse, we have confirmation from Lizard Squad that they have connections to the "Guardians of Peace."

The pieces are starting to come together for the claim being made in this book that the Sony hack was not North Korea, but the group I like to call "Lena and the Sony Five." The able assist of Lizard Squad was necessary for this hack, and they clearly gave it.

The BBC looked at this information and provided a new twist on it, suggesting that the American intelligence agencies were going to work themselves into a logical pretzel to cover their apparently unjustified attack on the North Korean internet.

The information throws some doubt on the theory that North Korea was behind the attacks on Sony' internal systems. The state was accused of being behind the attack because *The Interview* is about a fictional American plot to kill North Korean leader Kim Jong-un, and Pyongyang has filed formal complaints about the film.

However, the Reuters news agency has reported that US investigators are exploring whether North Korea "contracted out" some of the work involved, which could explain how Lizard Squad formed links to GOP.[239]

Is the pivot by the United States becoming clear?

The FBI and the United States government initially said with some certainty that North Korea was behind the hack.

The private cyber-security industry, spearheaded by Norse, Eric, and Mr. Grey, suggested it wasn't North Korea, and the evidence points to an insider who made contact with the hacker group, Lizard Squad, who had been associated with previous Sony hacks.

The United States accepts the possible participation of Lizard Squad, but instead of them being contacted by a disgruntled former Sony employee, they were "contracted out" by North Korea, and its evil dictator, Kim Jong-un.

Lizard Squad remains at the center of the hack, but "Lena and the Sony Five" are swapped out with North Korea, as the mastermind of the hack. The fired Sony employees, and the brutal Japanese business practices are all shuffled quickly off the public stage.

Like a good magician, the U.S. government distracts the public with one hand, while the trick takes place with the other one.

Norse was ready to end this conflicted situation and sit down with the FBI to show their evidence.

Because of Eric's communication with the FBI regarding the original source code of the Sony hack, and the public insistence by Norse and other private cybersecurity companies that North Korea was an unlikely suspect in the crime, the FBI agreed to have a meeting with Eric and the Norse representatives at their Saint Louis, Missouri field office.

Eric recalled being very nervous at the meeting but was confident of the information Norse had gathered and the analysis he had done. Mr. Grey often said of Eric, "He was a guy who shouldn't come out from behind his computer," but that wasn't the full story.

Eric knew how to turn on the charm when needed, how to speak slowly enough for people to follow, and when to pause if they needed to catch up. He was a virtuoso behind the computer screen, and that was his preferred location on Earth. But he understood that in order to be effective he had to interact with important decision-makers, or else all of his knowledge and findings would be useless.

Eric had grown up on a remote farm in Norway, but he vividly recalled his family's stories of World War II and the Nazis. The world had been a terrifying enough place then, but that was before humanity possessed nuclear weapons.

It was intimidating to walk up to 1600 Summit Street in Saint Louis, Missouri, a small squat building, almost like a military bunker in a war zone, with an American flag flying from a tall pole, and guarded by an evil-looking black wrought iron fence with what looked like spear points at the top.

Eric led the three-hour meeting, going over the data in detail.

As Kurt Stammberger, a senior vice-president for market development told Fox News:

"They were very open" to the new information, Stammberger said.

Among other details, he said, Norse has data about the malware samples that point to "super, super detailed insider information" that only a Sony insider would have ...

Stammberger explained Tuesday that the information points to at least one American – the former Sony employee, who according to Stammberger lost their job earlier this year – as well as individuals from Canada, Singapore, and Thailand.

He acknowledged that the FBI could have a "smoking gun" piece of evidence that they haven't shared, but said that the private intelligence community has seen nothing connecting the attack to a nation state.

"The fact that nobody has seen any data that connected this to North Korea is a little strange," he said. "Also strange was the speed at which the FBI ... pinned it on them."[240]

When they finished, Eric felt he'd given a good presentation and that the agents had listened. One nagging thought was that the FBI hadn't shared any of their information, but he knew the investigative services could be jealous guardians of their data.

Norse was about to get a rude awakening that the FBI wasn't open at all to the new information.

Although Norse handed over everything they had on the hack, going over the information in a three-hour briefing, and the FBI provided no additional information such as signal intelligence, to support their claims, the FBI went swiftly to the press to confirm their original conclusions.

As *CNN* reported on December 30, 2014, less than a week after *The Interview* hit theaters:

> Despite seeing evidence from data scientists pointing to individuals who may have been behind the hacking of Sony last month, the FBI isn't wavering on its original assessment that North Korea is the culprit, an FBI source tells CNN.

> FBI officials and data scientists with the U.S. cybersecurity firm Norse met Monday in St. Louis, according to Norse Vice President Kurt Stammberger and an FBI source.

> During the three-hour briefing, which was requested by Norse, representatives of the cybersecurity firm shared information they say links several people, including a former Sony employee, to the hack, Stammberger told CNN.

> The former employee had worked for Sony in Los Angeles for 10 years before getting laid off in May, Stammberger said.[241]

Norse felt they'd built an airtight case for "Lena and the Sony Five," but of course this conclusion could be undercut if the FBI provided additional intelligence, suggesting the hack originated from North Korea. As the CNN article explained:

> However, the FBI source said, the bureau continues to hold to its original assessment, based on information "from the FBI, the U.S. intelligence community, the Department of Homeland Security, foreign partners and the private sector."

> The FBI source said the agency didn't share any of its information with Morse due to "sensitivity of sources/techniques."[242]

One of the best ways to keep a lie going is to say, "I have the information, but I just can't tell you." It's almost like Tom Cruz in the original *Top Gun* movie saying in answer to a question about the flight capabilities of a Soviet MIG fighter, "I could tell you, but then I'd have to kill you."

In order to take the meeting, Norse was required to sign non-disclosure agreements, valid for five years. Think about how the controversy could have been avoided.

The FBI could have simply said, "Here's the signals intelligence we have about where the hack originated. You can't repeat this information, but we'd love it if after the meeting we have a joint press conference, and you say the evidence we showed convinced you." Would that have been so difficult? Norse had a history of collaborating with government agencies.

But even though Norse was a trusted entity and there were non-disclosure agreements signed, the FBI didn't want to share their intelligence with Norse. The FBI and the United States government continued their campaign against the Norse findings. As *Politico* wrote:

> After FBI agents were briefed yesterday, they concluded the security company offering the alternate theory did not have

an accurate understanding of all the evidence, a U.S. official familiar with the matter told POLITICO today.

The three-hour meeting with FBI investigators by cyber intelligence firm Norse "did not improve the knowledge of the investigation," according to the U.S. official.

Investigators are open to new information brought forth by researchers, the official said, but it became clear in the meetings yesterday that Norse's evidence was "narrow" and not an accurate analysis of the information, the official said.[243]

This was a public statement of disrespect by the FBI towards the information which had been provided by Norse.

And yet, on the other hand, the government was subtly changing their narrative, as was reported in a different article.

In a related report, Reuters spoke with an unidentified US official who's close to the government's investigation of the Sony Pictures attack. The source said the US government now believes that North Korea "likely" worked with outside parties to launch the attack. It's not clear if the source is referencing an outside government or other party, just that the act may have been "contracted" out.[244]

The campaign against North Korea would continue, despite the confession by Lizard Squad that they'd assisted the hack, and despite the presentation by Eric and Norse Corporation. The US government had no use for a theory the hack was an attack by "Lena and the Sony 5," a former employee of Sony who contacted some notorious hackers, striking Sony Pictures as a way of getting back at the cutbacks authorized by Sony's corporate masters in Japan.

It's almost as if the government had made up its mind about the hack and didn't want to be distracted by the facts.

The only question is, why?

Was it because Sony was hemorrhaging money and in need of an infusion of cash?

Was it because the government and its military contractors benefitted from increasing tensions with North Korea?

Was there a deal possible in which Sony could have access to additional funds, and the government and its defense contractors would have an argument for additional spending?

The French emperor Napoleon once said, "History is a set of lies that people have agreed upon."

If a lie is convenient to powerful interests, what chance would Norse and the private cybersecurity industry have at convincing them of the truth?

Norse was about to find out the answer to that question in a meeting in the White House situation room that Eric and Mr. Grey would forever after refer to as "the barbecue."

Chapter Ten

The Barbecue at the Pentagon & a 2018 Confession from Seth Rogen

What happens when one contradicts a story which benefits the military-industrial complex, while at the same time casting doubt on the claim that the United States is a beacon of artistic freedom and democracy?

The likely response is that powerful interests will seek to discredit you, even if they had not been the initial authors of the propaganda. Nobody likes to be embarrassed.

How much credibility would President Obama have lost around the world, if after pointing the finger of blame at North Korea, he had to back down, name a former disgruntled employee at Sony as the guilty party, and apologize to Kim Jong-un?

The narrative proposed in this book is that most of the main actors in the 2014 Sony hack are inherently unreliable. We start with the hackers themselves, a Hollywood studio, our own intelligence agencies, as well as the North Koreans and other foreign actors.

As far as I can determine, the only honest actors in this international drama which might have precipitated a nuclear exchange between the United States and North Korea, were the investigators at Norse. (And I'm sure there are those who might question whether the stories provided to me for this book are all part of an elaborate disinformation campaign.)

I'll let you be the judge of what you believe and find credible.

As the writer, all I can do is listen to the stories told to me by those who were involved, gather the necessary evidence, and give you my best opinion as to the truth.

In January of 2015, Eric went to the Pentagon to present Norse's evidence regarding the Sony hack.

I was provided copies of presentations which what had been prepared for this meeting and handed over to the Pentagon at the time.

One of the first slides gave what Norse believed to be a compressed timeline of the hack, highlighting the important dates. As best as Norse was able to determine, the initial Sony malware used in the attack, named Destover (version 1) was compiled on July 7, 2014, and the code was all in English.[245]

That means the hackers were likely English-speaking, not Korean, Russian, or Chinese.

The malware appeared to have been compiled with Sony internal information, using embedded USB drivers, and telemetry which was four months old, which was consistent with the time frame in which a number of Sony computer specialists were laid off.

The malware showed up on Sony's servers on August 28, 2014, stealing data from Sony and the information appears to have been fully extracted by October 22, 2014.[246]

The movement of these hackers through the Sony system suggested to Eric that the hackers were intimately familiar with the system and knew exactly where to go. These actions made it highly unlikely that the hackers were foreign state actors. The digital clues of droppers and timers used were well-known by various hacker groups, including Lizard Squad, JKT48, A Team, Syrian Electronic Army, Coupe de Main (a Turkish group pretending to be French), which also promotes a state sponsored group called Shadow Griefers.

The leveraged command and control structure used in the attack was one used by game hackers, as well as the malware infrastructure.

On October 31, 2014, Norse met with Sony and told them of the vulnerabilities of their system. (Norse claims they were only given limited access to the system and thus were not able to detect whether any hackers might be lurking on the network. (What Norse presented to the Pentagon was an analysis performed after the hack was announced to the public.)

Eric told the approximately thirty members of the defense and intelligence agencies assembled at the Pentagon, that on November 13, 2014, a variant of the malware was compiled, Destover II, utilizing both English and Korean.[247]

On November 21, 2014, the first email threats were received by Sony executives, but many of these emails ended up in their spam/junk folders.

On November 22, 2014, a variant of the malware Destover III, was placed on the system, and the code was 100% Korean in nature. This is also the date that the Sony attack went public, and their computers were disabled.

On November 24, 2014, an article appeared in *The Verge*, (an entertainment industry publication) claiming to be based on emails from the hackers. This is how the article opened:

> The hackers who took down Sony Pictures' computer systems yesterday say that they are working for "equality" and suggest that their attack was assisted or carried out by Sony employees. In an email responding to inquiries from The Verge, a person identifying as one of the hackers writes, "We Want equality [sic]. Sony doesn't. It's an upward battle." The hackers' goals remain unclear, but they used the attack yesterday to specifically call out Sony Entertainment CEO Michael Lynton, referring to him as a "criminal" in a tweet.

The hackers claim to have taken sensitive internal data from Sony. In an email from an address associated with the hack, a hacker who identified as "Lena" was vague about how the attack was carried out. "Sony doesn't lock their doors, physically, so we worked with other staff with similar interests to get in," Lena writes. "I'm sorry I can't say more, safety for our team is important [sic]."[248]

The hack, at least in its earliest stages, did not seem to be an attack by a foreign state actor, but read as the more mundane complaints of a disgruntled former employee (or employees), who wanted to strike back at management.

The email address in question is an open account, which allows anyone to send mail from it without entering a password. That means it's possible the message was sent by someone with no relation to the attack itself. Still, because the address was included in the initial .zip file and Lena identified as part of the group behind the attack, the message raises real questions about the political motives behind Sony's recent troubles. The account has also sent similar messages to other outlets, suggesting a consistent voice.[249]

Many may understand the concept of an email open account, but some may not. What this means is that an email was created which did not require a password. In essence, it was an "open" account, accessible to anybody who knew it existed.

But there is a catch.

Somebody had to know the email existed in order to access it.

The email was listed in the initial attack communications (and not released to the general public), then further messages were sent from it. In theory, it's possible somebody else gained access to this email, but in the opinion of Norse, highly unlikely.

From that point a chain of events followed, as I have detailed, from the illegal download of Sony movies, embarrassing emails, movie scripts, and medical records. There were comments about President Obama's taste in movies, derogatory comments about certain actors, and details about sexual activities.

From that point, the federal government swung into action, with the FBI launching an investigation on December 1, 2014.

On December 3, 2014, the Destover Version III was seen in the wild, wiping hard drives, backups, and generally causing internet mayhem.

On December 15, a class action lawsuit was filed by ex-Sony employees. An article from *Variety* detailed the claims made in the lawsuit:

> "At its core, the story of 'what went wrong' at Sony boils down to two inexcusable problems: (1) Sony failed to secure its computer systems, servers, and databases ... despite weaknesses that it has known about for years, because Sony made a 'business decision to accept the risk" of losses associated with being hacked; and (2) Sony subsequently failed to protect timely confidential information of its current and former employees from law-breaking hackers who (a) found these security weaknesses, (b) obtained confidential information of Sony's current and former employees stored on Sony's network, (c) warned Sony that it would publicly disseminate this information, and (d) repeatedly followed through by publicly disseminating portions of the information that they claim to have obtained from Sony's network through multiple dumps of internal data from Sony's network."[250]

Everything which was alleged in the lawsuit by ex-Sony employees is consistent with what I've been told by Norse, Eric, and Mr. Grey, as well as abundant documentation developed in the writing of this book.

What's left out of this account is the greater potential questions about the role of intelligence agencies in hyping up North Korean guilt, as well as what passive or active role Sony, Michael Lynton, or

Amy Pascal may have played in this deception, and whether that deception was witting or unwitting.

In a sense, Sony was simply on the hook for letting the studio be robbed for its intellectual property. The lawsuit made no claim as to the identity of the hackers, nor does it seek to answer that question. (The lawsuit was settled in October of 2015, with Sony required to pay up to $8 million in damages to the affected employees, with no answer to the question as to the identity of the hackers.[251])

From December or 2014 until January of 2015, several important events took place, all with the seeming intent of clouding the issue of an insider hack of Sony and supporting the North Korean narrative. There appeared to be a fake message from the "Guardians of Peace" left on Pastebin by a DHS reporter and fake malware hashes from a Russian named Kapersky with Sony certificates.

The private cybersecurity industry, however, messed up this narrative, as six of them released independent reports on the fake malware, demonstrating that some entity was laying a false trail. It was at this time Norse came to public attention, as it had the most thorough account of the alternative narrative with supporting data.

On December 19, 2014, the FBI formally accused North Korea of being responsible for the Sony hack.

A draft of the "Cyber Threat Analysis Summary of the 2014 Sony Breach, January 2, 2015," was provided to the author. From the Executive Summary:

> Norse has been examining the security posture, and cyber threat landscape around Sony Pictures Entertainment since August 2014 because we were prospecting them as a customer. In our view, to accomplish such a hack like the recent one disclosed by Sony and widely reported in the news media, it would take an insider that has intimate knowledge of the network. Given the security that Sony already had in place at the time of the breach an insider is the only option to accomplish such a hack. These summary findings below

are supported by the analysis detailed in this report and included link analysis artifacts.

1. Observed lack of physical security controls at SPE facilities.

2. It is obvious from dissecting the data that Sony had put all their "eggs" in one basket, meaning there was little to no segmentation and de-militarized zones in their network.

3. Analysis of malware and attack infrastructure shows direct linkage between a person of interest and illustrates that deep technical knowledge inside Sony was necessary to design/develop the malware.

4. Analysis of the malware does not indicate a match with previous malware used by North Korea *(note: Sony made Norse aware of the North Korean threat back in October and it appeared to our team that DPNK was the big elephant in the room already at Sony.)*

5. The Korean version of malware compiled AFTER data was exfiltrated from Sony servers.

6. Examination of the attack infrastructure reveals a tangled web of hacker groups, individuals, and shared malware resources.

7. Norse has identified 3 people of interest and included those details in this report and included artifacts

   a. Person of interest 1 – is a former Sony employee who moved from Sony Pictures in 2009 to Sony Electronics, she was terminated in May 2014.

b. Person of interest 2 – is a former Sony employee who has links to the South African and US hacker group Anonymous, and connection to Thailand.

c. Person of interest 3 – is a former employee who had worked close with ANTI-PIRACY while at Sony and had dealings with MPAA on behalf of Sony.[252]

As Eric continued his presentation, he could sense the assembled members leaning forward as he continued projecting his slides on the overhead. Eric noted five important pieces of evidence underlying the Norse analysis.

First was the lack of physical security controls over the computer system at Sony Pictures. Somebody could have literally walked into the computer room, plugged in a flash drive, and started downloading data.

Second, an analysis of the malware and attack infrastructure showed a direct linkage between a suspect, as well as illustrating the deep technical knowledge of the Sony computer system needed to design and develop the malware.

Third, analysis of the malware did not indicate a match with previous malware used by North Korea. (Norse also revealed to them that they had worked on the South Korean *Dark Seoul* attack, analyzing the samples of that malware, which had been blamed on North Korea.)

Fourth, Norse believed that the Korean version of the malware has compiled AFTER the data had been exfiltrated from the Sony Pictures servers. From their report:

The English version of the malware was compiled by July 7, 2014. The Korean version of the malware was not seen before Dec. 3rd. But was compiled November 22, which we believe to be AFTER the data was exfiltrated.

We estimate the date of data exfiltration to have been between Oct 21/Oct 22, 2014. This is based on data in the leaked Sony archive regarding payroll systems that was automatic writing to server files. Also the latest stamp file is Oct 21.[253]

The assembled experts at the Pentagon may not have been able to follow all the technical details Eric was providing, but timelines were easy to comprehend.

The hackers had been in the system for some time before July 7, 2014, when they had completed their first, 100% English version of the malware, designated Destover I. The theft of the data had been completed by October 21 or 22, as it included some data from October 21.

The 100% Korean version, Destover III, was completed by November 22 and left on the system, where the FBI would analyze it as coming from North Korea. The FBI investigation was so bad that it raised the question of whether it was incompetence or something else. Eric was trying to tiptoe gently through the information, but it was often difficult to conceal some of his amazement at the poor conclusions they'd drawn.

Fifth, Eric reviewed the creation of the code of the first malware detected on the system, and how it was built. This is what he presented in the report.

The first version of the malware used in the Sony attack, is sharing infrastructure with other known malware.

The same droppers and infection vectors that were used in the Sony attacks have been used in the past by several internet online gaming related groups such as Lizardsquad, JKT48, and groups affiliated with Syria.

Command and control nodes, as well as dropper sites used for distribution of the SPE data leak files, have been eastern European connections (e.g. the Trojan Sality Gen 3 Custom appears to be a piece of Romanian malware repurposed from a Russian code base)

The Thailand Hosting company which shares DNS records with the original malware dropper site, has been detected by the Norse global sensor grid, as having a deep history of clear compromise and has been attacking our honey grid enterprise in the US, Italy, and Portugal. Norse crawler data reveals very vulnerable servers with an outdated and vulnerable version of PHP.[254]

Eric felt he was hitting many of the same points, but believed it was important for the group to understand the strength of the data. There were multiple independent pieces of information which were all pointing in the same direction. The malware looked as if it had been assembled by Western hacker groups involved in gaming, rather than those operating out of North Korea, where their skills were much more primitive.

The initial hack had come from a server in Thailand, which Norse had previously identified as being a front for hackers. He had given them a clear roadmap as to how the attack had been planned and executed.

It was time to move in for the kill, revealing the identity of the hacker and the reasons he suspected her.

Eric displayed a slide listing the three suspects he had identified, as well as the evidence implicating each one of them.

While suspects #1 and #3 both possessed the requisite knowledge of the Sony computer network, it was suspect #2, who had the connections to the requisite hacker groups, as well as connections to Thailand, where the hack had originated.

Eric named Shahana Manjra as the prime suspect in the 2014 Sony hack which was blamed on North Korea.

Her Linked-In profile, (married name is Shahana Manjra Hardeman) accessed in 2023, described the seven years and nine months she worked at Sony Pictures Entertainment, from November 2006 to July of 2014. She entered the company as an Accounts Payable Analyst, a position in which she worked for six months. Her next position at the company was as a Procurement Administrator, which according to her account required her to:

"Manage and maintain 10,000+ AmEx P cards, accounts, controls, allocations, authorizations, reconciliations, and reporting.

Skills: Account Reconciliation – Financial Reporting – Financial Analysis – Business Process Improvement – Budgeting – Project Management – Management – Ad Hoc Reporting."[255]

Shahana must have impressed her bosses in this position. She was promoted in September of 2008 to the job of Senior Business Analyst/Systems Administrator. She would continue to work in that position for five years and eleven months until she was fired in the Sony downsizing of 2014, described earlier in this book which happened prior to the hack. Her Linked-In account describes her work in as follows:

- Administer Finance, ERP, CRM, MCM systems integration, updates and upgrades/enhancements.
- Run predictive financial models with customized dashboards and reports (billings, costs, labor, profitability, budget vs actuals, etc.)
- Optimize and document process flows for financial controls, visibility and forecasting by leading or lending to various dept/div/company-wide process improvement projects as a resource, SME, UAT, PM or CM (within GAAP/SOX/IFRS/Union/Guild guidelines)

Skills: Account Reconciliation – Financial Reporting – Financial Analysis – Change Management – Business Process Improvement – ERP Implementations – Budgeting – System Administration – Database Administration – Troubleshooting – User Acceptance Testing – Project

Management – SQL – Management – Ad Hoc Reporting
– FPA.[256]

Shahana's work at the company made it clear she had intimate familiarity with the computer architecture of Sony's system, which would give her the skills necessary to guide an attack on the system. And in the early days of the hack, the Guardians of Peace hijacked a few Twitter accounts linked to Sony to post some curious messages, which didn't quite seem as if they would come from a communist hacker group.

One of the Twitter accounts hijacked by the Guardians of Peace was called "Starship Troopers" (a 1997 science fiction film produced by Sony) and they posted the following message, *"You, the criminals including Michael Lynton will surely go to hell. Nobody can help you."*[257]

An article in *The State-Journal Register* from December 7, 2014 detailed what this strange message might mean.

That image is significant because it gives us a clue about the motives of Guardians of Peace. It accuses Sony Pictures of being "criminals," with Sony's logo Photoshopped onto a gravestone, and a photo of Sony Entertainment Inc. CEO Michael Lynton has been modified to make him look like Dracula. Guardians of Peace seem to be saying that Sony is killing the entertainment industry and that its corporate practices are criminal.

The images posted by Guardians of Peace suggest a similar motivation to the anti-capitalist ethos of groups like Anonymous and LulzSec. LulzSec famously hacked into Sony Pictures in 2011, a revenge attack for Sony's legal action against a man who hacked into and modified the PlayStation 3 video game console.[258]

The intelligence agencies of the United States government, as well as the mainstream media appeared united in blaming the hack on the communist dictatorship in North Korea. It's a clear division, easily understandable in people's minds, North Korea is evil and repressive, while the United States is good and has freedom.

But it doesn't make for such a clear story if the group responsible for the hack were citizens of the supposedly free Western world, protesting the deceptive business practices of large corporations. There are shades of grey in the telling of that tale, suggesting that the free press of the West has been hijacked by powerful corporate interests, who seem to be allied with the intelligence services of Western governments, creating panic to feed the bottom line of defense contractors.

As long as nobody gets too worked up about the situation and fires off a couple nuclear missiles, the scam can continue.

The government gets to claim they're virtuously defending Western values, the corporate fat cats line their pockets, the Pentagon and intelligence budgets grow even larger, a Hollywood studio sells a few more tickets, and the public carries on as if business is normal.

There were some other elements of the story, suggesting the hackers were savvy in the ways of the Western media, rather than the bumbling, tone-deaf messages which often arise from the "Hermit Kingdom" of North Korea. The article continued with some of the contradictions of the story:

> It's not just Photoshopped images that have been posted by the Guardians of Peace hackers, though. They have also talked via email to a small number of journalists. Salted Hash spoke to someone who claimed to represent Guardians of Peace and who made a bizarre claim that alluded to "The Interview," the Sony movie that angered North Korea:

>> *We are an international organization including famous figures in the politics and society from several nations such as United States, United Kingdom and France. We are not under direction of any state.*

*Our aim is not at the film The Interview as Sony Pictures sug-
gests. But it is widely reported as if our activity is related to The
Interview. This shows how dangerous film The Interview is.
The Interview is dangerous enough to cause a massive hack
attack. Sony Pictures produced the film harming the regional
peace and security and violating human rights for money.*[259]

It's difficult in a situation like this to separate the truth from
the lies. Was this a genuine message from the hackers? One cannot
say for certain. But does it seem plausible that whoever did gain
access to the computer system of Sony, had inside help? The article
suggests it is likely the hackers did.

A comment posted on Reddit by a former Sony Pictures
employee who says he has friends within the company says
that it "100% makes sense" that an unhappy employee let
hackers into Guardians of Peace. He also says that "in the
last year they have cleaned house, and not in a way most
employees are happy about...everyone has been on edge
there, morale is terrible, and good people were getting fired
left and right."[260]

It's as if the intelligence agencies and the United States government were ignoring the earlier series of layoffs as a possible
motivation.

The only question was why?

Eric continued his presentation to the assembled members of
the military and intelligence community, even though they continued to seem skeptical. He saw many of them shifting uncomfortably
in their seats and exhaling, waiting for what was coming next.

First, Shahana had worked at Sony in a position with gave her
access to the computer system, and her firing gave her motivation
to exact revenge on Sony.

Second, she belonged to a Facebook group called "South
Africans in LA," which had as one of its members a notorious hacker

named Chingy Whande, who was associated with the "Anonymous" hacking group, as well as Lizard Squad.

Third, Shahana was good friends with the sister of Chingy Whanda, who lived in the Los Angeles area.

Fourth, evidence existed that Shahana was familiar with Thailand, where the hack had originated.

Fifth, Shahana was also active in many on-line gaming groups, associated with hackers.

Eric was not suggesting that the case against Shahana had been proven beyond a reasonable doubt.

But it was a much better match for the evidence than the claim for North Korean responsibility.

Eric finished, giving all the usual warnings that this was evidence they'd developed, based on what they'd reviewed, and it was possible there was other information which they had not found, which might change their assumptions. But at the very least, Eric felt he had made the case that at least part of the government's investigation should focus on some of the recently fired technical staff at Sony.

"Who is this guy?" one of the assembled group asked. "And why should we believe him?"

Eric was about to respond when another member of the group spoke up. "I can vouch for them. They analyze about a quarter of the traffic for the NSA. They've done some very good work for us."

At least there was one vote of confidence in the room.

There was some more back and forth, questions why the analysis of Norse differed so much from that of the FBI, and the meeting wound down. Eric was thanked for the presentation, but knew he was being dismissed.

He gave them the report and started to walk out, feeling their eyes upon him as he left.

When he left the Pentagon he called Mr. Grey, who immediately asked, "How'd it go?"

"Like talking to a brick wall," said Eric. "They've got their minds made up."

"Maybe they just need some time to digest the information," Mr. Grey offered.

"No, something weird was going on in that room," Eric replied. "I don't know what it was, but we're out of the game. They're not going to talk to us. And what they made us sign to take the meeting means we can't talk about it for five years, either. We're bound by national security oaths until then."

"But the other cyber-security companies are saying the same things we are," Mr. Grey reminded him.

"It won't matter. For us, it's case closed. We move on."

In April of 2018, the actor Seth Rogen gave an interview in *Vulture* magazine, which should have flipped the mainstream media and FBI narrative about the Sony hack on its head.

What thoughts get kicked up when you see North Korea in the news these days?

It does kick some stuff up for sure. Honestly, I don't think North Korea hacked Sony.

Why's that?

When the trailer for *The Interview* came out [Author's note - June 11, 2014] we were called into a meeting at Sony, where they told us that North Korea had probably already hacked into their system and seen the movie and the statements they'd put out were their response. Then, months later, when the movie itself finally came out, all this hacking shit happened. This was months after North Korea had already probably seen the movie. Why would they wait? And they never did anything like that before and haven't done anything like it since. So things just never quite added up. The guy I'd hired to do my cybersecurity even told me, "There's no way this was a hack. It had to be a physical act." The amount of stuff that was stolen would have had to have physical mass to it.

In the sense that whoever stole the information needed to have his or her hands on the server at some point?
Yeah, it wasn't something you could've hacked remotely. It required plugging shit into other shit. And the hack also seemed weirdly targeted at Amy [Pascal], which seems fishy – of all the people to target? Why not me? Why not Michael Lynton?

Has anyone given you a plausible theory for who else might be responsible?
I've heard that it was a disgruntled Sony employee. I've also heard people say that they think someone was hired to do the hack as a way of getting Amy Pascal fired. I don't know if I subscribe to those theories, but I kind of don't think it was North Korea.[261]

These are some remarkable revelations by Rogen and cast an entirely new light on the first meeting Norse had with Sony in August of 2014, when one of the Sony executives had asked Norse what they knew about North Korea.

At least some of the top executives at Sony believed North Korea had already hacked into the computer system of the studio and watched *The Interview*. That makes it all the more curious that *The Interview* was not one of the five films that had been stolen from the company and placed on the internet, along with the embarrassing emails and other company data.

If North Korea had already stolen the film, why not release it, as they did the five other films?

The initial communications by the alleged hackers did not seem to be focused on *The Interview*, but with the corporate practices of Sony.

The cyber-security professional hired by Rogen didn't believe Sony had been remotely hacked, but that somebody had physically walked into the corporate offices and seeing the lack of security observed by Norse in August of 2014, plugged a device directly into the Sony network.

Rogen was cautious to say he didn't believe one story over another but questioned why the hackers seemed particularly interested in demolishing the reputation of Amy Pascal (who parted ways with Sony in February of 2015) and not going after her partner, Michael Lynton, who was arguably more powerful than Amy. There were some other remarkable revelations from the article.

> …When I look back at the whole situation, the thing I regret is that Sony convinced me to pretend to the press that we didn't know what we were doing when we made *The Interview*. They wanted us to act like we were just trying to make a silly comedy and didn't know we were making something controversial.

They were asking you to play naïve?
They were asking us to look like these dumb stoner filmmakers who just happened to make a movie about Kim Jong-un without really thinking about it. Like, *we had no idea North Korea might be mad!*

So why'd you play along?
Look, I mean, it was all happening in real time. They [Sony] were not protecting us very well. They pulled the movie from theaters when I was in a green room about to go on *Colbert*. No one from Sony came up to me being like, "Yo, we're doing this." They totally floated us out on our own. They just kept saying, "Say [*The Interview*] wasn't meant to be controversial. Say the controversy was an accident." And that's what we did! Just because it was all happening so fast and we didn't know what the fuck was going on. So that's what I honestly regret: not just saying, "We knew exactly what we were doing with *The Interview*."[262]

With the passage of nearly a decade, as well as the fact that a miscalculation by either side during this crisis could have precipitated a nuclear war, perhaps we should consider, as Rogen so eloquently asked "what the fuck was going on?"

From Rogen's own testimony, we know that sometime in the early summer of 2014, he was told by Sony executives that North Korea had likely hacked into the studio's computer network. That this information did not come out at the time of the November 2014 hack can only be considered an act of concealment at best, and an outright lie, at worst.

Did the government know this information, or did Sony withhold it from them as well?

And yet, when Norse met with Sony executives in August, there didn't seem to be a sense of urgency, except on the part of Amy Pascal. One gets the impression she wanted to proceed, but was stymied by her superior, who in the chain of command could only be Michael Lynton.

The quality of the second significant lie, that Rogen and his team didn't know they were making a provocative film, deserves some discussion. Who exactly told him to lie? It doesn't seem likely to have been Amy Pascal. Although she was co-head of the studio, her duties seemed to have been more with the creative talent. The larger decisions seem to have been made by Michael Lynton.

As the hackers did in their post, it seems the finger of blame points again at Michael Lynton.

The actions Rogen describes, being kept in the dark, then unceremoniously dropped when things go wrong, sounds suspiciously like the plot of a typical Hollywood thriller, where the intelligence agencies recruit unsuspecting civilians, making them believe they are virtuously pursuing one course of action, then when things fall apart, abandoning them, and leaving the hapless heroes to fend for themselves.

I'm not saying that's what happened with *The Interview*.

It's simply the most compelling narrative which lines up with all the known facts.

❧   ❧   ❧

Seth Rogen may have begun his career with stoner comedies, but his recent work suggests an interest in pursuing more adult themes.

In my opinion, if Seth Rogen continues on his current trajectory, he may end up as one of the most interesting and important filmmakers of our time, somebody on the level of Oliver Stone, best known for his films such as *Platoon, Wall Street,* and *JFK.*

While *The Interview* was his fledgling effort to discuss political issues (albeit in a comedic manner), he followed up with several interesting projects, indicating he wants to continue to provoke audiences. In the 2015 film, *Steve Jobs,* he portrayed Apple co-founder, Steve Wozniak, he appeared in the well-reviewed 2017 film, *The Disaster Artist,* (the real-life story behind the worst film ever made), and in 2019 he co-starred in *The Longshot,* with Charlize Theron, in which he played a journalist who awkwardly falls in love with his former babysitter, who is running to be President of the United States.

But nothing suggests Rogen's future ambitions more than *The Boys,* a series he has been connected with for many years. After many false starts at Sony, (originally planned to be a standalone movie), it premiered as a series on Amazon in 2019. In my opinion, it is the most slyly subversive and entertaining show in all of television. Rogen is a producer on the series, having first brought the graphic novel on which the series is based, to Sony in 2006.

In the world of *The Boys,* superheroes are real, but they're nothing like the characters in the Marvel or DC movies.

For the most part, they're genuinely messed up, often psychotic individuals.

There's "Homelander," a Superman-like figure, with blonde hair who acts like a fascist and doesn't mind killing people. Another is "Queen Maeve," who resembles Wonder Woman, but is an alcoholic, depressed lesbian. Then there's "A Train," who has super-speed like The Flash, but is addicted to performance-enhancing drugs to keep his edge. "The Deep" is an aquatic superhero like

Aquaman, who can communicate with the animals of the waters, but is a creepy sexual predator, whose greatest sexual attraction is not for superhero groupies, but dolphins.

The superheroes, known collectively as "The Seven," are owned by a corporation, Vought [Bought?] Industries, which manages their public appearances, as well as movie and film adaptations. (In the series there are several hundred with superpowers, but the public only cares about those who make it to "The Seven.") In the first season we're led to believe that these superheroes just appeared coincidentally among American children in the 1980s. But in the second season, we learn that these American heroes were the result of Nazi technology, stolen by Vought at the end of the Second World War, and given to unsuspecting children in the 1960s and 1970s.

The actual heroes of the series are not the superheroes, but a group of regular citizens, led by Billy Butcher, who oppose "the Supes." However, these regular citizens often veer dangerously in vigilantism, and the viewer will often find their actions as distressing as that of "the Supes."

Both the superheroes and the citizens who oppose them have conflicting impulses for good and evil, and whether the better angels of either side's nature will win out, is forever in doubt.

In 2021 the series received five Primetime Emmy nominations, including one for Outstanding Drama Series, and another for Outstanding Writing in a Drama Series.

More than anything else, the series suggests that the reality which is packaged and presented to the public by powerful entities, is far from the truth.

One wonders if Rogen's experiences with *The Interview*, have affected the tone of his popular series.

How did Bruce Bennett respond to the Sony hack? After all, he was the RAND Corporation expert who had been privately advising

Sony Pictures CEO Michael Lynton on *The Interview*, since the North
Koreans had first complained in the summer of 2014?

Bennet responded by blaming North Korea even before the
United States government did and suggesting a series of actions to
be taken against the North Korean regime.

In a December 11, 2014, commentary in *Newsweek*, Bennett first
dismissed the claims of many private cybersecurity companies that
an insider was the most likely suspect. He wrote:

> Some experts quoted in the media believe Sony insiders
> were to blame, because of the personal information that was
> released and because the attack didn't match the pattern
> of previous North Korean cyber-attacks. That is possible,
> though the number of current or former Sony personnel
> with sophisticated cyber capabilities must be very small. The
> apparent ongoing disclosures of information would make
> it difficult for a current disgruntled employee to avoid dis-
> covery. Moreover, North Korea is not the typical adversary
> state, and does adapt to achieve its objectives.[263]

Even if I wasn't suspicious of Bennett's ties to the military-
industrial complex, and his behind the scenes advising of Sony
chairman, Michael Lynton, his long-time hostility towards North
Korea suggests he might not be able to objectively review information which runs counter to his strongly held views. (It must also be
noted that Norse did find evidence of North Korean intrusion into
the Sony network, but this happened after the data had already
been exfiltrated. A good analogy would probably be something like
horse thieves walked into a barn with no horses, then got arrested
by the sheriff.)

However, even Bennett seems to be without a good answer as to
what should be done. He wrote:

> The United States must act to defer future cyber attacks
> against its people and corporations, but how? Culturally,

North Korea is unlikely to be deterred by a weak U.S. response. A weak U.S. response will only embolden North Korea and lead to more serious attacks, even if it is not proven to be the culprit.

So what might a strong U.S. response look like? Deterrence is achieved by convincing adversarial leaders that they have more to lose than gain by carrying out such attacks. There are many ways that the United States and even Sony Pictures could affect North Korean internal politics.

Slipping DVDs of at least parts of *The Interview* into the North, including a narration describing what their "god" Kim is really like, is one way. Leaking damaging information into the North is another. Such leaks might ask why the Kim family has absconded with perhaps $4 billion in state funds while many of its people are starving.[264]

Bennett's advice calls into question the quality of the intelligence upon which the U.S. government makes decisions of war and peace. Are military assets of the United States to be called upon to punish North Korea, "even if it is not proven to be the culprit?"

Isn't an unprovoked attack upon another nation a war crime?

Is it now an accepted practice of international diplomacy that we can engage in propaganda designed to affect the internal politics of another nation?

If that's the standard, are other nations allowed to do the same thing to the United States?

And if they do, can we reasonably complain?

However, it's only at the end of Bennett's piece that he provides the marching orders to the public and our leaders.

But deterrence is not just about punishment; it is also about denying the effectiveness of future attacks. While the details of North Korean cyber threats are uncertain, the

United States and its allies should seek to monitor, attack, and disable North Korean hacking capabilities. There is evidence that North Korean hackers work from China and use Chinese IP addresses. If this is true, then China's role should be publicly revealed and it should be pressured to terminate this assistance.

The United States must enhance its cyber defenses, both for its government and its commercial world. The United States currently strives to do so but likely needs to increase the resources devoted to this vital task. These defenses will never be perfect, but they almost certainly can be better.[265]

The best games to play are the ones where the rules are rigged in your favor. Heads I win, tails you lose. Does the truth matter? Not if you can scare the public, or at the very least confuse them.

The private cybersecurity companies look at the data and point the finger of blame at an insider? Bring the best one in for a talk, the one who was actually prospecting for work with Sony and acquainting themselves with their computer network, invite them to give a presentation at the Pentagon to see what they know, then remind them they signed a five-year secrecy oath.

The government wins.

All of the other companies see that, and know that if they keep talking, the government will just say they don't have all the data, which is classified because of "national security."

The government wins.

The actor at the center of the controversy reveals years later some of the lies told during the crisis? Simply ignore him. For Christ's sake, he's just some stoner actor.

The government wins again.

The message is what's important, not the details or the truth.

And the message is, the military-industrial complex needs more money. And if a company like Sony, plays ball with them, needs some money as well to cover some of their bad financial decisions, that can probably be arranged as well.

When investigating an unsolved crime in ancient Rome, the question was always *cui bono*, who benefits?

The answer in modern America, especially when it involves the government and big business, seems to be that they all benefit.

CHAPTER ELEVEN

THE IMPORTANCE OF FINDING

THE TRUTH BEHIND A FAKE

HOLLYWOOD ENDING

How does one develop an accurate picture of reality?
As a lawyer I was trained to look closely at the evidence on my side, as well as the other side, evaluate the strength of both positions, and come to my own conclusions. I was also strongly cautioned that simply because a person was sitting in my office, sharing a compelling story, didn't mean they were telling the entire truth. A common saying in the legal profession about the importance of verifying everything is that "If a client tells you his mother loves him, be sure to get a second opinion."

On the other side of the question of whether North Korea hacked Sony Pictures in 2014 is a 2018 book entitled: *The Perfect Weapon: War, Sabotage and Fear in the Cyber Age*, by David E. Sanger,[266] the national security correspondent for the *New York Times*. It takes the position that North Korea did hack Sony Pictures and release the information, as claimed by the United States government. The book has received glowing reviews from the *Washington Post*, the *Financial Times*, the *New York Times*, and has been turned into a documentary film for HBO. (In my mind, that gives it the Good Housekeeping seal of approval from the mainstream media, whether that matters to you or not.)

I was taught that a skilled attorney does their best to understand the other side, seeking to discover areas of agreement, and when that can't happen, working to understand the strength of the other side's different conclusion. I've found there's often agreement on the facts of a certain event, but each side may differ in what the information means, or whether the evidence is capable of a different interpretation. Sanger and I both agree on the importance of understanding cyber threats, and he adds a critical, terrifying piece of information about the potential harm of a cyber miscalculation.

A year into Donald J. Trump's presidency, his defense secretary, Jim Mattis [author's note - known by his colorful nickname "Mad Dog Mattis"], sent the new commander-in-chief a startling recommendation: with nations around the world threatening to use cyberweapons to bring down America's power grids, cell-phone networks, and water supplies, Trump should declare he was ready to take extraordinary steps to protect the country. If any nation hit America's critical infrastructure with a devastating strike, even a non-nuclear one, it should be forewarned that the United States might reach for a nuclear weapon in response.

Like most things in Washington, the recommendation leaked immediately. Many declared it a crazy idea, and wild overkill. While nations had turned their cyberweapons against each other dozens of times in recent years, no attack had yet been proven to cost a single human life, at least directly.[267]

The passage raises some immediate questions: How many times have we turned cyberweapons against our adversaries, and were those U.S. sabotage efforts against what another country might consider their "critical infrastructure?"

The answer, according to Sanger, is quite a few. How this came about was first revealed to the public by whistleblower, Edward

Snowden, and a piece of software called a "web-crawler," which could move stealthily through a computer network.

> This particular web crawler was deposited in the NSA's networks in the spring of 2013 by Edward J. Snowden, a Booz Allen Hamilton contractor working at an NSA outpost in Hawaii. Perhaps the most astounding aspect of his effort to steal a huge trove of the agency's documents – a move considered treasonous by many, but long overdue and patriotic by his supporters – is that it worked so well: the world's premier electronic spy agency was completely unprepared to detect such a simple intruder swimming in a sea of top secret documents...

> If you take Snowden at his word, his goal in revealing the inner secrets of the NSA was to expose what he viewed as massive wrongdoing and overreach: secret programs that monitored Americans on US soil, not just foreigners, in the name of tracking down terrorists who were planning to attack the United States. The vast databases at NSA Hawaii disgorged several examples of programs that bolstered Snowden's case that the NSA had used the Foreign Intelligence Surveillance Court, and compliant congressional committees, to take its surveillance powers into the domestic phone and computer networks that at first glance seemed off-limits by law.[268]

While the citizens of America were rightfully concerned that their Fourth Amendment rights against unlawful search and seizure had been bulldozed, there was another important revelation in the Snowden documents.

The US government had developed and deployed some highly sophisticated cyberweapons against Iran, North Korea, and China. This was in 2013, a year before the alleged North Korean hack of Sony Pictures.

...From Hawaii, not far from Pearl Harbor and the US Pacific Command, the NSA was deploying its very best cyberweapons against its most sensitive targets, including North Korea's intelligence services and China's People's Liberation Army. The weapons ranged from new surveillance techniques that could leap "air gaps" and penetrate computers not connected to the Internet to computer implants that could detonate in time of war, disabling missiles and blinding satellites. While the American public and much of the media were transfixed by the image of a "Big Brother" – tracking not only the numbers they call but the trail of digital dust left by the smartphones in their pockets – the most revealing documents in Snowden's trove showed the vast ambitions of the nation's new cyber arsenal.

If the revelations of Operation Olympic Games [George Bush's 2006 plan to attack Iran's nuclear facilities with cyberweapons to disrupt the spinning of their centrifuges] had given the public a peek through the keyhole at America's most sophisticated offensive cyber capabilities, Snowden offered the Google Satellite view, from miles above. From there, it was a remarkable sight. It was immediately clear that, over the past decade, the United States had tasked thousands of engineers and contractors, working under tight secrecy, to build a range of experimental weapons. Some of these weapons merely pierced foreign networks and offered another window into the deliberations and secret deals of adversaries and allies – basically a cyber-assisted form of traditional espionage. But other tools went much further, by burrowing deep into foreign networks that one day the United States could decide to cripple or destroy.[269]

Who seems to have the bulk of these scary new cyber-weapons? Apparently, it's the United States.

This might make you feel safer if you're a citizen, or more concerned if you live in another country. However, if you're one of the Americans who worry the powers of your own government, and their willingness to use such weapons against their own citizens, it may absolutely terrify you.

In the chapter entitled, "The Kims Strike Back," Sanger took a look at the 2014 Sony hack. While the North Koreans, unlike the Iranians, already had nuclear weapons, the effort by Obama would focus on going after North Korean missiles, one of the key plot points of *The Interview*.

> For Kim-Jong-un, the ability to reach an American city with a nuclear warhead was all about survival – but it was also about future power. He accelerated the effort drastically, turning it into the North Korean version of the Manhattan Project. That meant putting equal effort into a missile program that could get the weapons to the other side of the Pacific. And by 2013, for the first time, the missile program looked genuinely terrifying.

> "I heard more than once that he would have no problem decapitating Kim Jong-un's leadership circle if he had the chance – and thought it wouldn't start a war," one of Obama's aides later recounted. No one could provide that assurance, and because Obama was cautious to a fault even some of his own aides wonder whether he would have pulled the trigger. But he was certainly willing to do what he could to slow the North's nuclear program.[270]

As I've detailed in this book, the North Korean regime has some strong historical justification for looking with suspicion at the Western powers, with incidents beginning in the 19th century.

Whether it is true or not today, the North Koreans believed that nuclear weapons were the only thing likely to stop aggressive Western powers.

If one is to negotiate effectively with your adversaries, it's a good idea to understand their worldview, even if you don't agree with it.

President Obama acted with what must have been a confusing passive-aggressive stance towards North Korea. On the one hand, he mused to an aide how much he would "have no problem decapitating Kim Jong-un's leadership circle if he had the chance," while at the same time his aides questioned whether he would ever launch such an assault on North Korea.

However, Obama was willing to take certain actions, patterned after the successful Operation Winter Games attack on Iran's nuclear program. As Sanger reports:

> Early in 2014, Obama presided over a series of meetings to explore a range of options. The Pentagon and American intelligence agencies, he decided, should step up a series of cyber and electronic-warfare strikes on Kim's missiles, starting with an intermediate-range missile called the Musudan. The hope was to sabotage them before they got into the air, or to send them off-course moments after launch. The further hope was that the North Koreans, like the Iranians before them, would blame themselves for manufacturing errors.
>
> It would take a year or two, Obama was warned, before anyone would know if the accelerated program could work. Only in retrospect is it clear that in 2014, Obama and Kim were using cyberweapons to go after each other. Obama's target was North Korea's missiles; Kim's was a movie studio intent on humiliating him. Eventually, each would begin to discover what the other was plotting.[271]

Sanger does an admirable job in revealing the actions of the United States government regarding the North Koreans in 2014.

From what I read in this section, Sanger does not address the claims of the numerous private cybersecurity companies who disagreed that the hack was perpetrated by North Korea, and instead thought it more likely to have been a Sony insider, perhaps one who had been recently fired. In addition, the revelations of Seth Rogen in 2018, were unlikely to have been known to Sanger at the time the book was submitted.

However, I find Sanger's unquestioning trust in the same American intelligence apparatus which lied us into Vietnam and Iraq, to be a curious lapse for a national security correspondent, especially one working for the *New York Times*. Sanger wrote:

> ...Even today, the US government has never revealed its evidence – because it does not want to tip its hand about what kind of monitoring may be ongoing. But it seems clear the United States uncovered some intercepted voice communications or written instructions straight from the North Korean leadership.
>
> The evidence was persuasive enough that President Obama was briefed on it almost immediately.
>
> "I never thought I'd be here briefing on a bad Seth Rogen movie, sir," one of Obama's aides told him as the plot became clear.
>
> "How do you know it's a bad movie?" Obama asked.
>
> "Sir, it's a Seth Rogen movie..." Laughter broke out in the Oval Office.[272]

I find Sanger's account to be lacking in curiosity about the facts which underlay what was supposed to be "persuasive" evidence.

Couldn't Sanger get that information from his sources?

As a writer, I'm also aware of how easy it is to misdirect the reader. In one sentence, Sanger tells you that the government has not released the evidence upon which it based its conclusion, ignores the abundant contemporaneous press accounts of how private cybersecurity companies were doubtful of North Korean responsibility, then adds this sentence, "But it seems clear the United States uncovered some intercepted voice communications or written instructions straight from the North Korean leadership."

What is the justification for this sentence, other than to make me think the United States has some "intercepted voice communications or written instructions straight from the North Korean leadership?"

If that is what he was told by somebody in the military or intelligence agencies, then it's a lie to say the United States has released no evidence. The justification Sanger gives later in the section, that the United States did not want to reveal any of its sources or methods, falls apart when one realizes that such an innocuous statement reveals nothing of the sources or methods used to gather it.

The only other explanation is that Sanger made it up, possibly because it was just a hunch on his part.

Regardless of whether he was told the information, or it's his hunch, he needed to tell us the truth. This oversight makes me suspicious, as there is a lot of information he does provide, suggesting he had high-level sources for his reporting.

"This was a destructive attack," said Robert Litt, the general counsel for the director of national intelligence. "But you couldn't argue that it hit a vital sector of the US infrastructure. It wasn't exactly taking out all the power from Boston to Washington. So the issue was: is this the government's responsibility to defend?"

That was only one of the questions hanging in the air as Obama and his aides descended into the Situation Room on December 18. In a spirited debate, some of Obama's aides argued whether or not the target was "critical," the United States had just been attacked.

"I remember sitting there while some of our colleagues argued that this was just like planting a bomb inside Sony, which we definitely would have categorized as terrorism," said one national-security aide who was sitting along the back bench as the argument raged.[273]

Some in the Situation Room on December 18, 2014, were arguing that the hack was best compared to a bombing, which when it takes place between nations, will often precipitate military action. If this logic had been followed, there's no telling how the situation might have turned out, and how many might have died in the ensuing conflict, both Americans, as well as citizens of North and South Korea.

The calm person in the room appears to have been President Obama, who was wary of taking the action some in the room demanded.

Ever cautious, Obama came to the conclusion that it wasn't terrorism; it was more like "cyber-vandalism," as he said a few days later. (He soon came to regret the line.) Obama did not want to escalate. But he also did not want to go through another country's networks to get inside North Korea.

"The problem," one participant in the meeting later told me, "was that the only way to go into the North Korean networks was through China, and no one wanted to have the Chinese thinking that we were attacking them or using their networks to attack someone else."[274]

Maybe it was Obama's legal mind that made him able to thread the eye of a very delicate needle and some highly questionable military and intelligence agencies conclusions. A more aggressive

President might have made a completely different decision, and our history might look much different.

Whether that would have made for a better or worse world, is difficult for any of us to say.

Sanger's chapter on the Sony hack doesn't begin with Kim Jong-un, or his father, but with Sony Pictures CEO, Michael Lynton.

As I've mentioned before, Sanger's account contains a number of curious omissions, such as the summer 2014 hack reported by actor Seth Rogen after the first trailer for *The Interview* was released, while also failing to mention the consulting role played by long-time RAND Corporation Korea hawk, Bruce Bennett, or the slightest mention of the suspicions of many private cybersecurity companies that the hack was most likely the work of an insider. However, like me, Sanger places Michael Lynton at the center of this drama.

> Michael Lynton, the lean, European-born chief executive of Sony Pictures Entertainment, remembers well what happened when he called the State Department in the summer of 2014. He was worried about a torrent of threats from North Korea, all designed to force the studio to halt the release of a forthcoming comedy called *The Interview*. "I had never seen a country demand that we kill a project," Lynton told me.

> It wasn't hard to understand why the North Koreans were upset about the imminent release of a farce starring Seth Rogen and James Franco. The plot was not exactly subtle: Two bumbling, incompetent journalists score and interview with Kim Jong-un, but before they leave for the Hermit Kingdom, they are recruited by the CIA to blow him to smithereens. The plot was completely improbable, but the North Koreans were not known for their finely honed sense of satire.[275]

I'm aware as any writer of the creation of good and evil characters for engaging storytelling. But I can't help noticing that by referring to Lynton as "lean" and the "European-born chief executive," Sanger is creating a foil to the North Korean dictator who lacks a "finely honed sense of satire." While Sanger believed the film to be something of an inconsequential farce, Bennett, the RAND Corporation expert on North Korea advising Lynton, wanted to use scenes from the movie for DVDs that would be secretly shipped to North Korea. (The film is either useful propaganda to foment a revolution in North Korea, or it's not. It can't be both.)

Further in the section, Sanger criticized the North Korean protests to the United Nations as worthy of mockery (would the same be said of a movie protesting the life of the prophet Mohammed?), while Lynton's actions are depicted as those of a conscientious and capable CEO, although unfamiliar in matters of foreign affairs.

> ...As a business executive and then a Hollywood studio executive, he wasn't accustomed to doing geopolitics. And the more noise the North Koreans made, the more nervous he became-in part because his bosses at the headquarters of the Tokyo-based parent company, Sony Corporation, were terrified. Its chief executive Kazuo Hirai was so anxious that Lynton and his co-chair, Amy Pascal, ordered the studio to tone down a scene at the end of the movie in which Kim's head appears to explode during a gruesome assassination. Soon the name "Sony Pictures" disappeared from all of the film's posters and promotional materials as the corporate leadership in Tokyo did all it could to distance the parent company from the film.[276]

As I've detailed in this book, the Japanese have a terrible history when it comes to their brutality in the Korean Peninsula, before and during World War II, exacerbated after the Korean War by placing the United Nations General Command in Tokyo, the government capital of their former masters.

The assertion by Sanger that Lynton was unfamiliar with geopolitics is quite a claim, considering he served on the Broadcasting
Board of Governors from July 2, 2010, and headed the group for
more than a year as the interim presiding governor, resigning on
May 23, 2013. On September 23, 2012, he met with Secretary of
State Hillary Clinton to discuss the board's work. This is from a
press release by the *US Agency for Global Media*:

> In a meeting today with the Broadcasting Board of Governors,
> Secretary of State Hillary Rodham Clinton encouraged the
> Board in their strategic efforts to restructure and increase
> the impact of U.S. international broadcasting.

> BBG Presiding Governor, Michael Lynton led the Board's
> delegation to the State Department, which included
> Governors Victor Ashe, Dennis Mulhaupt, Susan McCue,
> and Michael Meehan, as well as Richard M. Lobo, Director
> of the International Broadcasting Bureau. Undersecretary
> of State, Tara Sonenshine, the Secretary's representative to
> the BBG, took a leading role in framing the discussion …

> … "Change will not happen overnight," Lynton said. "But
> the reforms we are enacting will strengthen the agency's
> ability to deliver on its mission in support of U.S. national
> interests: to inform, engage and connect with people
> around the world in support of freedom and democracy."[277]

It's wonderful to know that in America, where we value free
speech so much, that there is a *U.S. Agency for Global Media*, which
allows the government to tell us the truth, lest we fall victim to "fake
news". If you drew the conclusion that the United States was involved
in propaganda because it has a *U.S. Agency for Global Media*, that would
be a big mistake. They just want to give us the facts, namely that the
Broadcasting Board of Governors simply wants to "deliver on its mission in support of U.S. national interests," and nothing more.

And just in case you aren't quite convinced that the *U.S. Agency for Global Media* is a completely legitimate news outlet, and not a propaganda tool at all, when Michael Lynton stepped down as Presiding Governor of the Broadcasting Board of Governors on May 23, 2013, the *U.S. Agency for Global Media* published his entire resignation letter to his boss, President Obama. It reads as follows:

May 23, 2013

The President
The White House
Washington, DC 20500

Dear Mr. President:

With this letter, I submit my resignation from the Broadcasting Board of Governors (BBG) effective May 23rd, 2013.

It has been an honor to serve our country by taking part in the work of this board, which was established to oversee an agency with a complex and vital calling. Time and time again, we have seen the journalists and other staff of the BBG are dedicated to the agency's mission: to inform, engage and connect people around the world in support of freedom and democracy. They prove it around the clock and against steep odds, in many cases amid some of the most difficult circumstances imaginable.

In an effort to sustain this mission, I was proud to work with fellow board members on promoting long-needed reforms of the agency's structure and governance – among them, enhancing collaboration between the broadcasters and establishing the position of a Chief Executive Officer with day-to-day operational responsibilities. I wish the current members and our successors the very best in seeing these reforms through.

And once more I'd like to thank fellow board members for asking me to take the reins more than a year ago. Circumstances kept me from taking part in their recent formal meetings, but it is my hope that the BBG board will enjoy a full and productive membership soon.

Respectfully,
Michael Lynton[278]

Does that resignation letter to President Obama sound to you like somebody who is unfamiliar with geopolitics? By his own admission, he worked to, "inform, engage and connect people around the world in support of freedom and democracy."

If I was of a suspicious nature, I might conclude that Lynton is one of the most important propagandists for the United States government around the world.

If I was of a less suspicious nature, I'd simply view him as an incredible brown-noser and suck-up to the powerful.

I'd like to return to Sanger's book and his account of Lynton's actions in light of North Korea's protests against *The Interview.*

That's when Lynton called Danny Russel.

Russel was then the State Department's top Asia diplomat, a wry and experienced hand who had, by the time he turned sixty, seen just about every form of bizarre North Korean behavior. He had worked behind the scenes to get American hostages released, designed sanctions regimes and helped draft diplomatic initiatives over the North's weapons programs that he knew the Kim family would reject.[279]

I had to read that final sentence a few times to make sure I'd properly understood it. Danny Russel designed diplomatic initiatives for North Korea that he knew would fail.

Is that the person you go to for a solution?

It seems to me that's the person you go to for an escalation.

And that's exactly what happened.

It makes one wonder if that was the plan all along.

✤ ✤ ✤

How much damage did the hack of Sony Pictures cost the company?

Estimates varied widely, not just because of the amount stolen, or the size of Sony Pictures, but also because of the damage to its reputation. A December 5, 2014 article on the question framed it this way:

> "These attacks are pretty devastating," said Kurt Baumgartner, principal for security research at Kapersky Lab. The investigation into the situation could run on for months, and the cleanup will likely cost millions "if not tens of millions," he said.

> Baumgartner cited examples such as retailers TJ Maxx, which he says reported over $250 million in cleanup costs from a 2007 hack, and the Target breach from last year, which he expects will run over $400 million in cleanup costs. In 2011, Sony's Playstation Network was hacked [author's note – By Lizardsquad, the same hacker group this book argues committed the 2014 hack], costing the company an estimated $170 million.

> The cost to the hack against Sony Pictures is complicated to calculate. The company will have to bring in cybersecurity firms to investigate what happened and invest substantial efforts to get their networks up and running again. The studio will suffer lost revenue from films that were stolen and released online by hackers, and it might face legal costs responding to the needs of former and current employees whose personal information has been exposed. Documents allegedly released by the perpetrators of the digital heist

may also put a damper on deals in process, or make some Hollywood stars – some of whom appear to have had their personal data exposed by the attack - - less inclined to do business with the company.[280]

While Sony Pictures is not the size of the retailers, TJ Maxx or Target, a previous hack of the Sony Playstation Network had cost approximately $170 million dollars. This was a crime which caused a significant financial loss. The article continued with strong criticism of the inadequate cybersecurity preparations at Sony Pictures.

> ...In the case of Sony, the company has not disclosed how long attackers were in the system before the attack wreaked havoc on the company. Baumgartner believes that they may have been inside the system for months, adding complexity to the restoration process as investigators ensure that their network backups are clean of an attacker's code.

> Sony Pictures' internal approach to security may have contributed to the devastating nature of the attack. "It's clear they did not have their networks well-segmented, and the attackers could move freely and destroy data," said Baumgartner. Reports indicate the company didn't follow many industry best practices: For instance, passwords may have been saved in clearly labeled files without encryption.

> Fusion reports that documents leaked after the recent attacks show the company had just 11 people assigned to its information security team: "Three information security analysts are overseen by three managers, three directors, one executive director and one senior vice president." (Sony Pictures did not respond to for requests for comment to this story.)[281]

The contemporaneous accounts of the hack I've been able to review are consistent with the story told to me by Eric and Mr.

Grey about the findings of Norse Corporation. A more thorough article published eleven days later on December 16, 2014 in *The Intelligencer* came to similar conclusions about the size of the likely damages and the continuing problems it would cause for Sony Pictures.

> It's still too early to know how badly the hack might hurt Sony's bottom line, especially given that the hackers keep on putting out new leaks and new threats. But some early estimates of the corporate damage have started to trickle out. And $150 or $300 million does not seem like a bad guess at the moment, meaning the hack might wipe out half of the Sony Pictures unit's 2013 profits.[282]

These estimates make the damages from the hack appear even larger, perhaps more than a quarter of a billion dollars. As far as the level of legal representation available to Sony, they were represented at the time by David Boies,[283] the attorney who had represented the Al Gore campaign in the 2000 Presidential campaign over the Florida vote going to eventual winner, George W. Bush. It seemed the ultimate question of how much Sony would suffer from the hack came down to a question of insurance.

An article from *International Business Times* in late December 2014 sketched out a picture of how the problem might be resolved, as well as why there might have been a rush to judgment by the government to blame North Korea.

> Sony Pictures was added to parent Sony Corporation's insurance coverage in August, which included security and privacy liability coverage, event management, network interruption, cyber extortion and regulatory action for a total policy limit of $60 million, according to CSO Online.

> Sony's insurers include American International Group and Marsh Insurance. It is not clear of Sony's film projects

specifically are insured. The company turned down a request for comment from International Business Times.

Depending on how the attack is ultimately classified, the insurers may be in line for federal assistance if the damages exceeded more than $100 million under the terms of the Terrorism Risk Insurance Act (TRIA). The problem is that the TRIA was not renewed by Congress and is scheduled to expire on Dec. 31.[284]

Could the rush to blame North Korea for the hack, and the refusal to consider other malign actors, be because the government wanted to make sure their good friend, Michael Lynton and Sony Pictures, got the money he needed to keep the company going? The Terrorism Risk Insurance Act TRIA) was passed in the wake of the September 11, 2001, terrorist attacks, and by 2014 there were calls for it to be abolished.

As the clock ticked on the expiration of the Terrorism Risk Insurance Act, the Public Broadcasting System (PBS) NewsHour swung into action on behalf of the insurance company with its prize-winning reporter, Judy Woodruff, interviewing Leigh Ann Pusey, president and CEO of the American Insurance Association on December 17, 2014.

It seemed that a certain United States Senator was asking some very inconvenient questions about the government sponsored terrorism insurance business, holding up a vote, and why it was important for the program to be reauthorized.

Judy Woodruff: Let me read you what one – one comment that Senator Tom Coburn, the senator from Oklahoma, the one who is responsible for holding this up, said this week.

He said, "This program has made the insurance industry $40 billion in the last 12 years." He said, "American taxpayers take all the risk, except for 35 percent, and the insurance industry takes the money."

Leigh Ann Pusey: Well, what the insurance industry is doing is stepping in and providing for an orderly economic recovery that otherwise the taxpayer would be on the hook for the first dollar of.

So, have we charged a premium for that risk? Sure. That's a market force I would think Senator Coburn and other Republicans and pro-market voices would like to see happen. And the more we can get comfortable with this risk over time, the more we can learn about it, we can take on more of it. It will never be a risk that can be totally borne by the private market. And it shouldn't be.[285]

A United States Senator observes that this federal program has made the insurance industry $40 billion dollars over the previous twelve years, or a little more than $3 billion per year.

I'm no economist, but that seems like a pretty good business.

Since the 9/11 attacks of 2001, the United States has done a pretty good job of protecting the country from terrorism. We want the insurance companies to make money, but $40 billion over twelve years probably means they've overstated the actual terrorism risk to American businesses. If one wasn't worried about a North Korean dictator lobbing nuclear missiles at the West Coast, you might look a little more closely as to whether the insurance companies are correctly pricing the possible terrorism risk to American businesses.

Maybe $40 billion in profits for the insurance industry is worth it for the peace of mind of the American business community.

Judy Woodruff asked Pusey, the insurance industry representative why the insurance companies shouldn't bear the full risk since they're the ones collecting the premiums.

Leigh Ann Pusey: Well, because it's associated – it's national security. Terrorism is a national security issue. It's the responsibility of the federal government, who has the data, the knowledge, the know-how.

You just ran a piece about them confirming what they may or may not know about these threats related to Sony. Well, that – they have that knowledge. Nobody insuring Sony has that knowledge. They have that knowledge. We don't want that knowledge, by the way, but what it means is that insurers are limited in how much they can try to underwrite this and how much exposure they can take on.

The current TRIA program covers – provides $100 billion. There's not $100 billion of private market capacity. If you want to provide economic stability and economic growth, then you need a partnership.[286]

However, they need not have worried about the concerns of Senator Tom Coburn that terrorism insurance seemed to be a $40 billion dollar boondoggle for the insurance industry.

On January 7, 2015, Congress passed (the House vote was 416 to 5, and in the Senate, it was 93 to 4) the reauthorization of the Terrorism Risk Insurance Act (now called the Terrorism Risk Reauthorization Act of 2015, H.R. 26) and President Obama signed the program into law on January 12, 2015.[287] An article which reflected the insurance industry's approval of this legislation had this to say of the reauthorization. (And Leigh Ann Pursley was cheerleading the effort!)

"A well-functioning private terrorism insurance marketplace has been preserved because Congress and the Administration made TRIA's reauthorization an immediate priority," said Leigh Ann Pursley, president and chief executive officer of the *American Insurance Association (AIA)*. "The program, which has overwhelming bipartisan support, will continue to protect our nation's economy against major acts of terrorism. AIA thanks Congressional leadership and the Administration for moving so quickly to reauthorize TRIA."

TRIA was first signed into law in 2002 by President George W. Bush. It was later extended as the Terrorism Risk Insurance Extension Act of 2005 and in 2007 the president signed into law the Terrorism Risk Insurance Program Reauthorization Act of 2007 (TRIPRA). The law, which is administered by the U.S. Department of the Treasury created a "temporary federal program that provides for a transparent system of shared public and private compensation for certain insured losses resulting from a certified act of terror," according to the Department of the Treasury.[288]

It certainly was fortunate for those who wanted the "private terrorism insurance marketplace" to be continued with government partnership that there was a cyberattack blamed on North Korea so close to the reauthorization deadline.

Reality rarely serves up such a coincidental chain of events.

On January 14, 2015, Sony CEO Michael Lynton, was singing a happier tune than he had in weeks. Less that two months after the hack, his optimism on making the company whole because of insurance, strikes one as premature. It's almost as if somebody had privately assured him that everything was going to work out in his favor.

Sony Pictures CEO Michael Lynton revealed this week that the cyber attack would be completely covered by insurance and will not mean any more cost-cutting for the company.

"I would say the cost is far less than anything anybody is imagining and certainly shouldn't be anything that is disruptive to our budget," Lynton told Reuters. Though declining to reveal the exact cost of the breach, he confirmed it is "well within the bounds of insurance..."

All told, some experts have put the cost of the breach at $100 million. That figure could include computer repair or replacements, lost productivity and any steps taken to improve security and prevent a future attack. According to Lynton, cyber insurance will cover all such expenses.[289]

How much did the hack cost Sony and who paid for it? The answer is difficult to find. A February 4, 2015, article reported Sony estimated the cost as being $35 million dollars,[290] a far cry from the $300 million dollars suggested by some experts.

The trail of the insurance money, which Lynton was so confident of getting approximately six weeks after the hack, is absent from the public record for several years.

I found a reference about the Sony insurance issue from an April 2019 article in the *New York Times*. The article was not directly about Sony, but about the effort to recover insurance money by a Ukrainian snack company, Mondelez International, on a cyberattack insurance policy, for a hack blamed on Russia.

The question was whether a common, but rarely used exclusion in many insurance policies, the so-called "war exclusion," applied to cyberattacks blamed on a foreign government. The article suggested Obama had skillfully avoided that problem in the Sony hack.

In the past, American officials were reluctant to qualify cyberattacks as cyberwar, fearing the term could provoke an escalation. President Barack Obama, for example, was careful to say the aggressive North Korean cyberattack on Sony Entertainment in 2014, which destroyed more than 70 percent of Sony's computer servers, was an act of "cybervandalism."

That label was sharply criticized by Senators John McCain and Lindsey Graham, who called the hack a "new form of warfare" and "terrorism."

The description of the Sony attack was deliberate, said John Carlin, the assistant attorney general at the Justice

Department at the time. In an interview, he said the Obama administration had worried, in part, that the use of "cyber-war" would have triggered the liability exclusions and fine print that Mondelez is now challenging in court.[291]

The *New York Times* confirms that the Obama administration's designation of the Sony hack was based at least in part on insurance considerations. But many questions remained.

Was a payout even made?

If so, what companies or entities made the payments, what were their findings, and what was the amount of the award?

A partial answer to this mystery came in September of 2019, (nearly four years after the hack) but even then, the cryptic announcement from the San Francisco based law firm of Jones Day, was maddeningly vague about specific details.

Jones Day represented Sony Pictures for the 2014 cyber-attack by North Korean hackers, from 2015 to 2019. This unprecedented attack resulted in destruction of data and disruption of network systems. The Jones Day team advised the client on insurance coverage and pursued claims under three lines of coverage. The team achieved significant recoveries from nine different insurers to reimburse the client for breach response costs, business interruption losses, and class action litigation costs.[292]

The unanswered questions to me revolve around the identity of the nine different insurers, and whether payments had been made to Sony under the umbrella of the Terrorist Response Insurance Act, in concert with private insurers.

I have requested information on this question from the lawyers at Jones Day, as well as the Department of the Treasury, but have received no response as I write this account.

So much for the promise of "transparency."

However, an article from *Deadline* in April of 2015, five months after the hack, depicts 2014 as having been a good year for Sony Pictures.

> Sony Pictures Entertainment saw operating income increase 13.4% to $488M, the parent company said while reporting its full fiscal year results this morning in Tokyo. The jump was due to the favorable impact of the depreciation of the yen against the greenback. The period also benefitted from the stronger performance of the film slate, including hits like *The Amazing Spiderman* and *22 Jump Street*, as compared to the under-performance of White House Down and After Earth during the previous year. The reporting also noted $41M in costs related to "investigation and remediation expenses" stemming from the hack attack last November.[293]

Do we have our happy Hollywood ending? The hack cost $41 million dollars, and yet Sony still had a very good year, despite the layoffs, including getting rid of Amy Pascal.

But again, we are in the dark, as in 2014, Sony decided to stop producing an annual report, the type which can be vetted by those interested in such questions.[294] Sony Japan continues to report earnings, including those of Sony Pictures Entertainment, but does not produce an annual report.

And more questions remain unanswered.

I've spent a good number of pages in this book questioning the role of Sony Pictures CEO Michael Lynton in this series of events.

But a few things have been troubling me.

At one point in my research, Mr. Grey said, "You know, Kent, the dirty little secret of American business is that at some point, any company which becomes successful and prominent will be approached by our intelligence agencies. They'll want to 'partner' with you, and although you can say no, it's not a good decision. If you say no, you'll spend the rest of your life looking over your shoulder, wondering if they'll one day decide to take you down. It may never happen, but you worry it could. You want the intelligence agencies on your side, even if you may not trust them."

The second idea was realizing the limitations of your own understanding of an issue, despite the number of facts you may have at your fingertips. A former cyber-investigator for Norse had explained to me, "We can do research for a client, and confirm the facts we present to be 100% accurate. But then when we do the analysis, we're guessing. They're well-founded guesses, but one should assume your accuracy will only be about 60%. You can be certain of the facts. But always understand that what you believe to be true of an individual or situation, may be wrong."

It can be easy to point the finger of blame at Michael Lynton.

He was the CEO of Sony Pictures Entertainment when the hack happened, allowed his computer network to be vulnerable, and yet it was his second-in-command, Amy Pascal, who took the fall. And consider this description of Michael Lynton from the *New York Times* in the midst of the hack crisis:

Hurt by a misstep when it announced the cancellation of a Christmas Day release for "The Interview," Sony was knocked about by criticism by the White House, Hollywood stars and others who accused it of capitulating to extortionist threats. The studio's ultimate success in showing its film in the face of a terror threat came after Mr. Lynton's natural reserve fell more in line with the passion and grit of the studio's co-chairwoman, Amy Pascal, who was undermined early in the attack by the disclosure of embarrassing personal emails.

The son of a German Jew who served in British intelligence during World War II, Mr. Lynton, 54, had weathered past corporate crises, including an inherited accounting scandal when he ran the Penguin publishing house and a recent attempt by the activist investor Daniel S. Loeb to force change at Sony.[295]

What can we say with certainty about Michael Lynton?

Michael Lynton's father was a spy for British intelligence.

Lynton served on the Board of Directors of the RAND Corporation, a military and intelligence contractor for the United States government.

Lynton served as President of the Broadcasting Board of Governors, where he reported to both Secretary of State Hillary Clinton and President Barack Obama.

We also have the Wikileaks cache of Sony emails, with publisher, Julian Assange, asserting his suspicions about the close connection of Sony to the United States government.

All of these are established facts.

Add to that the claim of Seth Rogen in the 2018 *Vulture* interview that Sony management told him North Korea had hacked the network in the summer of 2014, possibly viewing *The Interview*, which formed the basis of some of their complaints to the United Nations, and the question of why Sony management did not aggressively move to secure their network by hiring a company like Norse, or one of the many other well-known cybersecurity firms. Both Mr. Grey and Eric were adamant to me that in late December of 2014 they'd located the Canadian server on which the embarrassing emails of Sony, along with the other stolen data was housed. Mr. Grey and Eric had explained this to Amy Pascal and told her they could render the site unusable, thus containing the damage.

Pascal reportedly called Lynton for permission to have the server rendered unusable. "I can still remember Amy being on that call, and hearing Lynton say 'no," Mr. Grey recalled.

The easiest conclusion to draw is that Sony is at least in part, a witting agent of the United States government, as well as the military and intelligence agencies, with Lynton as managing partner.

However, I could use the same facts to present another picture, which while not absolving Lynton of blame adds a shade of gray to our understanding.

Lynton's father was a British spy, which might make him more open to government "assistance," thinking that would be a good thing.

It would explain why he might easily accept appointment to the RAND Corporation board, as well as serving on the Broadcasting Board of Governors, and the generally close relationship the studio had with the Obama administration.

However, if one is familiar with the intelligence world, one also knows how deceptive people in that community can be. The analysis cuts both ways. Yes, you are an insider, but at the same time, you also have a better understanding of the inadequacies.

Could the intelligence agencies have come to Lynton in the summer of 2014, told him of the hack, and said that they would handle it? One explanation for Lynton's gross negligence in the summer and fall of 2014, is that somebody told him to stand down.

And then everything went to hell.

The intelligence agencies may have been tracking North Korea's efforts, but they missed the attack by LizardSquad, with the able assistance of their former, fired technology administrator, Shahana Manjra (Hardeman).

The question in my mind becomes, after everything happened, what did Michael Lynton think about the hack, and whether it was actually from North Korea?

Lynton did not respond to a request to be interviewed for this book, so I'm left with a curious interview he gave in the *Harvard Business Review*, for their July-August 2015 issue, a little more than six months after the hack. I ask you whether he sounds like a man convinced by what the Obama administration told him, or whether he's signaling his belief that the truth has not yet been revealed:

Do you accept the theory that North Korea did the hacking?

I actually haven't been concerned about who did this. I've been more concerned about getting the business up and running and making sure folks here feel calm enough and secure enough to keep on with their jobs. What the FBI and others in the government have told me, and what the president of the United States has said, is that it was North Korea. I have to believe them. They did the forensics; they did the intelligence work.

As you know, some people think that's not true for a number of reasons, including the fact that the hackers said nothing about *The Interview* in their earliest communications.

The U.S. government has access to more information about this than anyone else, and I have no reason to disagree. Experts have told me that the level of destruction and sophistication suggests it was a very expensive operation requiring a lot of people. I personally don't know whether it was the North Koreans or another entity, but I don't think it was some disgruntled employee. It was way too sophisticated.[296]

Maybe I'm biased, but as I read that section it doesn't sound like a ringing endorsement from Lynton about the quality of the evidence provided to him by the United States government. If anything, he appears to be saying he hasn't seen anything different than what the rest of the public has, which is exactly nothing.

Maybe Lynton was a willing collaborator with the intelligence community, as his father's work with British intelligence, and his service on the board of both the RAND Corporation and the Broadcasting Board of Governors, would suggest. But his interview in the *Harvard Business Review* raises the possibility he has not been treated well by these intelligence agencies who "had access to more information than anyone else." One might be tempted to fall back on the old expression, "He was treated like a mushroom; kept in the dark and fed shit" as a description of the relationship.

It is just as easy to conclude Lynton was a willing participant in an intelligence agency scheme to frame North Korea, thus potentially giving President Obama a reason to follow-through on his long-held hope that an incident would arise which would allow him to decapitate the North Korean leadership without risking a nuclear war.

But that doesn't account for the missteps between Lynton and President Obama, which the *Harvard Business Review* detailed in their summary of the conflict.

> The attack pushed a reluctant Lynton to the forefront of U.S. foreign relations when the hackers threatened retaliation if *The Interview*, a Sony Pictures comedy set in North Korea that includes the assassination of Kim Jong-un, was released. Fearing reprisals, many theaters declined to screen the film, and Sony had to look for alternative distribution. President Barack Obama weighed in, chastising Sony for what he viewed as caving to Pyongyang's pressure. The R-rated bro film had suddenly become a First Amendment icon.[297]

One might conclude that President Obama was also treated like a mushroom by the intelligence community, just as President Kennedy claims to have been by the CIA in the run-up to the disastrous Bay of Pigs invasion of Cuba in 1961.

However, Obama's natural caution seems to have prevented an escalation. In retrospect, his response may have saved millions of lives. What if a decapitation strike against the North Korean leadership had been attempted and failed? Would Kim have responded with a nuclear attack on American bases in Asia? Or even decided this was the time to see if one of his nuclear-armed missiles could hit the West Coast of the United States, as happens at the climax of *The Interview?*

It is good that these are hypothetical questions.

But the worry is that the same situation might arise again in the future if we do not have a clear understanding of what happened in this fiasco.

The *Harvard Business Review* interview tried to answer some additional questions:

I read that the eventual cost to the company was $15 million.

The $15 million Sony reported was the cost as of December 31. But the bottom line – and it's a testament to the people here – is that we didn't miss a single day's start on a single television show or on a single movie.

Wikileaks, meanwhile, is keeping the stolen data public and cataloging it for ease of search. I think Julian Assange's argument is that Sony is a big, influential public company and thus these documents deserve to be publicly accessible. I take it you don't agree.

I don't agree, particularly because there's so much personal information in there. I think people have a right to their privacy. And anyway, the emails were stolen. For that matter, I don't agree with the way the press has been looking through the emails.[298]

I'm not sure the above passage gives much new information, other than it shows how much information is being concealed under the guise of a "hard-hitting" interview.

In response to the first question, why didn't the reporter ask for the actual cost of damages from the breach?

No answer was provided by Lynton.

Was it $15 million or $300 million?

Six months after the hack, he should be answering the question of whether the insurance he was so certain would cover the damages, had been awarded. That's what a businessperson is interested in, the bottom line.

Similarly, when a question was asked about the Wikileaks/ Julian Assange assemblage of the hacked materials, Lynton focused on employee privacy. That seems like a non-responsive answer to me. And what of the questions raised by the emails, showing Sony's close ties with the RAND Corporation, as well as their strong political ties to the Democratic party?

However, instead of questions of responsibility for the hack, troubling relations with elements of the United States government, the damages suffered by his company, and whether Sony had been made whole, we get this at the end of the interview:

What did this experience teach you about leadership?

You have to be incredibly optimistic at all times about getting through a crisis – even if you're not quite sure how you're going to get through it. You need to be a thousand percent convinced in your own head, or you won't get across the finish line.

Isn't that just temperament? Aren't you just an optimistic person?

I'm actually not very optimistic, for the most part. But in times of crisis I become unreasonably so.

You mean falsely optimistic?

No, it's not about false optimism, because – and this will sound like bad movie dialogue – failure just isn't an option. You need to project a sort of cheerleading optimism, or you're not going to find your way.[299]

We are now ten years past the Sony hack and the United States government has still not released their evidence to support the claim of North Korean involvement. Nor have they refuted the evidence provided by private cybersecurity companies or responded to the allegations of Seth Rogen that Sony knew of a possible hack in the summer of 2014, but did nothing.

Additionally, in that time frame no other similar incident has involved North Korea.

Perhaps the Korea hawks of the RAND Corporation will respond by saying, "You see? We taught those North Koreans a lesson with our response," although they will be vague as to what that response might have been, other than taking down the North Korean internet for a few hours.

Although Amy Pascal was "fired" from Sony, she got a sweet deal, allowing her to form her own production company, Pascal Pictures.[300] The company has produced several successful *Spiderman* movies, *The Post* with Tom Hanks and Meryl Streep (2018 Academy Award nominee for Best Picture), *Little Women* (2020 Academy Award nominee for Best Picture), and most recently the *Venom* series with actor Tom Hardy.[301]

Michael Lynton currently works as the CEO of Snap (valued at 25.85 billion dollars as of June 1, 2024),[302] the parent company of the popular Snapchat mobile application, as well as serving as the chairman of the Warner Music Group (valued at $15.28 billion as of June 1, 2024).[303]

And Julian Assange, who cataloged all the Sony and RAND Corporation emails, as well as other data released in the hack, sat in a British jail until June of 2024, until he pled guilty to a single charge, ending a fourteen-year-long legal battle. Much of this same information was printed in newspapers around the world. In June of 2012, Assange took refuge in the Ecuadorian Embassy to escape what he believed to be malicious prosecution, and remained there until April 11, 2019, when he was taken into custody by the British government. The U.S. government has charged Assange with espionage, among other crimes, even though he is not an American citizen. For many in the world, the imprisonment of this Australian journalist by British and American authorities are the clearest sign that the intelligence agencies are in effective control of these governments.

And the private terrorism insurance marketplace continues to be strong, backed by you, the American taxpayer.

The sixteenth century political writer John Harrington wrote, "If it prospers, none dare call it treason." The question remains how this blindness serves humanity in the age of cyberweapons and nuclear bombs. And why do we continue to reward those who support the comfortable lies, while punishing those who tell the unsettling truths?

The time for "cheerleading optimism" is over.

We need the truth.

I suspect there will be more than a few surprises when, and if, the hidden information in this story is ever shared with the public.

Author's Note
Getting to Know "the Boys"

I began this book citing "the writer's dilemma," specifically that I do not know if what I am being told by anybody is true.

The best I can do is try to verify the claims made, tell you my response to the logic and credibility of what's asserted, and be honest about my own possible biases.

Let me tell you the story of how I came to know Mr. Grey*, Eric*, and the former employees of Norse Corporation, and the details of my continuing relationship with them.

In 2020 I published a bestselling book with Dr. Judy Mikovits, *Plague of Corruption*, which was purchased by a film company to make a documentary. However, before the company spent a couple hundred thousand dollars on the movie, they wanted to do a background check on me and Dr. Mikovits. When the director told me this fact, about halfway through production, I was intrigued. "What did they find?" I asked.

"The two of you don't have any suspicious financial transactions, troubling associations, and while we don't know if your claims about the medical establishment are true, you seem to genuinely believe them."

"Fair enough," I replied, then after a minute I asked, "Can I meet these guys?"

"Why do you want to meet them?" the director asked.

"You described them as doing cybersecurity, investigations, trying to find out what's true for the clients who hire them," I replied.

"They sound interesting. Because with my writing, I'm trying to find out what's true as well."

I guess it's unusual for the "target" of an investigation to want to meet the people who investigated him, as it took a couple months to set up the meeting. I had to remind the director several times of my interest, and finally we set a time for me to go to their office.

The director met me outside the office, we went in, and I shook hands with Mr. Grey and Eric. Then for the next fifteen minutes I was completely ignored, as the three of them held a long conversation about some other issues.

I was amused as I sat there, looking at Mr. Grey who was leading the discussion, and thinking, *Who's this big, swinging dick, and what's his reason for acting like I'm not here?*

After a few minutes I realized, *Oh, I get it, we're playing the silent game. Whoever talks first, loses. Mr. Big Swinging Dick wants to see if I have self-control.*

I simply sat there quietly, listening attentively, until after about fifteen minutes, Mr. Grey finally turned to me and said, "What can we help you with?"

I had a couple ideas I shared with him, most centered around the 2021 recall election in California against Governor Gavin Newsom, and whether it might be worthwhile to throw my hat in the ring to raise my visibility as an author, or whether a case might be made for a more well-known figure like Robert F. Kennedy, Jr, who had kindly written the foreword to my book, *Plague of Corruption*. (Four of my books have been published under Kennedy's book imprint, Children's Health Defense, at Skyhorse Publishing.)

I found out during that meeting Kennedy had already looked into and turned down that idea of running against Newsom, and as for me, in a race with more than a hundred people (cost to register about $4,000) it probably wouldn't do much for me.

Next, I suggested to Mr. Grey that I might hire his company to do investigations for books I write, in much the same way he does investigations for lawyers with legal cases. "You might be able to find information I can't or tell me when something I believe is mistaken."

That seemed to intrigue him. We talked for a while longer, and he walked me outside, which I took to be a good sign. "You're a creative," he said near the end of our conversation, a slight smile on his face, as if he'd just placed me into my proper tribe.

"Yeah," I replied. "Most people miss that because I'm a non-fiction writer. They don't realize that even if it's a true story, I'm making a lot of decisions about how to tell the story, and how I want people to feel when they're done reading it."

I got a good feeling from Mr. Grey at the end of that meeting, and a few months later I did hire him to help me with my book on *CNN*, the cable news giant.

"You should know that when we do research, we're like Switzerland," Mr. Grey warned me as the investigation began. "We're not on anybody's side. We just tell you what we find. And we might not find anything."

"I understand that," I said.

"And we'll never do anything illegal," warned Mr. Grey. "That's a line we will not cross. We've had some political figures ask us to do some things and we've said, 'That's fine. Where's your warrant?' They usually don't call us after that. But with that said, there's a lot we can find legally, and we know how to find it."

"I'd never want you to do anything illegal," I replied. "That's a line for me, too."

I put them on the question of whether CNN was taking orders from the Biden Administration. An exhaustive investigation didn't come up with much, but they'd stumbled over two other interesting pieces of information.

"CNN's got a computer department that looks like a cyber-warfare unit, complete with leaders who have military training," said Mr. Grey. "The tech department is suspiciously large. It's several times larger than is necessary for a company that size."

"That's troubling," I said.

"The other thing is they've got twenty-one top employees, including some on-air journalists, who have intelligence clearances. In our world, that broadcasts to everybody that you're a spook. The worst is Jim Sciutto. He headed up our embassy in Beijing, China from 2011 to 2013. He got to see all the secrets, and now they're trying to pass him off as a national security correspondent and anchor, working for the American people? Give me a break."

"Sounds like Operation Mockingbird never died," I said, referencing the program, revealed in the 1977 Church Committee hearings in the Senate, that more than 400 members of the press were on the payroll of the Central Intelligence Agency.

"Bingo. Now it's an open program, hiding in plain sight. Journalists go into government for a year or so, maybe work in some embassy or consulate, or some government job that gives them access to secret documents, then go back to work in the news."

I published that information in my book, *This Was CNN: How Sex, Lies and Spies Ruined the World's Worst Network*. My publisher was so nervous that we had the information vetted by one of the country's top constitutional lawyers, as well as a thirty-year FBI agent, who'd actually been the liaison to CIA stations in his foreign postings.

They both told me the information Mr. Grey and his company had provided was credible.

During the time writing that book I got to spend a lot of time with Mr. Grey, hearing stories about his life as a record producer and manager, starting in the early 1970s, and many of the people he'd met. "You know what I wanted to do when I was young?" he said during one of our times together. "I had this fantasy that I'd have two floors of attorneys whose only job was to secretly go after the world's bad guys." By this time, we'd become close, and I think he considered me somebody who would appreciate his desire to create a real-life Justice League. "Why couldn't you have been born a billionaire, Kent?" he asked. "Then we could just do it and not worry about working for anybody else."

"I probably would've been an asshole if I'd been born a billionaire," I replied, which made him laugh in return, as he'd worked for more than a few billionaires. "Maybe we're both just where we're supposed to be, me a writer, and you with a cyber-investigation company that can find me the information I need."

I've continued to hire Mr. Grey and his company for other books, but the Sony story kept coming up. I found the cyber-investigators to be like cops I've known, a little stand-offish at first, maybe even suspicious, but once trust has been established, my God, do the stories flow.

"You can't ever write about that story, Kent," they'd tell me time and again after one of their stories, and I'd promise to keep the confidence. That's what good friends do.

The world has the right to know some stories, and others they don't.

But the Sony story was different than their typical stories of cyber-investigations, like what was really going on with the marriages of certain Hollywood stars, how an executive came up with an almost untraceable way to embezzle money from his company, or an old, rich guy who was sending out pictures of his junk.

The Sony hack was still a mystery, and whether it was North Korea, or a disgruntled employee working with known hacker groups, it had enormous consequences for the world.

And since Sony had never hired them, there wasn't a duty of confidentiality to a client.

An additional factor was that by the time they talked to me about it, the five-year secrecy clause they signed with the government to take that meeting at the Pentagon had passed. "You should let me tell that story someday," I said to Mr. Grey.

When my father passed away, I even decided to invest some money into Mr. Grey's company, the one he and Eric founded after Norse Corporation. This was in 2023, about two years after I'd first met him and had hired his company for my own investigations.

I tell you this because I think it's important you understand my potential bias in favor of Mr. Grey and his star investigator, Eric. In my defense, all I can do is what you do every day in your lives, make judgments about whom you can and cannot trust.

I'm doing the best I can, and if you'll forgive the indulgence, I'd like to believe I'm working with a small group of people who are genuinely trying to make the world a better place.

And based on the growing number of whistleblowers, independent media voices willing to push back against government narratives, and individuals hungry for information, maybe we have something even more powerful than two floors of lawyers secretly going after the bad guys.

I like to think that all of us working together, are creating something we once used to only dream about, a real-life Justice League.

ENDNOTES

1   Geraldine Fabrikant, "Deal is Expected for Sony to Buy Columbia Pictures", *New York Times*, September 26, 1989, www.nytimes.com/1989/09/26/business/deal-is-expected-for-sony-to-buy-columbia-pictures.html.

2   Kenneth Noble, "A Clash of Styles: Japanese Companies in U.S. Under Fire for Cultural Bias," *New York Times*, January 25, 1988, www.nytimes.com/1988/01/25/us/a-clash-of-styles-japanese-companies-in-us-under-fire-for-cultural-bias.html.

3   Sam Biddle, "Leaked Email Alleges Racism and Sexual Harassment Horror at Sony," *Gawker*, December 12, 2014, www.gawker.com/leaked-email-alleges-racism-and-sexual-harassment-horro-1670318085

4   David Francis, "Did North Korea Finally Get revenge for 'Team America: World Police'?". *Foreign Policy*, December 3, 2014, www.foreignpolicy.com/2014/12/03/did-north-korea-finally-get-revenge-for-team-america-world-police/.

5   Bradford Evans, "Seth Rogen to Direct and Star in a Movie called 'The Interview'; James Franco May Co-Star," *Vulture*, March 21, 2013, www.vulture.com/2013/03/seth-rogen-to-direct-and-star-in-a-movie-called-the-interview-james-franco-may-co-star.html.

6   Law Offices of Michael Shapiro, "About Us," (Accessed January 17, 2023), www.mrshapirolaw.com/aboutus.

7   Interview with Michael Shapiro by Kent Heckenlively, March 27, 2023.

8   "About Us" Big Deal Records, (Accessed January 17, 2023), www.bigdealrecords.com/wordpress1/about-us/.

9   "Our Approach," Ohr HaTorah Synagogue, (Accessed March 30, 2023), www.ohrhatorah.org/about.

10 Interview with Michael Shapiro by Kent Heckenlively, March 27, 2023.

11 Ibid.

12 "Norse Expands Threat Intelligence to Include Detection of Malware in Development and Identification of Devices," *Dark Reading*, December 13, 2013, www.darkreading.com/risk/norse-expands-threat-intelligence-to-include-detection-of-malware-in-development-and-identification-of-devices.

13 Telephone Interview with Eric* by Kent Heckenlively, April 15, 2023.

14 Ibid.

15 Ibid.

16 Ibid.

17 Colin Schultz, "The Net's Dark Side: Watch People Try to hack Each Other, Live," *Smithsonian*, June 23, 2014, www.smithsonianmag.com/smart-news/nets-dark-side-watch-people-try-hack-each-other-live-180951823/.

18 Ibid.

19 Alexandra Cheney, "Sony CEO: I'm Not Entertaining Even the Notion of Selling Our Entertainment Assets," *Variety*, February 24, 2014, www.variety.com/2014/biz/news/sony-chief-kazuo-hirai-im-not-entertaining-even-the-notion-of-selling-our-entertainment-assets-1201118888/.

20 Ibid.

21 Ibid.

22 Alexandra Cheney, "Sony Lays Off 216 Workers Including 70 in Interactive Division," *Variety*, March 17, 2014, www.variety.com/2014/biz/news/sony-cuts-over-70-jobs-more-layoffs-expected-1201136617/.

23 Jane Martinson, "Amy Pascal: An Untypical Leading Lady Who's Taken Sony to the Top," *The Guardian*, May 18, 2006, www.theguardian.com/business/2006/may/19/4

24 Ibid.

25 "Eight Reasons the Sony Hack was Even Crazier Than You Thought," *Yahoo News*, June 26, 2015, www.yahoo.com/entertainment/sony-hack-the-interview-122508494457.html.

26 Bill Brownstein, "Review: Animal House Meets Rambo in The Interview," *Montreal Gazette*, December 29, 2014, www.montrealgazetta.com/entertainment/movies.animal-house-meets-rambo-in-the-interview/.

27 Ibid.

28 Tim Walker, "The Interview Film Review: Controversial Gross-Out Satire is Broad, Bawdy and Bad – But Undeniably Entertaining," *Independent*, December 26, 2014, www.independent.co.uk/arts-entertainment/films/reviews/the-interview-controversial-grossout-

satire-is-broad-bawdy-and-bad-but-undeniably-entertaining-9945801.html.

29   Ibid.

30   Ibid.

31   The Interview, Sony Pictures, 2014, (Accessed June 8, 2024), www.sonypictures.com/movies/theinterview.

32   Erin Blakemore, "The Korean War Never Technically Ended. Here's Why," *National Geographic*, June 25, 2020.

33   "The Korean War Armistice," *BBC*, March 5, 2015, www.bbc.com/news/1065796.

34   Donald Kirk, "South Korea Isn't Likely to Sign a Peace Treaty – Nor Should It," *The Hill*, December 22, 2021, www.thehill.com/international/586252-south-korea-isn't-likely-to-sign-a-peace-treaty-nor-should-it/.

35   "South V. North Korea: How Do the Two Countries Compare? Visualized," *The Guardian*, April 8, 2013, www.theguardian.com/world/datablog/2013/apr/08/south-korea-v-north-korea-compared?ref=quillette.com

36   Ibid.

37   Ibid.

38   Ibid.

39   Ibid.

40   Ibid.

41   Ibid.

42   Ibid.

43   Ibid.

44   Ibid.

45   Stephen Losey, "Here's What it Costs to Keep US Troops in Japan and South Korea," *Military.com*, March 23, 2021, www.military.com/daily-news/2021/03/23/heres-what-it-costs-keep-us-troops-japan-and-south-korea.html.

46   "Korea Under Japanese Rule," Encyclopedia Britannica, (Accessed January 30, 2023), www.britannica.com/place/Korea/Korea-under-Japanese-rule.

47   Monir H. Moni, "Japan's Fresh Bid for a UNSC Permanent Seat: Prowess, Problems and Prospects," *World Affairs*, Vol. 11, No. 4 (Winter 2007), p. 118-140, www.jstor.org/stable/48531773#metadata_info_tab_contents

48   "Extraordinary Press Conference by Foreign Minister Taro Kono," December 15, 2017, Ministry of Foreign Affairs of Japan, www.mofa.go.jp/press/kaiken/kaiken4e_00048.html.

49   Jiji, Kyodo, "Japan to be Tested as Nonpermanent U.N. Security Council Member," *Japan Times,* January 2, 2023.

50   "Variety Top 500 Entertainment Business Leaders – Michael Lynton," *Variety,* December 2017, www.variety.com/exec/michael-lynton/.

51   Ibid.

52   "Eight Reasons the Sony Hack was Even Crazier Than You Thought," Yahoo News, June 26, 2015, www.yahoo.com/entertainment/sony-hack-the-interview-122508494457.html.

53   Jiji, Kyodo, "Japan to be Tested as Nonpermanent U.N. Security Council Member," *Japan Times,* May 23, 2023, www.japantimes/co.jp/news/2023/05/23/national/politics-diplomacy/security-council-membership/.
      "Variety Top 500 Entertainment Business Leaders – Michael Lynton," *Variety,* December 2017, www.variety.com/exec/michael-lynton/.

54   Chalmers Johnson, "The RAND Corporation: America's University of Imperialism," *Global Policy,* April 30, 2008, www.archive.globalpolicy.org/empire/intervention/2008/0430rand.htm.

55   "About CFR," Council on Foreign Affairs website, (Accessed February 2, 2023), www.cfr.org/about.

56   Ibid.

57   "About the Expert – Richard Haass," Council on Foreign Relations, (Accessed February 2, 2023), www.cfr.org/expert/richard-haass.

58   Ibid.

59   Ibid.

60   Elsa Bertet, Amy Pascal Timeline," *Variety,* September 6, 2007, www.variety.com/2007/film/features/amy-pascal-timeline-1117971486/#!.

61   Ibid.

62   "Amy Pascal Extends Long-Term Employment Agreement with Sony Pictures," Columbia Pictures Press Release, December 7, 2010, www.sony.com/content/en/en_us/sca/company-news/press-releases/columbia-pictures-2010/amy-pascal-extends-longterm-emplyment-agreement-with-sony-pictures.html.

63   "Ideas in Action – 60 Years of RAND," RAND Corporation Press Release, 2005, www.rand.org/pubs/corporate_pubs/CP501.html.

64   Email from Bruce Bennett to Michael Lynton, July 15, 2014, WikiLeaks – Sony Archive, (Accessed February 22, 2023), www.wikileaks.org/sony/emails/emailid/134870.

65   Ibid.

66   Ibid.

67   David E. Sanger and Martin Fackler, "N.S.A. Breached North Korean Networks Before Sony Attack, Officials Say," *New York Times,* January

18, 2015, www.nytimes.com/2015/01/19/world/asia/nsa-tapped-into-north-korean-networks-before-sony-attack-officials-say.html.

68   Ibid.

69   Luis Martinez, "How Clapper's Secret Mission to North Korea Came About," *ABC News*, November 9, 2014, www.abcnews.go.com/international/clappers-secret-mission-north-korea/story.

70   Ibid.

71   Rick Gladstone, "Kenneth Bae, Longest-Held U.S. Prisoner of North Korea, Reveals Details of Ordeal," *New York Times,* May 2, 2016, www.nytimes.com/2016/05/03/world/asia/kenneth-bae-longest-held-us-prisoner-of-north-korea-reveals-details-of-ordeal.

72   Ibid.

73   Luis Martinez, "How Clapper's Secret Mission to North Korea Came About," *ABC News*, November 9, 2014, www.abcnews.go.com/international/clappers-secret-mission-north-korea/story.

74   Ted Thornhill, "Intelligence Chief James Clapper was Treated to Lavish 12-Course Meal in North Korea as He Negotiated Release of Americans – Before Pyongyang Officials Presented Him with a BILL for the Banquet," *Daily Mail*, January 7, 2015, www.dailymail.co.uk/news/article-2900824/US-spymaster-dined-N-Korea-general-responsible-Sony-hack.

75   Bill Chappell, "Clapper Apologizes for Answer on NSA's Data Collection," *NPR*, July 2, 2013 Clapper Apologizes for Answer on NSA's Data Collection, www.npr.org/sections/thetwo-way/2013/07/02/198118060/clapper-apologizes-for-answer-on-nsas-data-collection.

76   Ibid.

77   Luchina Fischer "Could Seth Rogen and James Franco's New Film Start a War?" *ABC News*, June 26, 2014, www.abcnews.go.com/blogs/entertainment/2014/06/could-seth-rogen-and-james-francos-new-film-start-a-war.

78   Ibid.

79   Jennifer M. Wood, "Dan Sterling, The Interview Writer at the Center of the Sony Hack, Speaks Out," *Esquire*, December 17, 2014, www.esquire.com/entetainment/movies/interviews/a31646/dan-sterling-the-interview-sony-hack.

80   Steph Bazzle, "Sony Pictures Hacked by #GOP – What is It and What Does It Mean?" *Yahoo News*, November 24, 2014, www.yahoo.com/news/sony-pictures-hacked-gop-does-mean-185110289.

81   Todd Spangler, "FBI Leading Probe Into Sony Pictures Hacking Incident," *Variety*, December 1, 2014, www.variety.com/2014/digital/

news/fbi-leading-probe-into-sony-pictures-hacking-incident-1201368110/.

82   Sam Biddle, "Sony Hack Reveals 25-Page List of Reasons It Sucks to Work at Sony," *Gawker*, December 3, 2014, www.gawker.com/sony-hack-reveals-25-page-list-of-reasons-it-sucks-to-w-1666264634.

83   Ibid.

84   Ibid.

85   Brandon Bailey and Youkyung Lee, "Experts: The Sony Hack Looks a Lot Like Previous Attacks on South Korea," *Business Insider*, December 4, 2015, www.businessinsider.com/experts-the-sony-hack-looks-a-lot-like-previous-attacks-on-south-korea-2014-12.

86   Ibid.

87   Ibid.

88   Ibid.

89   David Robb, "The Sony Hack One Year Later: Just Who Are the Guardians of Peace?" *Deadline*, November 24, 2015, www.yahoo.com/entertainment/sony-hack-one-year-later-just-230633534.

90   Aly Weisman, "A Timeline of the Crazy Events in the Sony Hacking Scandal," *Business Insider*, December 9, 2014, www.businessinsider.com/sony-cyber-hack-timeline-2014-12.

91   "Sony Investigator Says Cyber Attack 'Unparalleled' Crime," *Reuters*, December 6, 2014, www.cnbc.com/2014/12/06/sony-investigator-says-cyber-attack-unparalleled-crime.html.

92   Ibid.

93   Jose Pagliery, "Conan O'Brien & Sylvester Stallone's Personal Information Exposed in Sony Hack," *CNN*, December 5, 2014, www.money.cnn.com/2014/12/05/technology/security/conan-obrien-sylvester-stallone-sony-hack/index.html.

94   Ibid.

95   Ibid.

96   "North Korea Denies 'Righteous" Hack Attack on Sony," BBC, December 7, 2014, www.bbc.com/news/world-asia-30366449.

97   Ted Johnson, "Sony Hackers Apparently Demand Studio Pull *The Interview*," *Yahoo News*, December 8, 2014, www.buzzfeednews.com/article/matthewzeitlin/hackers-tell-sony-not-to-release-the-interview.

98   Beatrice Verhoeven & Matt Donnelly, "Greatest Hits of Leaked Sony Emails: Angelina Jolie, 'Aloha,' David Fincher, and More," The Wrap, November 11, 2015, www.thewrap.com/greatest-hits-leaked-sony-emails-angelina-jolie-aloha-david-fincher/.

99   Ibid.

100 Phillip Caulfield & Cory Siemaszko, "Sony Email Hack Shows Scott Rudin, Amy Pascal Making Racist Jokes about Obama: Producer Apologizes," *New York Daily News*, December 11, 2014, www.nydailynews.com/entertainment/gossip/rudin-pascal-made-racist-jokes-obama-sony-hacks-article-1.2041618.

101 Brent Lang, "Obama's Got a Friend at Sony: Studio Leaders Big Donors in Past," *The Wrap*, April 21, 2011, www.thewrap.com/obamas-got-friend-sony-studio-leadership-big-donors-past-26697/.

102 Tufayel Ahmed, "What the Former President and First Lady's Deal is Worth and What They're Producing," *Newsweek*, September 19, 2019, www.newsweek.com/obama-netflix-deal-worth-trump-films-tv-shows-1459571.

103 Ibid.

104 Sam Biddle, "Leaked: The Nightmare Email Drama Behind Sony's Steve Jobs Disaster," *Gawker*, December 9, 2014, www.defamer.gawker.com/leaked-the-nightmare-email-drama-behind-sonys-steve-jo-1668882936.

105 Dave McNary, "Seth Rogen Thanks Sony's Amy Pascal for 'Having the Balls' to Make 'The Interview,'" *Variety*, December 11, 2014, www.variety.com/2014/film/news/the-interview-seth-rogen-amy-pascal-1201377101/.

106 Telephone Interview with Mickey Shapiro by Kent Heckenlively, March 27, 2023.

107 "Cybersecurity Firm Identifies Six in Sony Hack – One a Former Company Insider," *Yahoo News*, December 29, 2014, www.yahoo.com/entertainment/former-sony-staffer-among-six-suspects-hack-says-023241354.

108 Ibid.

109 William Turton, "An Interview with Lizard Squad, the Hackers who Took Down Xbox Live," *The Daily Dot*, December 26, 2014, www.dailydot.com/debug/lizard-squad-hackers/.

110 Ibid.

111 Ibid.

112 Ibid.

113 Martyn Williams, "Hackers Contacted Top Sony Executives Before Attack," *ComputerWorld*, December 8, 2014, www.computerworld.com/article/2857272/hackers-contacted-top-sony-executives-before-attack.html.

114 Ibid.

115 Michael B. Kelley and Armin Rosen, "The US Needs to Stop Pretending the Sony Hack is Anything Less than an Act of War,"

Business Insider, December 15, 2014, www.businessinsider.com/sony-hack-should-be-considered-an-act-of-war-2014-12.

116 Ibid.

117 "The Interview: Sony Shelves Worldwide Release," *BBC,* December 18, 2014, www.bbc.com/news/entertainment-arts-30528772.

118 Ibid.

119 Jon Sopel, "A Comedy of Terrors – In Four Acts," *BBC,* December 18, 2014, www.bbc.com/news/world-us-canada-30540527.

120 Dave Lee, "What is FBI Evidence for North Korea Hack Attack?", *BBC,* December 19, 2014, www.bbc.com/news/technology-30554444.

121 Ibid.

122 Ibid.

123 Ibid.

124 Ibid.

125 Michael B. Kelley, "FBI Blames North Korea for the Sony Hack," *Business Insider,* December 19, 2014, www.businessinsider.com/us-official-north-korea-hacked-sony-and-china-may-have-helped-2014-12.

126 "FBI: Sony Hackers 'Sloppy.' Used North Korean Servers," *Voice of America,* January 7, 2015, www.voanews.com/a/fbi-sony-hackers-sloppy-used-north-korean-servers/2589224.html.

127 Russell Brandom, "Project Goliath: Inside Hollywood's Secret War Against Google," *The Verge,* December 12, 2015, www.theverge.com/2014/12/12/7382287/project-goliath.

128 Ibid.

129 Mike Fleming, Jr., "Hollywood Cowardice: George Clooney Explains Why Sony Stood Alone in North Korean Cyber-Terror Attack," *Deadline,* December 18, 2014, www.deadline.com/2014/12/george-clooney-sony-hollywood-cowardice-north-korea-cyberattack-petition-1201329988/.

130 Ibid.

131 Ibid.

132 Ibid.

133 Oliver Laughland, "Sony Pulling The Interview Was 'a Mistake" Says Obama," *The Guardian,* December 20, 2014, www.theguardian.com/us-news/2014/dec/19/obama-sony-the-interview-mistake-north-korea.

134 "Update on Sony Investigation," FBI Press Office, December 19, 2014, www.fbi.gov/news/press-releases/update-on-sony-investigation.

135 Lisa De Moraes, "'The Interview' Release Would Have Damaged Kim Jong-un Internally, Says Rand Expert Who Saw Movie at Sony's

Request," *Deadline*, December 19, 2014, www.deadline.com/2014/12/
the-interview-kimg-jong-sony-hack-rand-corp-obama-1201331020/.

136 Linda Ge, "Sony Blames Movie Theaters for 'The Interview'
Decision: 'We Had No Choice,'" *The Wrap*, December 19, 2014, www.
thewrap.com/sony-blames-movie-theaters-for-the-interview-deci-
sion-we-had-mo-choice/.

137 Jon Stone, "North Korea Threatens Attack Against the White House,
Pentagon, and the 'Whole US Mainland' in Retaliation for The
Interview Hacking Accusations," *The Independent*, December 22, 2014,
www.independent.co.uk/news/world.asia/north-korea-threatens-
attack-against-the-white-house-pentagon-and-whole-us-mainland-in-
retaliation-for-the-interview-hacking-accusations/.

138 WikiLeaks Press Release, "The Sony Archive," April 16, 2015, www.
wikileaks.org/sony/press/index.html.

139 Email from Michael Rich to Bruce Bennett and Michael Lynton,
June 18, 2014, 5:52 pm, Wikileaks Sony Archive, www.wikileaks.org/
sony/emails/emailid/116595.

140 Michael D. Rich, RAND Profile, (Accessed March 1, 2023), www.
rand.org/about/people/r/rich_michael_d.html.

141 Ibid.

142 Email from Bruce Bennett to Michael Lynton, June 20, 2014, Wikileaks
Sony Archive, www.wikileaks.org/sony/emails/emailid/116595.

143 Ibid.

144 Samuel Cox, "The Battle of Ganghwa, Korea, 1871," Naval History
and Heritage Command, July 2021, www.history.navy.mil/about-us/
leadership/director/cirectors-corner/h-grams-0631.

145 Email from Bruce Bennett to Michael Lynton, June 20, 2014, www.
wikileaks.org/sony/emails/emailid/116595.

146 Ibid.

147 Ibid.

148 Ibid.

149 Ibid.

150 Rick Gladstone, "Tourists on Trial in a North Korea Angry at the
U.S.," *New York Times*, July 1, 2014, www.nytimes.com/2014/07/02/
world/asia/korean-anger-may-be-behind-trialof-tourists.

151 Email from Shiro Kambe to Nicole Seligman, Charlie Sipkins, et
al, Wikileaks Archive, July 2, 2014, Email ID 29859, www.wikileaks.
org/sony/emails/emailid/29859.

152 Ibid.

153 Yoko Wakatusi and Jethro Mullen, "Japan Eases Sanctions on North
Korea after Talks on Abductions," *CNN*, July 4, 2014, www.cnn.

com/2014/07/04/world/asia/japan-north-korea-sanctions/index.
html.

154 Email from Shiro Kambe to Charles Sipkins, Michael Lynton &
others, Wikileaks Sony Archive, July 3, 2014, Email 121175, www.
wikileaks.org/sony/emails/emailid/121175.

155 Email from Bruce Bennett to Michael Lynton Chain, Wikileaks
Sony Archive, July 17, 2014, Email ID 119396, www.wikileaks.org/
sony.email/emailid/119396.

156 Ibid.

157 Ibid.

158 Alastair Gale, "North Korea Takes Complaint About Assassination
Movie to White House," *Wall Street Journal,* July 17, 2014, www.wsj.
com/articles/BL-KRTB-6223.

159 Email Chain from Valerie Jarret to Michael Lynton and Kristen
Jarvis, Wikileaks Sony Archive, August 13, 2014, Email-ID – 131530,
www.wikileaks.org/sony/email/emailid/131530.

160 Brent Lang, "'The Interview' with Seth Rogen, James Franco, Pushed
Back to Christmas," *Variety,* August 7, 2014, www.variety.com/2014/
film/news/the-interview-delayed-release-date-1201277869/.

161 Tatiana Siegal, "Sony Altering Kim Jong Un Assassination Film
'The Interview' (Exclusive)," *The Hollywood Reporter,* August 13,
2014, www.hollywoodreporter.com/news/general-news/sony-altering-
kim-jong-assassination-725092/#!.

162 Email from Leah Weil to Aimee Wolfson, Wikileaks Sony Archive,
August 13, 2014, Email-ID 99168, www.wikileaks.org/sony/email/
emailid/99168/.

163 Ibid.

164 Email from Stephen Basil-Jones to Steven Odell and Nigel Clark,
July 8, 2014, Wikileaks Sony Archive, www.wikileaks.org/sony/
email/emailid/185314/.

165 Paul Fisher, "North Korea's Fear of Hollywood," *New York Times,*
July 3, 2014, www.nytimes.com/2014/07/04/opinion/sunday/north-
koreas-fear-of-hollywood.html.

166 Ibid.

167 Email from Michael Lynton to Valerie Jarrett, July 15, 2014,
Wikileaks Sony Archive, Email ID 136271, www.wikileaks.org/sony/
email/emailid/136271/.

168 Ibid.

169 Email from Michael Lynton to Valerie Jarrett Email Chain, July 23,
2014, Wikileaks Sony Archive, Email ID 116739, www.wikileaks.org/
sony/email/emailid/116739/.

170   "About Malcolm," Malcolm Gladwell website, (Accessed March 6, 2023), www.gladwellbooks.com/.

171   Email from Michael Lynton to Valerie Jarrett Email Chain, July 23, 2014, Wikileaks Sony Archive, Email ID 116739, www.wikileaks.org/sony/email/emailid/116739/.

172   Email from Valerie Jarrett to Michael Lynton, August 1, 2014, Wikileaks Sony Archive, Email ID -136549, www.wikileaks.org/sony/email/emailid/136549/.

173   Email Chain from Valerie Jarrett to Jay Carney and Michael Lynton, Wikileaks Sony Archive, June 18, 2014, Email-ID 129388, www.wikileaks.org/sony/email/emailid/129388/.

174   Ibid.

175   Email from Jay Carney to Michael Lynton, Wikileaks Sony Archive, June 23, 2014, Email ID 130480, www.wikileaks.org/sony/email/emailid/130480/.

176   Hadas Gold, "Sony CEO Tried to Recruit Jay Carney," *Politico*, April 17, 2015, www.politico.com/blogs/media/2015/04/sony-ceo-tried-to-recruit-jay-carney-205700.

177   WikiLeaks Press Release, "The Sony Archive," April 16, 2015, www.wikileaks.org/sony/press/index.html.

178   Paul Fisher, "North Korea's Fear of Hollywood," *New York Times*, July 3, 2014, www.nytimes.com/2014/07/04/opinion/sunday/north-koreas-fear-of-hollywood.html.

179   "State Department: 'No Specific Credible Threat' of North Korea Attack," NBC News, December 22, 2014, www.nbcnews.com/storyline/sony-hack/state-department-no-specific-credible-threat-north-korea-attack-n273236.

180   State Department Daily Briefing, CSPAN, December 22, 2014, www.c-span.org/video/?323449-1/state-department-briefing.

181   Ibid.

182   Ibid.

183   "Sony Pictures Entertainment Announces Limited Theatrical Release of The Interview on Christmas Day," Sony Pictures Entertainment, December 23, 2014, www.sonypictures.com/corp/press_releases/2014/12_14/122314_theinterviewtheatrical.html.

184   Fortune, "Sony Announces Limited Release of The Interview," TIME, December 23, 2014, www.time.com/3645866/sony-limited-release-the-interview/.

185   Associated Press, "Sony Announces Limited Release of 'The Interview' Beginning Christmas Day," *Los Angeles Daily News*, December 23, 2014, www.dailynews.com/2014/12/23/sony-

announces-limited-release-of-the-interview-beginning-christmas-day/.

186   Aly Weisman, "Obama Applauds Sony's Decision to Release 'The Interview,'" *Business Insider* December 23, 2014, www.businessinsider.com/obama-applauds-sonys-decision-to-release-the-interview-2014-12.

187   Alyson Shontell, "'The Interview' Raked in a Reported $1 Million from Theaters on Opening Day," *Business Insider,* December 26, 2014, www.businessinsider.com/the-interview-makes-1-million-in-opening-day-box-office-2014-12.

188   Ibid.

189   Adam B. Vary, "'The Interview' Has Made Nearly Seven Times More Online than at the Box Office," *Buzzfeed* News, January 20, 2015, www.buzzfeednews.com/article/adambvary/the-interview-tops-31-million-in-online-sales.

190   "Executive Order – Imposing Additional Sanctions with Respect to North Korea," The White House, Office of the Press Secretary, January 2, 2015, www.federalresgister.gov/documents/2017/09/25-20647/imposing-additional-sanctions-with-respect-to-north-korea/.

191   Sam Byford, "Sony Pictures Hackers Sent Ominous Email to Executives Warning of Attack" *The Verge*, December 8, 2014, www.theverge.com/2014/12/9/7356575/sony-pictures-hack-extortion-email/.

192   Russel Brandon, "New Evidence Points to North Korean Involvement in Sony Pictures Hack," The Verge, December 1, 2014, www.theverge.com/2014/12/1/7316401/new-evidence-points-to-north-korean-involvement-in-sony-hack/.

193   Doina Chiacu & Arshad Mohammed, "Leaked Audio Reveals Embarassing U.S. Exchange on Ukraine, EU," Reuters, February 6, 2014, www.reuters.com/article/us-usa-ukraine-tape-idUSBREA1601G20140207.

194   Russel Brandon, "New Evidence Points to North Korean Involvement in Sony Pictures Hack," The Verge, December 1, 2014, www.theverge.com/2014/12/1/7316401/new-evidence-points-to-north-korean-involvement-in-sony-hack/.

195   Jemima Kiss, "Xbox Live and Playstation Attack: Christmas Ruined for Millions of Gamers, *The Guardian*, December 26, 2014, www.theguardian.com/technology/2014/dec/26/xbox-live-and-psn-attack-christmas-ruined-for-millions-of-gamers/.

196   Dave Smith, "Alleged 'Lizard Squad' Member Reveals His Face in a TV Interview," *Business Insider,* December 27, 2014, www.buinsessinsider.com/lizard-squad-member-reveals-his-face-in-a-tv-interview/.

197   Ibid.

198   Ibid.

199   Gabrielle Levy, "American Airlines Flight Diverted After Hackers Make Bomb Threat," *UPI,* August 25, 2014, www.apnews. com/article/united-security-issue-flight-diverted-chicago-bomb-threat/.

200   Alyssa Newcomb, "Lizard Squad: Who is the Group Claiming Responsibility for the High-Profile Hacks?", *ABCNews,* August 26, 2014, www.abcnews.go.com/Technology/lizard-sqaud-group-claiming-responsibility-high-profile-hacks/.

201   Nicole Perlroth, "New Study May Add to Skepticism Among Security Experts that North Korea was Behind Sony Hack," *New York Times,* December 24, 2014, www.archive.nytimes.com/bitys.blogs.nytimes. com/2014/12/24/new-study-adds-to-skepticism-among-security-experts-that-north-korea-was-behind-sony-hack/.

202   Ibid.

203   Ibid.

204   Laura Hautala, "How US Cybersleuths Decided Russia Hacked the DNC," *CNET,* May 3, 2017, www.cnet.com/tech/computing/how-experts-decided-russia-hacked-dnc-election/.

205   Nicole Perlroth, "New Study May Add to Skepticism Among Security Experts that North Korea was Behind Sony Hack," *New York Times,* December 24, 2014, www.archive.nytimes.com/bitys.blogs.nytimes. com/2014/12/24/new-study-adds-to-skepticism-among-security-experts-that-north-korea-was-behind-sony-hack/.

206   Evan Perez & Daniella Diaz, "FBI: DNC Rebuffed Request to Examine Computer Servers," *CNN,* January 5, 2017, www.cnn.com/2017/01/05/politics/fbi-russia-hacking-dnc-crowdstrike/index.html.

207   Aaron Mate, "Hidden Over 2 Years: Dem Cyber-Firm's Sworn Testimony it Had No Proof of Russian Hack," *Real Clear Investigations,* May 13, 2020, www.realclearinvestigations.com/articles/2020/05/13/hidden_over_2_years_dem_cyber-firms_sworn_testimony_it_had_no_proof_of_russian_hack_of_dnc_123596.html.

208   Ibid.

209   Ibid.

210   Nicole Perlroth, "In Cyberattack on Saudi Firm, U.S. Sees Iran Firing Back," *New York Times,* October 23, 2012, www.nytimes. com/2012/10/24/business/global/cyberattack-on-saudi-oil-firm-disquiets-us.html.

211   Ibid.

212   Ibid.

213 Jim Finkle, "Exclusive: Insiders Suspected in Saudi Cyber Attack," *Reuters*, September 7, 2012, www.reuters.com/article/idUSBRE 8860CR/.

214 Jose Pagliery, "The Inside Story of the Biggest Hack in History," *CNN*, August 5, 2015, www.moneycnn.com/2015/08/05/technology/aramco-hack/index/.

215 Choe Sang-Hun, "Computer Networks in South Korea are Paralyzed in Cyberattacks," *New York Times*, March 20, 2013, www.nytimes.com/2013/03/21/world/asia/south-korea-computer-network-crashes.html/.

216 Ibid.

217 Ibid.

218 Ibid.

219 Marc Rogers, "Why I Still Don't Think It's Likely that North Korea Hacked Sony," Marc Rogers Org, December 21, 2014. www.marcrogers.org/2014/12/21/why-i-still-dont-think-its-likely-that-north-korea-hacled-sony/.

220 Ibid.

221 Ibid.

222 "Fauxtribution," Krypt3ia Word Press, December 20, 2014, www.krypt3ia.wordpress.com/2014/12/20/fauxtribution/.

223 Ibid.

224 Ibid.

225 Ibid.

226 Ibid.

227 Ibid.

228 Ibid.

229 Ibid.

230 Paul Roberts, "New Clues in Sony Hack Point to Insiders, Away from DPRK," *The Security Ledger*, December 28, 2014, www.securityledger.com/2014/12/mew-clues-in-sony=hack-point-to-insiders-away-from-dprk/.

231 Ibid.

232 Ibid.

233 Ibid.

234 Ibid.

235 Ibid.

236 Brian Fung, "A Q&A with the Hackers Who Say They Helped Break Into Sony's Network," *The Washington Post*, December 29, 2014.

237 Ibid.

238 Ibid.

239 "Sony Hackers 'Shared' Stolen Employee Log-in Data," *BBC*, December 30, 2014, www.bbc.com/news/technology-30632711.

240 Judson Berger, "Doubts on N. Korea Claim? FBI Briefed on Theory Sony Hack was Inside Job," *Fox News*, December 20, 2015, www.foxnews.com/politics/doubts-on-n-korea-claim-fbi-briefed-on-the-ory-sony-hack-was-inside-job/.

241 Pamela Brown and Mary Kay Mallonee, "North Korea Did it: FBI Not Budging on Sony Hack Culprit," *CNN* December 30, 2014, www.cnn.com/2014/12/30/justice/fbi-sony-hack/index/.

242 Ibid.

243 Tal Kopan, "FBI Rejects Alternate Sony Hack Theory," *Politico*, December 30, 2014, www.politico.com/story/2014/12/fbi-rejects-alternate-sony-hack-theory-113893/.

244 Ben Gilbert, "FBI Maintains that North Korea Hacked Sony as Detractors Mount," *Engadget*, December 30, 2014, www.engadget.com/2014-12-30-sony-pictures-maybe-not-north-korea/.

245 Norse Presentation to Pentagon, January 2015.

246 Ibid.

247 Ibid.

248 Jacob Kastrenakes & Russell Brandom, "Sony Pictures Hackers Say They Want 'Equality,' Worked with Staff to Break In," *The Verge*, November 25, 2015, www.theverge.com/2014/11/25/7281097/sony-pictures-hackers-say-they-want-equality-worked-wth-staff-to-break-in/.

249 Ibid.

250 Ted Johnson & Brent Lang, "Sony Hit with Class Action by Ex-Employees," *Variety*, December 16, 2014, www.variety.com/2014/film/news/sony-hit-with-class-action-lawsuit-by-ex-employees-1201380668/.

251 Mark Walton, "Sony Pictures Settles Employee Class Action Lawsuit of *The Interview* Hack," *Ars Technica*, October 21, 2015, www.arstechnica.com/tech-policy/2015/10/sony-pictures-settles-employee-class-action-over-the-interview-hack/.

252 "Cyber Threat Intelligence Analysis Summary of the 2014 Sony Breach," Norse Corporation, January 2, 2015.

253 Ibid. at 14.

254 Ibid. at 11.

255 Linked-In Account of Shahana Manjra-Hardeman, (Accessed December 20, 2023), www.linkedin.com/posts/shahana365_activity-6843607175072489473-Y5kv/.

256 Ibid.

257 James Cook, "Here's Everything We Know About the Mysterious Group that Hacked Sony Pictures," The State-Journal Register, December 7, 2014, www.businessinsider.in/Heres-Everything-We-Know-About-The-Mysterious-Hack-Of-Sony-Pictures/.

258 Ibid.

259 Ibid.

260 Ibid.

261 David Marchese, "In Conversation: Seth Rogen," *Vulture*, April 2018, www.vulture.com/2018/04/seth-rogen-in-conversation/.

262 Ibid.

263 Bruce W. Bennett, "Did North Korea Hack Sony?" *Newsweek*, December 11, 2014, www.newsweek.com/did-north-korea-hack-sony-292050/.

264 Ibid.

265 Ibid.

266 David E. Sanger, "The Perfect Weapon: War, Sabotage, and Fear in the Cyber Age," (New York: Broadway Books, an Imprint of Random House, 2018).

267 Ibid. at vii.

268 Ibid. at 56.

269 Ibid. at 56-57.

270 Ibid. at 132.

271 Ibid, at 133.

272 Ibid. at 142.

273 Ibid.

274 Ibid. at 143.

275 Ibid. at 124-125.

276 Ibid. at 125-126.

277 "BBG Meets with Secretary of State Clinton," *U.S. Agency for Global Media*, September 13, 2012, www.usagm.gov/2012/09/13/bbg-meets-with-secretary-of-state-clinton/.

278 "Presiding Governor Lynton Steps Down from BBG Board," May 23, 2013, *US Agency for Global Media*, www.usagm.gov/2013/05/23/presiding-governor-lynton-steps-down-from-the-bbg-board/.

279 David E. Sanger, "The Perfect Weapon: War, Sabotage, and Fear in the Cyber Age," (New York: Broadway Books, an Imprint of Random House, New York, 2018), 126.

280 Andrea Peterson, "Why It's So Hard to Calculate the Cost of the Sony Pictures Hack," *The Washington Post*, December 5, 2014, www.washingtonpost.com/news/the-switch/wp/2014/12/05/why-its-so-hard-tocalculate-the-cost-of-the-sony-pictures-hack/.

281 Ibid.

282 Annie Lowrey, "Sony's Very, Very Expensive Hack," December 16, 2014, *New York Magazine*, www.nymag.com/intelligencer/2014/12/sonys-very-very-expensive-hack/.

283 Jeff Stone, "For Sony Pictures, North Korea Hack an Insurance Nightmare Before Christmas," *The International Business Times*, December 22, 2014, www.ibtimes.com/sony-north-korea-hack-insurance-nightmare-christmas-1765098/.

284 Ibid.

285 Judy Woodruff, "What a Lapse in Terrorism Insurance by Congress Means for Business," *PBS Newshour*, December 17, 2014, PBS NewsHour, www.pbs.org/newshour/show/terror-insurance/.

286 Ibid.

287 Caroline McDonald, "TRIA Signed into Law by President Obama – Terrorism Risk Insurance Act," *National Law Review*, January 18, 2015, www.natlawreview.com/article/tria-signed-law-president-obama-terrorism-risk-insurance-act/.

288 Ibid.

289 "Here's How Insurance Will Respond to the Sony Cyber Attack," *Insurance Business America*," January 14, 2015, www.insurancebusinessmag.com/us/news/breaking-news/heres-how-insurance-will-respond-to-the-sony-cyber-hack/.

290 Tim Hornyak, "2014 Cyberattack to Cost Sony 35M in IT Repairs," *IDG News Services*, February 4, www.computerworld.com/article/1629515/2014-cyberattack-to-cost-sony-35m-in-it-repairs/.

291 Adam Satariano & Nicole Perlroth, "Big Companies Thought Insurance Covered a Cyberattack. They May Be Wrong," *New York Times*, April 15, 2019, www.nytimes.com/2019/04/15/technology/cyberinsurance-notpetya-attack/.

292 "Sony Pictures Obtains Insurance Coverage for Losses Arising from Liabilities from 2014 Cyberattack," September 2019, Jones Day website, www.jonesday.com/en/practices/experience/2019/09/sony-pictures-obrains-insirance-coverage-for-losses/.

293 Nancy Tartaglione, "Sony Earnings Improve: Picture Division Jumps in Full Year Results," *Deadline*, April 30, 2015, www.deadline.com/2015/04/sony-earnings-full-year-2015/.

294 "Sony Group Portal – Annual Report," (Accessed June 7, 2024), www.sony.com/en/SonyInfo/IR/ar/Archive/.

295 Michael Ciply & Brooke Barnes, "Sony Cyberattack, First a Nuisance, Swiftly Grew Into a Firestorm," *New York Times*, December 30, 2014, www.nytimes.com/2014/12/31/business/media/sony-attack-first-a-nuisance-swiftly-grew-into-a-firestorm/.

296 Ad Ignatius, "'They Burned the House Down': An Interview with Michael Lynton," *Harvard Business Review*, July-August 2015, www.hbr.org/2015/07/they-burned-the-house-down/.

297 Ibid.

298 Ibid.

299 Ibid.

300 Beatrice Verhoeven, "The Sony Hack's Key Players: Where Are They Now?", *The Wrap*, January 13, 2017, www.thewrap.com/the-sony-hacks-key-players-where-are-they-now-photos/.

301 "Amy Pascal," Independent Movie Database, (Accessed June 9, 2024), www.imdb.com/nane/nm1166871/awards/.

302 "Snap, Inc.," Companies Market Cap, June 2024, www.companies-marketcap.com/snap/marketcap/.

303 "Warner Music Group," Companies Market Cap. June 2024, www.companiesmarketcap.com/warner-music-group/marketcap/.